Praise for The Intuitive Mind ...

"When times are tough skilful intuition may be our most important asset. This book provides a sensible and readable guide to the intuitive mind – what it is, how it can be developed, and the ways in which it can be applied to advantage in work and business settings."
Rob Goffee, Professor of Organizational Behaviour, London Business School

"Your intuition is a powerful heuristic engine that is constantly learning from the past. The Intuitive Mind *is a fascinating and practical book that will maximize your intuition and help you make better decisions today and predictions about tomorrow! Sigmund Freud and Carl Jung would most assuredly approve."*
Steve W. Martin, www.heavyhitterwisdom.com
Heavy Hitter Sales Psychology: How to Penetrate the C-Level Executive Suite and Convince Company Leaders to Buy

"Time and time again, we see that analytic thinking can only take us so far. In this important book, Eugene Sadler-Smith gives needed attention to the 'other' way of thinking – intuitive – and reminds us that leadership is an art as well as a science."
Cindi Fukami, Professor of Management, University of Denver, USA

"From one of our prominent 'thinkers' in the management education arena, we learn in The Intuitive Mind *how to use our intuitive judgment to improve our managerial decision making. Eugene Sadler-Smith doesn't just argue for the need for managers to understand their intuitive responses, but, in a well-illustrated and absorbing account, he shows us when and how our intuitive judgments can be harnessed and applied and how to assess their utility and validity."*
Joe Raelin, The Knowles Chair for Practice-Oriented Education, Northeastern University, USA

"This timely, well researched and accessible book takes intuition out of the shadows and provides practical guidance to solve thorny problems."
Sebastian Bailey, Global Product Director, The Mind Gym

The Intuitive Mind

The Intuitive Mind

Profiting from the Power of Your Sixth Sense

Eugene Sadler-Smith

WILEY

A John Wiley & Sons, Ltd., Publication

This edition first published 2010
© 2010 John Wiley & Sons, Ltd

Registered office
John Wiley & Sons Ltd, The Atrium, Southern Gate, Chichester, West Sussex, PO19 8SQ,
United Kingdom

For details of our global editorial offices, for customer services and for information about
how to apply for permission to reuse the copyright material in this book please see our
website at www.wiley.com.

Library of Congress Cataloging-in-Publication Data

Sadler-Smith, Eugene.
  The intuitive mind: profiting from the power of your sixth sense / by Eugene Sadler-Smith.
    p. cm.
  Includes bibliographical references and index.
  ISBN 978-0-470-72143-8
1. Intuition. 2. Brain. I. Title.
  BF315.5.B45 2009
  153.4′4—dc22

                                                                    2009027976

ISBN 978-0-470-72143-8

A catalogue record for this book is available from the British Library.

Set in 11/16pt ITC Garamond Light by SNP Best-set Typesetter Ltd., Hong Kong
Printed in Great Britain by TJ International Ltd, Padstow, Cornwall, UK

CONTENTS

ACKNOWLEDGEMENTS

The ideas behind *The Intuitive Mind* are the product of many stimulating interchanges and collaborations with colleagues too numerous to mention individually in both the academic and business worlds, and including those at the University of Surrey (UK), TiasNimbas (Netherlands), Society for Organisational Learning (SOL-UK), and the European Learning Styles Network. I am very grateful to Cinla Akinci (University of Surrey) for her very careful reading of the typeset manuscript. My sincere thanks in particular go to Rosemary Nixon, Executive Editor at John Wiley and Sons, who not only commissioned the project and thereby demonstrated insight and intuition in abundance, she also thought of an inspired title for the book.

INTRODUCTION – YOUR MOST VALUABLE ASSET

In a world of uncertainty and unparalleled change people in general, and leaders and managers in particular, are forced to ask themselves fresh and searching questions about what it is that they can truly rely upon when times get tough – what are their most important and valuable assets? In the face of the 2008 credit crunch and subsequent recession of 2009 millions of ordinary people were forced to ask this very question. Was their most valuable asset the house they owned, their stocks and shares, or even their job? Regrettably events that surfaced in 2008–2009 brought home to millions across the world the fact that taken-for-granted supposed high-value assets such as property and financial wealth can nose dive out of the control of individual citizens, employees and company bosses, and leave governments standing by, virtually helpless. Shares can end up worth little more than the paper they're written on, a home can be worth less than the mortgage taken to buy it and businesses can downsize at the drop of a hat. The wider knock-on effects of company lay-offs, closures, bankruptcy, unemployment, threats of deflation and the spectre of civil unrest can be traumatic.

But the gloom of economic recession has brought about for many people the startling realisation that the most valuable asset that an employee, leader or manager can own actually is something that can't be taken away from them or owned by someone else; its multiplier effect can be extraordinary; it can be used to create other assets such as a new job or a business venture; it's perfectly natural and eminently sustainable; under the right conditions and with the right care and attention it can show real and permanent growth in value; moreover it's a guaranteed lifelong asset. It can empower and emancipate citizens and employees and loosen the grip of inept and immoral leaders. As a leader, manager, employee or citizen your most valuable asset isn't held in a bank vault, or in bricks and mortar or on a company balance sheet, it's held inside a much more secure but quite fragile place – your head – and is the twin portfolio of assets comprised of your analytical mind and your intuitive mind.

But why 'minds' rather than 'mind'? Recent scientific advances in psychology and cognitive neuroscience show that the human species has evolved two distinct systems of thinking ('two minds') which are the foundations not only of our reasoning processes,[1] but of our feelings and behaviours as well. Each of the two minds we all possess is a unique and valuable asset both in personal and professional life.

The analytical mind is the asset that our education and training sets out to nurture, condition and discipline from the time we start kindergarten to the time we leave college, and beyond; for example, many MBA courses are heavily – perhaps overly – analytical and hard-data driven. The analytical mind gives us the power to compute, reason and problem solve. However it's only 50% of the design spec that nature built into our species' capacities for thinking, problem solving, creating, judging and deciding. Alongside the analytical mind, there's the mental asset that goes largely unnoticed and, certainly in most businesses, largely untapped – the intuitive mind. But if we take a closer look at the commercial world we find that there are some very significant figures who have seen its potential and realised the value of this asset.

Sony Walkman, Starbucks Coffee and Virgin, as well as being highly successful, global brands, have at least one other thing in common: the senior executives in each of these firms have claimed that spontaneous intuition and business instinct – the products of the intuitive mind – have been crucial in the management and decision-making processes of their companies. For these executives their own and the intuitive minds of their employees are vital items in the human resource base of their businesses. Indeed it's not just these three, many other successful business leaders are singled out by the fact that they deploy their own intuition and that of their employees skilfully in the right place and at the right time in the management of their enterprises in the pursuit of profit and the creation of wealth.

The examples of Akio Morita of Sony, Howard Schultz of Starbucks and Sir Richard Branson of Virgin testify to the importance of the intuitive mind in creating new products and innovating new business ventures that have not only created wealth for individuals, companies and nations, but also impacted on the lives of millions of people worldwide by producing products and services that have shaped vital aspects of modern life. For these companies, and many others, the intuitive mind has been one of their most powerful assets. Akio Morita (Sony) described intuition as essential for the creativity that is the touchstone of technological innovation and new product development:

Machines and computers cannot be creative in themselves, because creativity requires something more than the processing of existing information. It requires human thought, spontaneous intuition and a lot of courage.[2]

Howard Schultz's (Starbucks) experience testifies to the emotional charge that comes with creative intuitions that if interpreted and followed through in the right way may signal a unique business opportunity:

> It happened in the spring of 1983. I had been at Starbucks for a year, and the company had sent me to Milan to attend an international housewares show. The morning after I arrived, I decided to walk to the show. During my stroll through the centre of the city, I noticed espresso bars on almost every street corner. What struck me emotionally was the ritual and romance of each coffeehouse. The bartenders, called baristas, had a strong bond with customers. All kinds of people gathered and chatted at the bars, which served as extensions of the front porch in each neighbourhood. Right then it struck me like a lightning rod: Why not bring the concept to America? Starbucks could be re-created to do just that. The vision was so overwhelming, *I began shaking.*[3]

Sir Richard Branson (Virgin) in his autobiography acknowledges that for him gut feeling is a vital ingredient in his entrepreneurial judgement and business venturing decisions:

> I make up my mind about someone within thirty seconds of meeting that person. In the same way that I tend to make up my mind about people within thirty seconds of meeting them, I also make up my mind about a business proposal within thirty seconds and whether it excites me. I rely far more on gut instinct than researching huge amounts of statistics.[4]

It isn't just highly successful business executives who have 'gut instincts' about people, events and situations and who use intuition to make important decisions. Nature, through the processes of evolution, has equipped *Homo sapiens* with a highly-sophisticated perceptual, processing and decision-making system that operates without effort and beyond our conscious awareness.

We all have intuition, we've all experienced its effects, and we've all lived with the consequences of listening to it or of ignoring it. It works in parallel with the analytical mind, and both minds are needed if we're to perform, profit and grow in our professional and personal lives.

The intuitive mind probably evolved as a neurobiological alarm bell that acted as an early warning radar, offering help in deciding what or what not to do next, who or who not to trust and if, when and how to take important decisions. As a result it's a guidance system which often errs on the side of caution because our well-being and survival are its number one priorities. Like a complex computer-based simulator the intuitive mind provides a window on the future, enabling users to hypothesise future problems and possibilities. But as well as signalling danger ahead, the intuitive mind also flags up opportunity and the signals it posts within conscious awareness can predict what might or might not happen, the rewards that may be reaped and the hazards that might be encountered on the road ahead.

Unfortunately the intuitive mind can't communicate directly with us in the normal language of our conscious awareness – words. To get its message across it speaks a different language – that of 'gut feeling' or 'hunch'. It's a biologically ancient body-mind system, but as is the case with even the most advanced digital technology, one of its drawbacks is that it isn't 100 % reliable. The intuitive blip that we sense on the screen of our consciousness can be misunderstood and misinterpreted, overlooked or ignored. Sometimes its predictions can take us to the wrong place and we may, at our peril, confuse its voice with other more feeble but potentially dangerous voices such as logical errors, bias, prejudice and wishful thinking.

How can we steer clear of these pitfalls? The answer, as with any sophisticated system, is that we need a users' manual to help us understand both how the system works and how to use it as effectively as possible. Some mystics take the view that the intuitive mind is the home of a sacrosanct 'sixth sense' which is inhibited and limited in its power by any attempts to understand it. This is one view, but the position adopted in this book is that the workings of the intuitive mind:

1. are neither magical nor paranormal;
2. can be explained scientifically.

Such a position gives us the capability to understand and harness the power of our 'sixth sense' in the world of business and management, whilst not conflicting with the spiritual perspective taken towards intuition and the mind in certain systems of philosophy and practice such as Buddhism. From the point of view of developing better intuitive judgement in professional or personal life, an appreciation of the principles which the designer – nature – built into the intuitive mind and which guide its operation is crucial. With this in mind this book is based on five fundamental assumptions:

1. The basic design spec of our species is that we have an intuitive mind and an analytical mind.
2. Western societies and business organisations in particular have privileged the analytical mind over the intuitive mind.
3. The intuitive mind can be powerful or perilous in its effects on the judgements we make and decisions we take.
4. Understanding the intuitive mind gives us the power to take more informed decisions in our personal and professional lives.
5. The intuitive mind is one of our most important and valuable but under-exploited assets.

Finally a word of caution: the terms 'intuitive mind' and 'analytical mind' are metaphors for systems that are the basis of two types of thinking each of which is useful and appropriate under different sets of circumstances. In the business world, if harnessed correctly, they're the most sustainable, hard-to-copy and therefore valuable source of competitive advantage. But any tendency on my part towards anthropomorphic language and the depiction of analytical and intuitive homunculi inside our skulls is a deliberate exaggeration for the purposes only of explication. Whether or not there are literally two minds, and in which specific brain regions they may one day be found, is interesting but not wholly relevant for our purposes. It's the effect of these two types of thinking on the ways we perceive, think, feel and act in managerial situations which is vitally important. The practice of intuition in business is as old as management itself, the study of intuition in management is in its infancy and the development of training techniques for developing managers' intuitive minds is only now being conceived of, systematised and evaluated.[5] The answer to the fundamental question of 'can intuition be developed?' is, from the perspective offered in this book, an unequivocal and resounding 'yes'. Professional experience, knowledge of the science of intuition and an informed self-awareness are the building blocks of one of your deepest and most durable assets – your 'intuitive intelligence'.

NOTES

[1]Evans, J. St. B.T. (2003) In two minds: dual process accounts of reasoning, *Trends in Cognitive Sciences*, **7**(10): 454–9.

[2]Morita, A. (1991) 'Selling to the world: the Sony Walkman story', In J. Henry and D. Walker (Eds) *Managing Innovation*, London: Sage Publications, p. 191.

[3]Interview 1998, 'King bean', *Your Company*, **8**(3), (emphases added).

[4]Branson, R. 2005. *Losing My Virginity: how I've survived, had fun and made a fortune doing business my way*, London: Virgin books: 120 & 152.

[5]For example: Sadler-Smith, E. & Burke, L.A. 2009. Fostering intuition in management education: activities and resources, *Journal of Management Education*, **33**(2): 239–62; Sadler-Smith, E. and Shefy, E. 2007. Developing intuitive awareness in management education. *Academy of Management Learning and Education*, **6**(2): 1–20.

Chapter 1

INTUITIVE MINDWARE

In this chapter I present the central idea of this book: that we each have two minds in one brain, an 'intuitive mind' and an 'analytical mind'. The chapter goes on to describe four distinctive features of the intuitive mind, namely that it speaks in the language of feelings; it's fast and spontaneous in its operation; it's a holistic 'pattern-recognition enabled system'; and it offers hypotheses rather than certainties.

Some years ago a man I'll refer to as 'Joe' featured in a BBC TV documentary called 'Brain Story'. Joe suffered from severe epilepsy which led to surgeons severing the connections between the left and the right hemispheres of his brain in order to treat his condition. After the surgery it soon became apparent that there had been an unintended consequence: as well as the beneficial outcome of his surgery Joe ended up, literally, with two separate brains. His party trick was to visualise two different shapes independently with each of his brains, for example a circle and a square, and draw one with each hand at the same time. Studies of Joe and hundreds more like him in a programme of scientific research that spanned half a century has revealed that the brain's two hemispheres control vastly different aspects of thought and action: for example, the left hemisphere is dominant for language and speech, while the right specialises in spatial tasks.[1]

The evidence for *Homo sapiens'* 'two brains' design is unequivocal: but what about *mind*? Is there more than one mind lurking inside our skulls? Can the 'two minds model' explain why reason ('head') and feeling ('heart') pull us in different directions, why we're often 'in two minds' and unable to 'make up our mind'? How can we reconcile and integrate these two systems of thinking and reasoning in a world where we can't prevaricate forever, in which options have to be narrowed down, and where decisions have to be taken?

In Two Minds

The idea of the human psyche (which is taken from a Greek word meaning 'soul') as having two sides isn't new. For example in ancient Greece – the god Apollo signified order, rationality and self-discipline alongside Dionysus – who represented the chaotic, instinctive and frenzied side of human nature. In ancient as well as modern-day Chinese wisdom the mental force of Yin signifies a 'front-of-the-mind' intellect which coexists alongside Yang – a 'back-of-the-mind' intuition.[2] Not only was this duality important to the ancient Greeks and Chinese, it also recurs throughout history. Humanity has witnessed the light and dark sides of political and business leadership and the two minds concept is a duality that's reflected in many of our cultural icons, for example Shakespeare's 'thing of darkness'[3] or R.L. Stevenson's *Dr. Jekyll and Mr. Hyde*. It's as relevant today as ever because:

1. it says something fundamental about the two-sidedness of human nature;
2. we can profit by balancing these two sides of our nature both in our professional and personal lives;
3. the analytical mind is no longer sufficient by itself in the face of the challenges that managers and business leaders are faced with.

The idea of two minds ('intuitive' and 'analytical'[4]) in one brain is a dominant theme in modern psychology. Apollo/Dionysus and Yin/Yang, not to mention the dark and mysterious sub-consciousnesses in the works of Sigmund Freud and Carl Gustav Jung, are old ideas that contain undoubted insights, but from the perspective of the 21st century they're the prehistory of the intuitive mind. Modern ideas about the two-sidedness of human consciousness draw on concepts ranging from evolutionary biology through to 'dual-mind' models from cognitive and social psychology; moreover for those interested in the micro-world of the intuitive mind the latest brain imaging techniques are beginning to pinpoint the neural geography of some of these processes. The modern view of *Homo sapiens* two minds is summarised below:

⚷ Key Facts No. 1: The Modern View of the Two Minds

Evolved at different times	The analytical mind is a modern 'up-grade' that came on the scene perhaps no more than 50,000 years ago coinciding with developments in tool making, cave art and religion.
Are under different degrees of conscious control	The intuitive mind has a strong and sometimes a-rational (not *irrational*) will of its own. The analytical mind, on the other hand, is the rule maker and rule follower, it's a personal mental 'enforcer' which can check the excesses but also inhibit the potential of the intuitive mind, often to excess in bureaucratic and rule bound business organisations.

Complement and conflict	Sometimes the analytical mind and the intuitive mind work together in balance and harmony, at other times they contradict each other and compete for attention and for control of our thoughts, feelings and actions.
Exercise a major influence on career, personal and life decisions	This is especially true in business management where many of the best companies seem to have developed the knack of treading the fine line between the intellectual rigour and discipline of analysis and the creative freedom of intuition.

We're aware of the analytical mind not only because it's under conscious control, but also because it 'talks' to us as inner speech in the language we're most familiar with – words. We associate the idea of 'the mind' itself with logic and rational thought. Its workings are the epitome of human 'intellect' and reason. We're perhaps not so familiar with the idea of an intuitive mind because it's not under our conscious control (we're not aware of the processes that lead up to an intuitive moment); it works effortlessly (having an intuition is easy, we don't will it to happen) and it hasn't got a voice (it can't speak to us in the language of words, but it uses 'hunch' and 'gut feeling' instead). Some go as far as to imbue intuition with a 'sixth sense' of magic and mystery, but these ideas are dismissed by many in the scientific community as naïve and fanciful. We associate the idea of 'intuition' with the heart rather than the head, and in management 'going with your gut' is seen in many circles as the antithesis of rationality and, for that reason, undesirable and to be avoided if at all possible.

As *Homo sapiens*, literally 'wise man', we pride ourselves on our distinctive capacity to be rational – whether we are in practice is a different matter. As many political psychologists will vouch for, when it comes to choosing a Prime Minister or President the heart often wins out over the head. In elections people tend to vote by going with their judgement of how a candidate makes them feel (in other words their 'gut'), and to many a candidate's cost the slightest slip of the tongue can undermine voters' feelings of trust. For example, in 1984 only a few months before the US elections President Ronald Regan was bidding for re-election. With an open microphone he prepared for a weekly radio address by doing a sound check with the following tongue-in-cheek assertion: 'My fellow Americans, I'm pleased to tell you today that I've signed legislation that will outlaw Russia forever. We begin bombing in five minutes'. Millions heard his words including the Russians who, not unreasonably, demanded an apology. Reagan's popularity plummeted; he won in the November election, but with a much-reduced margin of victory. Evolution has hard-wired human beings to gravitate to potential leaders who bring 'emotional dividends', those who inspire our hopes or assuage our fears.[5] Nowhere was this more apparent than in post-George W. Bush America with the election of Barack Obama.

From a purely practical point of view we need an analytical and an intuitive mind to get by day-in day-out. Without two minds life would be so effortful and demanding that we'd end up being unable to function, overwhelmed by the number, range and complexity of the tasks we face. For example, on a quite basic level the intuitive mind makes it possible to do fairly complex, but everyday, tasks in personal and professional life on 'auto-pilot'. Getting home from work by walking, driving the car, or taking train or bus is quite a complex activity done without much conscious thought at all (think about the first time you made what is now a familiar home to work journey). Giving over some of the basic 'housekeeping' of our lives to the lower reaches of the intuitive mind means we can devote our precious analytical thinking resources to other less mundane issues. But this is not to say that tasks completed on 'auto-pilot' use intuition as such; they don't, they're purely habituated responses that share some of the features of the type of intuition that is the focus of this book (for example, they don't take up much conscious thinking power).

It's the complex, informed intuitions which form the basis of managers' and leaders' business instincts and these work best when managers and leaders have the requisite amount of experience to draw on in order to be able to make judgements or come to decisions based on what worked well in the past. These judgements can manifest themselves in everything from how to close a sales deal or knowing when and where to invest on the stock market, to what's the right direction in which to take a business. The analytical mind is (re-)engaged:

1. when there's an unexpected turn of events, for example when an intuitive entrepreneur has to re-think when a business opportunity has suddenly become closed off;
2. if a manager needs to take decisions that haven't been encountered before, for example when moving into overseas markets where culture-specific intuitions may not work.

The intuitive mind comes into its own when we need to make complex personal and social judgements in all walks of life. Often the most complex decisions we face are people-related or job-related and many of these don't have a clear right or wrong answer at the time when they have to be taken. For example, what could be more important, or speculative, than deciding where to live, who to marry, who to hire, whether or not to take a job offer, or which business to invest in?

The Two Minds Model

The two minds model, which has been a dominant theme in psychology for several decades, has been given renewed impetus by scientific developments in a variety of areas, including evolutionary biology and cognitive neuroscience.

1. The analytical mind is a recently evolved powerful, general purpose system with the power to monitor, intervene and over-ride the intuitive mind – it's a cognitive heavyweight that can solve some of life's most demanding intellectual and computational problems.
2. The intuitive mind is a more ancient much nimbler, fleet-of-foot set of systems that operates effortlessly alongside the analytical mind. It's especially potent when we're faced with important social, aesthetic, creative and moral judgements – all of which are crucial aspects of decision-making in businesses that aspire to be people-centred, sustainable, responsible and ethical.

Research conducted by psychologists and others over the past decade and a half suggests that the differences between the intuitive and analytical minds can be summarised as follows:[6]

🔑 Key Facts No. 2: The Two Minds Model

Analytical Mind	Intuitive Mind
Narrow 'band width' ('serial processor')	Broad 'band width' ('parallel processor')
Controlled (effortful) process	Automatic (effortless) process
Works step-by-step	Works by whole pattern recognition

Conscious (processes open to direct introspection)	Non-conscious (processes not open to direct introspection)
'Talks' in language of words	'Talks' in the language of feelings
Faster formation (learns quickly)	Slower formation (learns slowly)
Slower operation	Faster operation
Evolutionarily recent (perhaps tens of thousands of years old)	Evolutionarily ancient (perhaps hundreds of thousands of years old)

The interplay between the analytical and the intuitive mind is an inherent tension in the human psyche. My experience of being 'me' is that my thoughts and actions are things which the conscious analytical 'me' determines and which I control. However, if I stick to this restricted view of 'me' I may in fact be fooling myself and operating under an illusion of control in spite of the fact that my non-conscious, intuitive mind may have its hand on the tiller guiding my thoughts, feelings and actions in ways that are unknowable to me.[7] The analytical mind operates on the assumption, or perhaps under the delusion, that it's in charge, when actually the intuitive mind may have a greater say in what goes on than we prefer to think.

THE SCIENCE OF THE INTUITIVE MIND – WHO'S IN CHARGE?

Researchers working at the Max Planck Institute in Leipzig found that by monitoring people's brain signals in decision-making experiments they could predict which button-pressing option they'd take a full seven seconds before they consciously took the decision. Normally researchers are interested in what happens when a decision is made or shortly after, the Leipzig scientists were interested in what happens immediately *before* a conscious choice is arrived at. They gave participants the freedom to choose whether they wanted to press a button with their left or right hand, and when to do so. Their aim was to find out what happens in the brain just before the person *felt* (was aware) they'd made their decision.

By scanning participants' brains the scientists were able to 'mind read' their intentions and able to predict participants' decisions seven seconds before participants themselves were aware they'd made a choice. The lead researcher John-Dylan Haynes commented that: 'Many processes in the brain occur automatically and without involvement of our consciousness. This prevents our mind from being overloaded by simple routine tasks. But when it comes to decisions we tend to assume they are made by our conscious mind'. The research has implications beyond simple decisions, for example it opens up the question of what is meant by 'free will' – and questions of who (the conscious analytical mind or the non-conscious intuitive mind) decides and when.

From the point of view of the two minds model the intuitive mind may sometimes unconsciously prepare a choice in advance. A big advantage of having two minds is that an intuitive choice can be reversed by the intervention of the analytical mind[8] (or vice versa).

Source: Soon, C.S., Brass, M., Heinze, H-J. and Haynes, J.-D. (2008) Unconscious determinants of free decisions in the human brain. *Nature Neuroscience*, **11**: 543–5.

Even though the non-conscious intuitive mind is an important influence on our day-to-day living we're for the most part blithely unaware of just how much power it has. So how do we know it's there and what should we look for? Four things stand out as the hallmarks of the intuitive mind:

1. Speaks in the language of feelings.
2. Is fast and spontaneous.
3. Is holistic.
4. Can offer hypotheses, but not certainties.

The Intuitive Mind Speaks in the Language of Feelings

Because the intuitive mind can't 'talk' it needs a compelling way to get its message across. One of the most forceful arguments that nature has at its disposal to influence any organism's behaviour, including humans, is feeling. From our own personal experiences and the accounts other people give we know that intuition is visceral – it's driven by inward feelings rather than conscious reasoning. Howard Schultz of Starbucks had the visceral sense that he was onto a big idea when he reported physically shaking at the thought of bringing the Italian style coffee experience to the United States. Allegedly so did Ray Kroc when he took on the financial risk in starting the McDonalds empire on the basis of a 'feeling in his funny bone' that ran counter to the advice of his financiers.

The feelings that come with intuition can be so powerful as to convince us that an intuitive judgement is valid and correct even if we can't explain why ('intuitions are sometimes wrong, but never in doubt'). As a result intuitive judgements usually fall into two groups:

1. Compelling and accurate, and it would be very convenient if this were to be the case 100% of the time, sadly life isn't like that.
2. Compelling and inaccurate, and therefore an invaluable skill is to be able to weed out inaccurate and feeble intuitions from those intuitions that have something potentially useful to say to us.

One of the facts of intuitive life is that intuitions have evolved to be hard to ignore. The conviction they carry comes from the powerful hold that any kind of feeling can take on our thoughts and actions. That said there's an important distinction to be drawn: the feelings that come with intuition are different from the feelings that come with a 'passionate' emotion like anger, love or hate:

1. When was the last time you experienced a really strong emotion, such as anger? What was it like? How intense was it? How long did the feeling of anger itself last for – seconds, minutes, hours, days, weeks, years?

2. Think about the last time you experienced a strong 'gut feeling' – you felt that you knew something but you couldn't explain why. What was it like? How intense was it? How long did the gut feeling last for?

Fast emotionally-driven responses can create intense anger, sadness, happiness, fear or disgust, but fortunately they tend to be short-lived (for example, most people are physically incapable of going around in a rage for days on end – it would simply be emotionally exhausting). Whilst emotions are fleeting, the subtle feelings that come with intuitive judgements are less intense but they can linger on and, once experienced, be called-upon again and re-imagined. Intuitions differ from emotions, and mixing them up can be perilous. For example, if we feel a romantic attraction to another person, or are passionately committed to what we feel is a great business venture our emotions may overwhelm our intuitive, and perhaps better, judgement. Given the fact that intuitions are charged with feelings but aren't emotionally-charged, a vital skill is to be able to disentangle intuition's subtle feelings from intense emotional feelings and the attachment and cravings that strong emotions bring.

THE SCIENCE OF THE INTUITIVE MIND – EMOTIONS AND FEELINGS

Psychologists often use the broad term 'affect', meaning a feeling, emotion or desire, from the Latin *affectus* meaning 'disposition' (not to be confused with 'effect'). The English word 'emotion', on the other hand, is derived from the French word *émouvoir* meaning 'excite'. As the world-renowned neurologist Antonio Damasio reminds us, emotions and feelings are not equivalent: an emotion is a pattern of chemical and neural responses produced by the brain; a feeling is a subjective mental representation of the physiological changes that come with an emotion. This is a nuanced distinction: emotions are targeted at the body (for example to enable 'flight' or 'fight'), whereas feelings are an awareness of the emotional state. The feeling of an emotion alerts the brain to threats and challenges,[9] or even opportunities, faced by the organism. We experience feelings as changes in the 'body landscape'. Human consciousness buys, in Damasio's words, an 'enlarged protection policy' because it enables us to not merely respond to threats and opportunities (as an animal might) but also to project, plan ahead and imagine.

Source: Damasio, A.R. (1994) *Descartes' Error: emotion, reason and the human brain.* New York: HarperCollins (p.133).

Intuition arrives in conscious awareness tagged with either a positive feeling or a negative feeling, and this affective 'tag' can work in two different ways:

1. Negatively-tagged intuitions are a signal for avoidance.
2. Positively-tagged intuitions are a signal for attraction.

Because intuition probably evolved to help our savannah-dwelling ancestors survive the natural and social hazards of Pleistocene life it errs on the side of caution and avoidance. Like biological reflexes, instincts and emotions, the intuitive mind 'kicks-in' on the basis of a snap-shot perception, before the analytical mind has the chance to intervene. After all, mistaking an innocent stranger on the savannah for a potentially life-threatening foe and therefore treating them with caution would have improved our ancestors' chances of survival, even if it eventually turned out that the stranger posed no threat.

Whether we like it or not some of these hangovers from our evolutionary past come into play in personal and professional life, the difference is that in the modern world we don't have to contend with the life-or-death situations that faced our ancestors. Therefore I can't, or don't need to, simply 'trust my gut' no matter how powerful the feeling is – I have an analytical mind which also may have something useful, if not vital, to say. For example, what does a manager do with two potential job hires – both with equally good résumés, great scores on a battery of psychometric and aptitude tests and work simulations, and excellent track records – one 'feels' right, the other doesn't but it's hard to say exactly why?

In this situation ignoring intuition might lead to a bad and very expensive decision, but blindly following it might lead to rejecting a good hire or legal trouble. So what to do? Following-up gut feeling by getting more objective data, for example from written references or making a phone call to a candidate's previous boss can help you to decide if gut-feeling is the basis for a good or bad judgement call.[10] Intuitions are invaluable early warning signals and filtering devices that can be combined with analysis to enable managers, leaders and business venturers to project the future and plan ahead.

In business organisations many of the situations that managers and leaders encounter are complex, messy and fluid, and high stakes judgements have to be taken on a daily basis. Unfortunately two of the inconvenient facts of intuitive life are that: firstly, we can never know what another person's intuition is like, for example how intense or compelling it is; and secondly, even people with highly-tuned intuition can find it difficult to convince others why they find their personal gut feeling compelling and important.

🔑 **Key Facts No. 3: The Significance of Gut Feeling**

Feelings speak volumes	Feelings are the language of the intuitive mind; words are the language of the analytical mind.
Words aren't the whole story	Words, even though they're good for putting together a logical argument, are only an approximation of a feeling – they aren't the feelings themselves.
Our intuitions affect others	As social beings we often have to share our intuitions with our family, friends and colleagues to give them a window into our thoughts, feelings, motivations and intentions.

When we use words to express gut feeling they may fall a little way and sometimes a long way short, and unfortunately things can get lost in translation.

INTUITION WORK OUT NO. I: WHAT HAPPENS WHEN YOU INTUIT?

The phenomenon of intuition is unique, personal and subjective. I can't know what intuition is like for someone else because I can't inhabit their body. The account I or anybody else, for that matter, offers of intuition is inherently subjective.

Have you ever experienced a situation in which you arrived at a compelling judgement about a person, object or situation but were unable to say *how* or *why* you arrived at that view? If you've had such an experience the chances are that it was your intuitive mind that was speaking to you.

Stop for a moment: what was the situation and what was the judgement that you arrived at?

How would you express the way the intuitive judgement presented itself if you had to explain it to another person? What was it like? Where was the intuition? Did you have any particular feelings? Did any particular metaphor or image come to mind?

Thinking more broadly, are there any aspects of your work or personal life where your intuition has proven to be particularly effective?

- Cast your mind back to intuitive episodes in your life, try to recall the experiences. What happens when you intuit?
- Has your intuition been friend or foe? Has it helped or hindered in judgement and decision-making?

Reflecting on 'what happens when you intuit?' and 'what happened when you followed your intuition?' are the two most important building blocks of intuitive intelligence.

The Intuitive Mind is Fast and Spontaneous

I've yet to meet anyone who can will an intuition into being on demand and on the spur of the moment. Intuition is something that happens involuntarily and unexpectedly. For example, on meeting someone for the first time we may have an instantaneous reaction to whether we like them, feel we can trust them, or feel attracted to or repelled by them – it can happen within seconds. Intuition's spontaneity is useful because there are many complex situations where we need to make fast judgements, for example whether to engage with someone socially, whether to grasp a business opportunity that's available momentarily, or what action to take when a quick-fire decision is needed.

In social domains such as management and leadership intuitive snap-shots of people's behaviour convey a wealth of information and, often unwittingly, we give away a great deal about ourselves in the first few seconds of any social interaction. These snap-shots, sometimes called 'thin slices' (the subject of Malcolm Gladwell's best selling book *Blink*), can be uncannily accurate. But we need to be vigilant and intelligent about such instinctive responses because fast intuitive judgements about a particular person, object or event may be influenced not only by emotions but also by our personal prejudices, expectations or moods.

One example is stereotyping. Whether we like it or not, stereotypes affect the way many people see others and especially how people who aren't in the same social group as ourselves (the 'out group') are judged.[11] One of the perils of poorly-developed social intuition is that it can lead to people being evaluated in terms of social categories that we personally happen to approve or disapprove of. Poorly developed social intuition is feeble because it's biased and prejudiced. Preferring or favouring someone because they're in our own social class, race or gender isn't intuition, it's race, class or gender prejudice and discrimination. Judging a situation in the hope of an outcome we desire or that we feel is deserved isn't intuition, it's wishful thinking. On top of this our general emotional tone also complicates the picture – if we're in a positive mood we're likely to put greater faith in intuition.

One way to weed out good intuition from bad intuition is to consciously reflect on your motivations and moods, and if in serious doubt deploy the safety net of the analytical mind, or ask someone else to act as a sounding board. The tempting and easy reaction to a gut feeling might be to follow it unthinkingly, but often this can be a dumb way to use intuition. On the other hand, if an intuition can stand up to your own and other people's scrutiny this should give you more confidence in it. Before you 'go-with-your-gut' you can ask yourself if it's really an intuitive judgement or is it one of the four enemies of intuition:

⚒ Application No. 1: The Four Enemies of Intuition

An emotional judgement?	If it's emotional what are the tell-tale signs (for example, intense, short-lived)?
A prejudiced judgement?	If it's prejudiced who are you being prejudiced against and why (for example, gender, class, ethnicity)?
A biased judgement?	If it's biased what's the source of your bias (for example, are you seeing what you want to see, ignoring the facts)?
Un-warranted wishful thinking?	If it's wishful thinking what's behind it (for example, desire, hope, and craving)?

There's also an important paradox at work: the intuitive mind is fleet-of-foot, but it's a slow learner and, unless we're hard-wired to be able to perform certain skills intuitively, it requires repeated exposure, experience and feedback in order to develop good intuitions. While some people may be naturally gifted, many have good social intuitions because it's a skill they've been developing all of their lives. Work-related intuitive judgements, on the other hand, are acquired in adulthood. If we change the direction of our careers we may need to unlearn old intuitions and develop new ones. Unlike the intuitive mind, the analytical mind, even though it's relatively slow and deliberate in its workings, can absorb new knowledge very quickly, from listening, reading, watching and so forth. In the work situation learning and practice inside and outside one's comfort zone, allied to feedback on performance, build what the psychologist Robert J. Sternberg refers to as 'street smarts' – the practical intelligence that is the bedrock of informed intuition.

The Intuitive Mind is Holistic

The intuitive mind is 'holistic' in two ways: firstly, its broad 'band-width' means that it can handle the bigger picture; secondly, it's a body-mind process in which thinking and feeling work together rather than separately.

For experienced professionals working in areas ranging from management to medicine or golf to gambling, the overall 'gist' of a situation can flag up when something is out of kilter, and whether or not a closer look is called for. For example, many experienced law enforcement officers put faith in their ability to recognise when something doesn't fit – sometimes referred to as a 'JDLR' – 'just doesn't look right'. This drug bust story illustrates the power of the JDLR:[12]

> Picture a summer evening in a large American city where under-cover narcotics officers are on a 'buy-bust' operation purchasing illegal substances from street dealers. Having successfully 'bought' they alert their colleagues, waiting in unmarked vehicles, of the dealers' descriptions. The unmarked cars approach the street corner to arrest the dealers. In the ensuing bust Officer A for some reason yells to his colleagues to 'get the one in the red shirt, he's got a gun' – not one of the individuals is identified as

a dealer – but to Officer A he's a 'JDLR' for sure. The guy in the red shirt begins to run down the sidewalk; he's chased, surrounded by narcotics officers, and has no choice but to surrender. Sure enough, underneath his red shirt is a .357 revolver.

But how did the officer 'know' the guy had a gun? In recalling these events later under detailed questioning it was clear that the officer had actually noticed-without-noticing a number of unusual but unobvious things which by themselves didn't amount to that much, but which taken as whole were instantly picked-up on by his intuitive mind. The suspect:

1. stood up and adjusted his waistband;
2. had a long sleeve shirt with the tails hanging out even though it was a warm summer evening;
3. turned away to walk in the opposite direction;
4. grabbed his waistband as if to secure a heavy object.

Not one of these four things amounted to very much in itself, but their combined effect was enough for the officer's intuitive mind to extract the gist of the situation as being: 'the guy in the red shirt may be armed and dangerous'. His gut feeling was swift, spontaneous, negatively-tagged and erred on the side of caution. It was only afterwards that his analytical mind, under questioning, had the time to make sense of events that had unfolded swiftly, spontaneously and holistically. This JDLR was an 'intuitive hit', but as we're all only too well aware it's possible for there to be tragic intuitive misses as well.

Good intuitive judgement in complex and time pressured situations often requires a great deal of information to be taken in all at once and parallel processed. Experience enables decision makers to sift relevant information from irrelevant information, making the parallel processing task easier. Decision makers with the experience to sort relevant from irrelevant information, even though they may not be able to explain fully what or how they do so (but simply 'feel'), are at a distinct advantage over novices and are less likely to make errors of judgement which may have serious consequences.

The archetypal view of the analytical mind is of a cool, calm, calculating machine unaffected by feelings. Machines, such as computers, process information dispassionately – affect is completely alien to them. The humble human being, by comparison, is a complex concoction of thoughts and feelings not designed for purely analytical thought, moreover the human mind and body aren't separate, they work together as one. If human beings had only an analytical mind to rely on for solving problems, making decisions and coming to judgements in many aspects of our lives would be much easier. It would be great to have a computer for a brain if all we ever had to do was compile spreadsheets, fill-out expense claims or do tax returns. But we don't, and whilst an analytical mind may be enough to get by with if you're a robot, it isn't enough for you or me. Our lives are much more varied, richer, passionate and complicated than the life of any calculating machine could ever be.

THE SCIENCE OF THE INTUITIVE MIND – MEMORY AND EMOTION

Memories are stored in our brains as separate components which are linked together in networks of associations to form an intricate web of interconnected facts, ideas, stories and feelings some of which are more easily available to our conscious mind than others. For one of these 'memory objects' to come into conscious awareness the level of activation of this across the web of associations has to reach a threshold level.

The different elements of the web each have 'weights' of varying strengths attached to them and some are tagged with feelings (they're affectively 'tagged'). The weight can be related to many things, including our emotional state when the memory was laid down. Emotional memories are often beneath the level of conscious awareness and not easily retrieved (Freud talked about them as 'repressed'), but they may be activated so that they exceed the threshold level in the presence of relevant cues from the environment. For example when you visit a certain place that has particularly fond or unpleasant feelings associated with it, memories of past events that took place there may be activated by any of the five senses and the scene vividly comes into conscious awareness.

Source: Le Doux, J.E. (1996) *The emotional brain: the mysterious underpinnings of emotional life,* New York: Simon and Schuster.

Emotional memories are strongly imprinted and once they're unleashed can have a fast and very powerful effect on our recall (for example, many people can remember exactly where they were and what they were doing when the news of Princess Diana's death was announced or on 9/11) and our judgement of a person, object or situation (we tend to feel good about and view favourably those places where we've spent happy times and feel bad about and be unfavourably disposed towards places where we've been less happy). If we experience a person, place, object or situation when we're in a highly emotional state it'll be remembered more vividly and the association will live on with the potential to be activated under the right conditions. Some have gone as far as to argue that the human gut, in which there are millions of nerve cells, has a 'mind of its own'. Even though gut feelings may manifest themselves in our bodies (including the gut) they don't originate there, they emanate from the brain as a result of the unconscious associative processes that take place in the complex web that is the basis of the intuitive mind.[13]

Contrary to what might be expected, having two minds, far from hindering us in making-up our mind, is not only beneficial, it's essential. The intuitive mind works together with the analytical mind in coming to a decision.

🗝 Key Facts No. 4: The Interplay of Intuition and Analysis

Infusion	Sending out 'gut feelings' that feed back into the brain and influence the way in which the analytical mind consciously weighs up the alternatives.
Anticipation	Influencing decision choices before the analytical mind is consciously aware or has time to weigh up the pros and cons – something which is indispensable in complex, people-related and time-pressured situations.

Visceral (bodily) experiences, including gut feelings, have a strong hold on how we think, judge and decide. The billionaire financier George Soros claimed that his body sends him an early warning signal when investment decisions may be about to go wrong:

> I used the onset of acute pain as a signal that there was something wrong in my portfolio. The backache didn't tell me *what* was wrong ... but it did prompt me to look for something amiss when I might not have done so otherwise.[14]

Intuition is the operation of a holistic system in which the body and the brain together process information – in this sense the 'intuitive mind' is actually a misnomer, but an acceptable one A better term might be the 'intuitive body-mind system'. This idea is found in a number of Eastern traditions such as Ayurveda, a medical system which integrates physical, mental, social and spiritual well being; and Buddhism in which mind and body are like 'two bundles of reeds supporting each other' and the 'self', if it exists at all, is nothing more or less than a series of impermanent cognitive (thinking) and affective (feeling) processes.[15] In a thought-provoking contribution to the debate about the nature of human consciousness the cognitive scientist Douglas Hofstadter considers 'I' to be a myth, but nonetheless indispensable, and the 'self' to be nothing more or less than 'a hallucination *hallucinated* by a hallucination'[16] and analogous to a video camera watching itself on a monitor with infinite regression of the images.

Along with the analytical mind, the intuitive mind isn't 'out there' disembodied from the brain or indeed other neural structures. It's not merely – to use a term from Descartes – 'lodged' in the body, it's a part of a highly-evolved and integrated psycho-physiological (body-mind) system. By accepting this and attuning ourselves to and being mindful of subtle changes in our 'body landscape'[17] or body-mind system it's possible to notice intuitions more lucidly, develop a heightened awareness of them, embrace them and use them more effectively.

The Intuitive Mind Offers Hypotheses

Benjamin Franklin's technique of 'moral or prudential algebra' is the forte of the analytical mind. Franklin offered it in his famous letter of 1772 to his nephew Joseph Priestly in order that young Joe should avoid any 'rash' steps. It goes like this:

> Take a decision that currently vexes you; write it at the top of a
> piece of paper; divide the paper into two columns; head one

column 'pro' and the other 'con'; over a three or four days' consideration make an exhaustive list of 'pros' and 'cons'; weigh them up, and where a 'pro' and a 'con' seem of equal value cross them both out; what's left in the balance sheet at the end of this process is the best answer.

You might like to try Ben Franklin's moral algebra next time you're faced with a complex, personal or people-related decision. As a many-time house hunter I've often been tempted to take his advice in order to help me to choose where to live. I'm naturally averse to cheating of any kind, but whenever I've tried formally weighing up the pros and cons I'm tempted to add in a 'fudge factor' so as to swing the balance of my evaluation towards my favoured option – the one I *like*. In house hunting and many other complex, judgemental decisions I often come to an instantaneous 'gut feeling' for what's right or wrong, and I'm not the only one, as this quote from a banking executive employed in an organisation that was largely immune from the excesses of the credit crunch testifies: 'I usually have a feeling before I start and when I try and analyse by putting down the pros and cons I tend to try and sway it towards my gut feeling'.[18] Whether it's right or wrong, or whether we like it or not, feelings figure prominently in decision making in spite of our best endeavours to be logical and analytical and the exhortations of others to be so.

Human beings in general have an aversion for uncertainty, and even though we may find it frustrating that we can't know if a decision will pay off it's a fact of life that we end up taking gambles of varying degrees of risk almost on a daily basis. This is true for many of life's major decisions – educational and career choices, marriage decisions, major purchases, family matters – we can never know for sure how things will turn out. Indeed, it's salutary to reflect on the fact that some of our most important decisions, although we may experience a feeling of certainty at the time, amount to little more than high-risk 'hypotheses' woven from the interplay of the intuitive and analytical minds.

Intuitive judgements, like any other hypothesis, are tested out only in the fullness of time as events unfurl and circumstances change. Managers who spend their professional lives confronted by choices are well aware of the risks associated with intuitive decision making, as another quote from a very experienced banking executive illustrates: 'I'd say that nearly all my decisions at work to a greater extent are based to some degree on gut feeling. There isn't always a right and a wrong answer; there are usually some answers which are definitely wrong and some which are definitely right, but there's usually never one right answer. The best answers tend to go on a gut feeling for which one you like the *feel* of'.[19]

THE SCIENCE OF THE INTUITIVE MIND – THE MAGIC AND MYSTERY OF THE INTUITIVE MIND

Psychologists examined whether or not a person's faith in intuition was related to their mood and their susceptibility to believing in ghosts and UFOs. In an experiment in which participants were shown seventeen-second video clips purportedly of UFO sightings and ghostly apparitions the researchers found that a more positive mood and greater faith in intuition together led participants to believe that the UFO or ghost in the video was real (tested by using a simple questionnaire). Too much faith in intuition may predispose people to interpret their experiences in paranormal ways especially when they're in a positive mood.

Non-rational beliefs (in things such as UFOs, ghosts and 'sympathetic magic' – making simple associations between objects and people, for example voodoo dolls, crystals, charms) may be rooted in a biologically ancient intuitive mind which learns about the world through powerful images and meaningful stories (such as fairy tales and myths) and simple intuitively appealing associations. Because they are intuitive such beliefs are difficult to counter with logic and rational argument[20] – a fact of life we see time and time again in superstitious behaviours and rituals, for example what possible direct effect can a 'lucky charm' bracelet or a superstitious ritual have on physical events? This might also help to explain why many people associate intuition with magic, clairvoyance, precognition, remote viewing and other psychic phenomena.

Source: King, L.A., Burton, C.M., Hicks, J.A. and Drigotas, S.M. (2007) Ghosts, UFOs and Magic: positive affect and the experiential system, *Journal of Personality and Social Psychology*, **92**(5): 905–19.

We're fortunate that we have two minds at our disposal and doubly fortunate that our analytical mind – the cognitive heavyweight – is consummate in not only formulating penetrating questions to interrogate how we feel about a particular choice but also in looking ahead:

1. Questioning can expose the reasons why a situation just didn't 'add up' in the intuitive mind's eye, and with insightful questioning the reasons might become clear.
2. Intuitive judgement can also be bolstered by hypothetically 'fast-forwarding' and inwardly watching the action unfold in your own Hollywood epic or TV soap opera in which you're the principal character.

But mental simulation on its own isn't enough. Mental simulations rely on consciously envisioning future states and upon the intuitive mind to provide an affective reaction to the envisioned future state. Experiment by running a mental simulation of a decision scenario you're faced with and watching events unfurl, in doing so ask yourself important questions such as: 'Can I imagine myself living in this place?', or 'How might I feel if I were to take this job offer?'. The skilful interweaving of thought and feeling, of the intuitive and analytical minds, is the foundation of an intelligent approach to intuition.

INTUITIVE INTELLIGENCE PRINCIPLE No. 1: ACKNOWLEDGE THE INTUITIVE MIND

We're one being with two minds – one analytical the other intuitive – both are products of our evolution. The intuitive mind extracts the 'gist' of a situation in order to produce judgements – 'intuitions', 'hunches' or 'gut feelings' – that are rapid, holistic, non-conscious and affective. At the end of the day neither the intuitive mind nor the analytical mind offers any guarantee for the accuracy of the 'advice' it offers in relation to the judgements and decisions that leaders and managers have to take. We're not forced to heed the intuitive mind's advice. The better we understand the 'back stage' processes the better-informed our intuitive judgements are likely to be. To get the best of both minds we need to be able to know when and how to use them. In complex judgemental situations we can combine informed intuitive judgement with mental fast-forwarding of the scenario, asking penetrating questions, and sensing how different outcomes might feel – how realistic and viable they are. The cornerstones of intuitive intelligence are the questions of 'what happens when you intuit?' and 'what happened when you intuited?'

NOTES

[1]Gazzaniga, M.S. (2005) Forty-five years of split-brain research and still going strong, *Nature Reviews: Neuroscience*, **6**: 653–9; 'The man with two brains' retrieved on 4th September 2008 from http://news.bbc. co.uk/1/hi/health/870311.stm.

[2]Anthony, C.K. (1998) *The Philosophy of the I Ching*, Stow, MA: Anthony Publishing Company; Wilhelm, R. (2000) The book of changes. In W. Bloom (Ed.) *Holistic Revolution: the essential reader*. London: Allen Lane, The Penguin Press, pp. 331–4.

[3]From *The Tempest* (Act V Scene 1), the magician Prospero's reference to his 'demi-devil' Caliban.

[4]'Dual process' theories use various names for the two minds depending upon their focus; my preferred terms are the 'intuitive mind/analytical mind'. See: Chaiken, S. and Trope, Y. (Eds) (1999) *Dual-process theories in social psychology*, New York: Guilford Press; Stanovich, K.E. and West, R.F. (2000) Individual differences in reasoning: implications for the rationality debate? *Behavioral and Brain Sciences*, **23**: 645–65.

[5]Begley, S. (2008) When it's head versus heart, the heart wins, *Newsweek*, February, retrieved on 4th September 2008 from http://www. newsweek.com/id/107601/page/1; 'Famous political faux pas', retrieved on 13th September 2008 from http://wcco.com/slideshows/political. faux.pa.20.688643.html.

[6]Epstein, S. (1994) Integration of the cognitive and the psychodynamic unconscious, *American Psychologist*, **49**: 709–24; Epstein, S., Pacini, R., Denes-Raj, V. and Heier, H. (1996) Individual differences in intuitive-experiential and analytical-rational thinking styles. *Journal of Personality and Social Psychology*, **71**, 390–405; Evans, J. St. B.T. (2003) In two minds: dual process accounts of reasoning, *Trends in Cognitive Sciences*, **7**(10): 454–9; Sloman, S.A. (1996) The empirical case for two systems of reasoning. *Psychological Bulletin*, **199**, 3–22; Smith, E. R. and DeCoster, J. (1999) Associative and rule based processing. In S. Chaiken and Y. Trope (Eds), *Dual-process theories in social psychology*, pp. 323–36. New York: Guilford Press; Stanovich, K.E. and West, R.F. (2000) 'Individual differences in reasoning: implications for the rationality debate?' *Behavioral and Brain Sciences*, **23**: 645–65.

[7] Bargh, J.A. and Ferguson, M.J. (2000) Beyond behaviourism: on the automaticity of higher mental processes, *Psychological Bulletin*, **126**(6): 925–45.

[8] Soon, C.S., Brass, M., Heinze, H-J. and Haynes, J-D. (2008) Unconscious determinants of free decisions in the human brain. *Nature Neuroscience*, 13th April 2008.

[9] Damasio, A.R. (2001) Fundamental feelings, *Nature*, **413**: 781.

[10] Luecke, R. (2007) When your gut speaks, should you listen? *Harvard Business Review: Harvard Management Update*, February: 3–4.

[11] Hinton, P.R. (2000) *Stereotypes, cognition and culture*. Hove: Psychology Press.

[12] Pinizzotto, A., Davis, E.F. and Miller, C.E. 'Intuitive policing', retrieved on 17th April 2009 from http://www.fbi.gov/publications/leb/2004/feb2004/feb04leb.htm#page_2.

[13] Flora, C. (2007) Gut almighty, *Psychology Today*, May/June: 68–75.

[14] Soros, G. (1995) *Soros on Soros: staying ahead of the curve:* 21, Chichester: John Wiley & Sons; Stewart, T.A. (2002) How to think with your gut, *Business 2.0*: **3**(11): 98–104 (emphasis added)

[15] Jayasinghe, S. (2003) Medical professionals in Asia have subscribed to Western thought, *British Medical Journal*, **326**(7389): 601.

[16] Hofstadter, D. (2007) *I Am a Strange Loop*. New York: Basic Books.

[17] The term 'body landscape' is from Damasio, A.R. (1994) *Descartes' error: reason, emotion and the human brain*, New York: HarperCollins.

[18] Hensman, A. and Sadler-Smith, E. (2008) Intuitive judgement in the banking industry. Proceeding of the British Academy of Management Annual Meeting, Harrogate, UK, September 2008.

[19] Hensman, A. and Sadler-Smith, E. (2008) Intuitive judgement in the banking industry. Proceeding of the British Academy of Management Annual Meeting, Harrogate, UK, September 2008.

[20] Why do some individuals treat intuitions as true and absolute, whilst others are more wary? One possible reason why some people treat intuitions as hypotheses to be supported or disconfirmed may be because of differences in working memory capacity (WMC). Individuals low in WMC may be more confident about the validity of their intuitions, treating them as facts; even where they detect uncertainty in their intuitions they may lack the cognitive resources to do the necessary

analysis. On the other hand, people higher in WMC may have the mental capacity to treat their intuitive beliefs as beliefs not certainties. See Feldman Barrett, L., Tugade, M.M. and Engle, R.W. (2004) Individual differences in working memory capacity and dual process theories of mind, *Psychological Bulletin*, **130**(4): 553–73. Researchers at the University of Georgia found that lower levels of working memory capacity amongst police officers increased the likelihood of shooting unarmed people among those officers who had higher levels of negative emotionality, see: Georgia State University (2009, April 1). Police with higher multitasking abilities less likely to shoot unarmed persons. *Science Daily*. Retrieved 14th April 2009, from http://www.sciencedaily.com/releases/2009/03/090330123223.htm. It should also be noted that the level of faith placed in intuitions may be attributable to individual differences in thinking styles that are independent of WMC (see Chapter 2).

Chapter 2

THE AMBIDEXTROUS MIND

Most people have a personal preference for relying on the intuit-ive mind or the analytical mind. In leadership and management both of these modes of thinking, reasoning, problem solving and deciding are necessary, but which one is most appropriate depends on the circumstances. This chapter will show you how to develop an awareness of your preferred mode of thinking, suggest some ways in which you can become more 'mentally ambidextrous' and explore the benefits of working with people who think differently.

A small number of famously gifted people are mentally ambidex-trous – they can excel not only in what they're best known for but also reach expert levels of performance in other fields in parallel. Sir Winston Churchill (1874–1965) is most famous as a politician and war-time Prime Minister of Great Britain, but he was also awarded the Nobel Prize for literature in 1953 for his mastery of historical and biographical description, was a senior officer in the British Army, a journalist and a gifted amateur painter. Another Nobel laureate Albert Schweitzer (1875–1965) was not only a medical missionary in central Africa but also a noted theologian and classical musician whose recorded performances of Bach's keyboard music are still available to this day. Brian May, famous to millions as the guitarist with the rock band Queen, as well as having sold over 100 million recordings worldwide is also an astrophysicist with a Ph.D. on the subject of interplanetary dust, is a visiting researcher at Imperial College, University of London

and has the honour of having a minor planet ('52665 Brianmay')
named after him.[1]

The majority of people aren't as cognitively versatile as these
famous polymaths but, nonetheless, being equipped by nature
with two minds means that we at least have the potential of two
mental 'gears' to choose from. The majority of people when averaged out don't deploy their intuitive and analytical minds with
equal facility; instead they have a preference for relying more on
analysis or intuition. This habitual preference could have arisen
for a number of reasons and combined together four factors influence the extent to which a person relies on their intuitive or
analytical mind: personality, family background, education and
training, and their job.

🗝 Key Facts No. 5

Personality	Some people are by nature conscientious with an eye for fine detail and a preference for routine and stability, whilst others are more open to new ideas and unfamiliar experiences.
Family background	The influence of a significant family member who was strongly intuitive or analytical.
Education and training	Certain types of education and training can encourage analysis and objectivity (such as science), whilst others permit more freedom, subjectivity and intuition (such as the arts).
Job	In certain jobs, the bosses, clients or shareholders who call the shots may – when averaged out – require a manager to be more analytical and less intuitive, or vice versa.

A word of warning: we set up children, students and employees for failure if we make the cardinal mistake of confusing thinking preferences with abilities. 'Preference' simply means that some people will tend to be more analytical thinkers who'll prefer and/ or excel in situations which require attention to detail and a methodical step by step approach; other people will tend to be more intuitive thinkers who'll tend to prefer and/or excel in situations where the bigger picture needs to be taken into account and where feelings are important. It's crucial that a person's performance (whether it's in school or college exams, or assessment or appraisal at work) is interpreted in the light of the fit between their thinking preference and the task they're being judged in relation to, or the situation that they find themselves in. The positive aspect of seeing thinking preferences in this way is that it opens up the opportunity for people to work to their strengths and also develop thinking strategies that can be deployed consciously to suit the demands of particular problems or decisions when their habitual preference doesn't suit. For example, in business and management the situations where intuition is appropriate include the following:[2]

Application No. 2

Sensing when a problem exists	When the data, situation or someone's story doesn't stack up and doesn't feel 'right'.
Performing well-learned behaviour patterns rapidly	Where we meet a situation that's familiar, we know what to do, there's no need to de-compress our expertise, we can simply go ahead and 'do' rather than 'think'.
When expectations are violated	In familiar situations we expect things to be and to turn out in particular ways, when this doesn't happen an intuitive alarm bell is sounded.[3]

Synthesizing a 'big picture'	Where we're confronted by multiple isolated bits of data and information; in this situation the intuitive mind allows us to stand back, avoid 'analysis paralysis' and see how the pieces of the jig saw fit together.
Checking on the results of rational analysis	Sometimes the results of analysis are clear and unequivocal and don't require any checking, but sometimes even when the data have been analysed there can be a sense that it's not right. In this situation intuition can sound the alarm for a re-analysis, perhaps revealing some basic computational error.
By-passing in-depth analysis and coming up with a quick-fire plausible solution	In business, managers often have to act quickly otherwise opportunities evaporate or are cashed in on by competitors. Intuition mode avoids planning paralysis; it gives first-mover advantage and enables experienced managers to anticipate the right strategic direction for a business.

None of this is to imply that intuition is infallible – it isn't, but neither is rational analysis. People who have a well developed intuition that's informed by learning, experience and feedback do make bad gut calls, but when averaged out the 'intuitive hits' tend to outweigh the 'misses'. Nor is it realistic to expect that every situation that a manager will come across will suit his or her thinking preferences – life would be predictable and mundane if this were the case. The world is much richer and varied, and by going outside of our cognitive comfort zone we extend ourselves and develop a more rounded set of thinking skills. Thinking preferences don't pigeon hole us and define the limits of our mind, they help us to understand ourselves more completely and develop new and different ways of interacting with the world.

THE SCIENCE OF THE INTUITIVE MIND – THE ANALYTICAL TEENAGE MIND

Psychologists Valerie Reyna and Frank Farley offer the counter-intuitive hypothesis that the thinking style of the teenage mind is 'too rational', that teenagers weigh up pros and cons but in a way that is biased in favour of risky options.

The Swiss psychologist Jean Piaget argued that we start off as intuitive children and become analytical adults. Reyna and Farley overturn this idea – they argue that as we become older, more experienced and more expert we are able to adopt a 'gist-based' approach that filters and disregards distracting details, especially in the case of risky choices:

1. A mature decision maker taking a gist-based approach will respond rapidly and won't deliberate about the degrees of risk and the magnitude of the benefits if there's the slightest chance of a catastrophic or health-compromising outcome.
2. Teenagers, on the other hand, will tend to take longer to respond (measured in milliseconds in the lab but a real differences nonetheless) to questions such as 'Is it a good idea to set your hair on fire?', and not only do they deliberate, they're 'risky deliberators' who weigh the benefits of a risky action more heavily than the costs.

This can lead to teenagers intentionally going ahead with risky actions that a mature decision maker would never contemplate, in everything from dangerous automobile driving to promiscuous sexual behaviour. Reyna and Farley recommend offering teenagers:

1. Factual information about the social norms that may be causing them to weigh benefits more heavily than costs and dispelling myths (for example, 'The notion that everyone your age is having sex just isn't true').

Hard-hitting bottom-line messages that will help them to derive the gist of a decision ('smoking does lead to lung cancer', 'lung cancer kills' and 'smoking kills').

Source: Reyna, V.F. (2004) How people make decisions that involve risk: a dual-processes approach. *Current Directions in Psychological Science*, **13**(2): 60–6.

The analytical teenage mind contrasts starkly with the more intuitive mind possessed by older, more experienced people. The clinical neurologist Elkhonon Goldberg, an expert on the degenerative diseases of the human brain, presents a positive view of aging:

1. As we get older our powers of attention, memory and computation decline.
2. As far as taking real-world decisions are concerned this is more than offset by a rise in expertise and competence accumulated through large numbers of experiences which are stored as mental patterns or 'cognitive templates'.

In Goldberg's words the older brain becomes increasingly 'pattern-recognition enabled'. The intuitive mind grows and develops with age under the guidance of one of the best teachers – experience.[4] We can build our intuitions over the course of our lives, and unlike other assets, they stay with us and can steer us through the most difficult and challenging of times.

Even though the concept of 'thinking' is associated normally with 'intelligence' or 'ability', the idea of thinking preference is quite different but just as important on two counts:

1. Thinking preferences aren't abilities, for example preferring the analytical mode doesn't necessarily mean you're more intelligent than someone who's more intuitive or vice versa.

2. Whilst one mode of thinking isn't intrinsically better than another, some modes are more suited to certain types of decisions or problems than others.

As far as taking decisions and solving problems in the real world is concerned the vital skill is being able to judge when it's better to deploy analysis rather than intuition or vice versa. An analogy is clothing: most people if invited to a Hollywood premiere have the good sense to realise that a pair of shorts and a T-shirt aren't appropriate to the context. This isn't because shorts and T-shirts are necessarily inherently bad, they're simply not suited to the occasion. In the same way, intuition wouldn't be a suitable approach to adopt for filling out an expenses claim, but it may be something to rely on when meeting someone for the first time or when a business decision has to be taken speedily. The two different modes of thinking are contextually appropriate (Figure 2.1).

FIGURE 2.1   The mode of thinking should fit the situation (be 'contextually appropriate')

THE SCIENCE OF THE INTUITIVE MIND – THINKING STYLES AND DOING BUSINESS

A 'style' is a habitual pattern or a preferred way of doing something. Thinking styles are individual differences in preferred ways of thinking, deciding and problem solving which are contextually appropriate and independent of ability. In business and management thinking styles are important in:

1. Recruiting and selecting employees so that an organisation has employees with the right thinking styles for a particular job or project; for example, a software engineer may need to be more analytical in his or her job, whilst an advertising executive may need to be more intuitive.
2. Deploying the style that's best-suited to the task; for example by using the intuitive mind for generating ideas for new products and services and the analytical mind for implementing them.
3. Giving employees career guidance and counselling according to their style so that they pursue career goals that are realistic and achievable; for example, intuitive judgement skills are needed for executive jobs, therefore for aspiring executives possessing or developing intuition is indispensable.
4. Training and developing employees in ways that both suit their preferences but also help them develop a wider toolkit of thinking styles and strategies.
5. Enabling groups of employees with the same or different styles to work together as an effective team, using the differences between analytical and intuitive thinkers constructively and maximising synergy.

Source: Cools, E. and Van den Broeck, H. (2007) Development and validation of the Cognitive Style Indicator, *The Journal of Psychology*, **141**(4): 359–87.

By understanding and valuing the diversity of preferences for the different modes of thinking that's bound to exist in any group of employees, leaders and managers can improve individual, team and organisational performance. By becoming more adaptable and flexible in their preferred ways of thinking, deciding and problem solving, all employees can be better-equipped to cope with and adapt to the demands and challenges of 21st century working life.

Different Strokes

What does it feel like to have a preferred way of doing something? Take the analogy of handwriting: apart from the small number of ambidextrous people, most of us are either right- or left-handed. When I write with my preferred hand (my right) it feels easy, relaxed, comfortable and effortless. If I try to write with my left hand it feels difficult and awkward, but when we do things in the mode we're accustomed to and have grown to prefer, things tend to be effortless and feel comfortable. When we do things in a mode to which we're unaccustomed things tend to be more effortful and feel more uncomfortable.

Everyone has personal preferences for different types of clothes, food, and music and so on. How does it feel to wear things, eat things or listen to things that are new and different and outside the comfort zone of your preferences? Similarly, in business and personal life:

1. What's the payoff to you for sticking to your preferred mode of thinking, or what's the payoff for adopting a new mode of thinking?
2. What happens when circumstances conspire against us and we can't do things in the way we prefer?

These are significant questions because managers and leaders have to adapt to an ever-changing world. By analogy, people who lose the use of their preferred writing hand can learn to use their other hand even if it's only a temporary measure. The Spanish tennis player and 2008 Wimbledon champion Rafael Nadal is naturally right-handed but his coach taught him to play tennis left-handed because he felt that this would give him an advantage against the majority of tennis players (who happen to be right-handed). Although it can be uncomfortable to start with there are potentially big payoffs for switching between the different modes when circumstances require, and with practice and training it's possible to become more cognitively versatile.

Managers need to have a command of analytical tools to deal with problems that are quantifiable and objective, but modern businesses equally need leaders who have the intuitive skills that will enable them to manage situations that are uncertain and unquantifiable and which require inspired, informed and nuanced judgements:

1. The analytically-minded manager who's a natural planner is likely to be an effective idea implementer, but without ideas to implement his or her analytical mind is going to be of little practical benefit.
2. The intuitively-minded manager who's a natural innovator is likely to be an effective idea generator, but without well thought through plans to implement new ideas his or her intuitive mind is going to be of little practical benefit.

As the Canadian management professor Henry Mintzberg once said, to be effective it's vital that businesses and their leaders and managers blend 'clearheaded logic and powerful intuition'. Leaders and managers must be able to lead, strategise and innovate, as well as communicate and empathise with followers; and to be effective across the sheer variety of problems and decisions faced in the modern business world requires cognitive ambidexterity. It's a fact that most people have over the course of their lives developed a preference for intuitive or analytical thinking, but having two minds in one brain means that we all have the potential to develop a complementary mode of thinking by developing an awareness of and confidence in our untapped reserves of intuition or analysis.

In the same way that most people have a preferred hand – we exhibit left- or right-handedness – most of us also have a preferred mind and as a result we're either more analytically-minded or more intuitively-minded. There are two important differences however between handedness and 'mindedness':

1. We can, in the main, get through life unencumbered by our handedness.
2. We can't get through life in the business world by being exclusively analytically-minded or intuitively-minded.

This second point, as noted earlier, is especially true for employees who occupy or aspire to jobs at senior levels. Most people's personal and professional lives, and certainly in business and management, are far too complex for someone to be successful by being one-track minded. Some management tasks need analysis, but others need intuition. Therefore, to be more effective across the range of business scenarios a manager or leader is likely to encounter, he or she has to be able to judge, decide and problem-solve using their intuitive as well as analytical mind. But before you can become more mentally ambidextrous you need to know where your personal thinking preference lies.

INTUITION WORKOUT No. 2: WHAT'S YOUR PREFERENCE?

Do you, in general, prefer to use your analytical mind or your intuitive mind?

From the table below read each pair X and Y, then circle one from each pair that you prefer the most (circle X or Y in the two right hand columns). For example, if you prefer 'being spontaneous' to 'being reserved' circle Y (or X if vice versa). Circle 10 letters in all. Don't deliberate too much – just give your immediate reaction.

1	X. Being reserved	Y. Being spontaneous	X	Y
2	X. Immediate gratification	Y. Delayed gratification	Y	X
3	X. Facts and figures	Y. Hunches and hypotheses	X	Y
4	X. Fine detail	Y. Big picture	X	Y
5	X. Being creative	Y. Being conservative	Y	X
6	X. My thoughts	Y. My feelings	X	Y
7	X. The future	Y. The present	Y	X
8	X. Things that are concrete	Y. Things that are abstract	X	Y
9	X. Reality	Y. Possibilities	X	Y
10	X. Being conventional	Y. Being unconventional	X	Y

TOTAL NUMBER OF X's:

TOTAL NUMBER OF Y's:

Mark your X and Y scores on Figure 2.2 by circling the appropriate number on each side (X on the left, Y on the right) then join them with a straight line.[5]

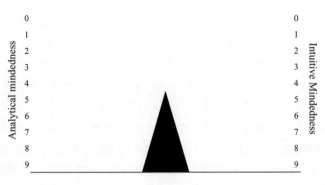

FIGURE 2.2   The thinking preferences scale

In terms of your personal preference:

1. A flat line on the diagram means no strong preference for being either analytically-minded or intuitively-minded.
2. A line which is up on the left and down on the right represents a preference for being intuitively-minded.
3. A line that's up on the right and down on the left represents a preference for being analytically-minded.
4. The tilt of the line indicates the strength of preference for intuition over analysis, or vice versa.

How tilted the line *needs* to be, and to which side, depends on the situation you're in and whether it requires you to be intuitive or analytical. For example, in complex people-related judgements the requirement is shifted more to the right, whereas in areas such as operations management or financial planning the requirement is shifted more to the left. The research that's been conducted over the past couple of decades suggests that the situations where managers tend to use intuition are where there's:

1. a high level of uncertainty: exactly what's going on isn't clear and there's no more data available, or there simply isn't time to gather any more information;

2. little previous precedent to go on: in uncharted waters there are no 'maps', nobody else has been there before, therefore informed intuition may be the only source of data;

3. unpredictability in the key variables: no one knows which way the situation will turn, the computer models don't help, and all a manager has to go on is experience and gut feeling;

4. a number of solutions to choose from: a judgement call has to be made between choices that are distinctly different and a decision has to be made (as opposed to indifferent choices where the choice is inconsequential but where many analysts get into a decision-making paralysis);

5. limits on the amount of time available to make a decision: there's a brief window of opportunity for you to make a decision, and if you don't someone else may step in and first-mover advantage could be lost forever.

Intuitively intelligent managers aren't mindless intuitors simply and naïvely 'trusting their gut', they know when to rely on their intuitive mind to sense problems, execute well-learned behaviour ('they do what normally works'), see the big picture, avoid planning paralysis and check out doubts about the validity of previous analyses.[6] The ultimate test of a manager's intuitive intelligence is to know when intuition (or analysis) has reached its limits and can no longer be relied on and when a different cognitive gear has to be found. The intuitively intelligent manager knows when and how to switch mental gear and create a balance between 'head', 'heart' and 'gut'.[7]

The Analytical Manager

The 'birth' of the analytical manager can be traced back to Frederick W. Taylor (1856–1915) and Henry Ford (1863–1947). The analytical manager came of age in the 1950s and 1960s when econometricians, computer scientists and operational researchers seized on the emergence of the computer as a 'hard', systematic, quantitative analytical tool and applied it, sometimes indiscriminately, to the softer domain of business management. As a consequence management became more a precise science than a judgemental art and concerned itself with the language of numbers, reducing problems to their smallest component parts in the search for convergence on a single right answer.[8] The analytical approach was, and still is, epitomised by the use of rational choice analytical tools, consisting in their simplest form of listing the 'pros' (for) and 'cons' (against) associated with a choice, weighing these and doing the math and coming up with a definitive and unequivocal answer. For example, suppose the choice is between holidaying at home or abroad. A rational approach to this choice might be to list an equal number of 'pros' of each (in this case 10) and then rank the attributes by allocating points to each (10 for the most important, nine for the next most important, and so forth).

Holiday at home	Points	Holiday abroad	Points
Cheaper	10	Better weather	1
Less travel	3	Change of scene	8
Safer	2	Excitement	9
Take the dog	7	Meet up with friends	4
Take family members	6	Novelty	5
Score	**28**		**27**

In this example, 'holiday at home' wins but, in this case, the one point victory isn't exactly clear cut and decisive; it's in what decision researcher Gary Klein calls the 'zone of indifference' where the alternatives have roughly equal strengths and weaknesses. Under these circumstances and in the absence of any gut feeling for which way to go tossing a coin might be the only way to decide between the two.[9] Other rational choice techniques include putting 'advantages' and 'disadvantages' in columns and following the same scoring method, or putting items to choose between in the columns (for example, models of computer) attributes in the rows (features, speed, capacity, prices, etc), allocate a score and a weight for the attributes, then calculate an overall score for each item, and 'winner takes all'. There's little doubt that the rational model can be invaluable in circumstances where:

1. all the attributes can be identified quickly, easily and unequivocally;
2. allocation of scores is straight forward;
3. agreement can be reached when more than one person is involved in the decision;
4. computation can be automated (for example by using an algorithm or computer) to overcome human error or fatigue.

The rational model is unmessy and gives a definite, if not always clear cut, answer, but sometimes it's not sufficient in itself because:

1. choice is involved in constructing the model in the first place (for example, why isn't 'don't take a holiday' an option in the example above?);
2. search for 'pros' and 'cons' could go on indefinitely (for example, why stop at some arbitrary number?);
3. ratings attached to each attribute aren't objective measurements (like mass, length or time) they are subjective choices (raters' opinions and trade offs);

4. ratings, and hence the final choice, might be different if the rater happened to be in a different mood or if new information came to light.

An alternative and novel approach to the 'holiday abroad versus holiday at home' dilemma goes as follows: take a coin, let heads be 'holiday at home' and tails be 'holiday abroad', flip the coin, and – this is the crucial step – focus attention on your bodily reaction at the outcome. Be mindful of your feelings – does your bodily 'felt sense' soar or take a nose dive at the outcome? Flipping a coin is one of the simplest and surest ways to test your feelings about something. Like a knee jerk reaction, it's instantaneous and you have no control over your body's instinctive reaction, all you can do is notice it. It can be a hot line into how you feel, and a window into your intuitive mind.

Subjectivity and feelings are inherent in all but the simplest and most inconsequential of human decisions, which means that whether we like it or not there's an intuitive dimension to human thinking and decision making. As has been stressed many times already developing 'intuitive intelligence' doesn't mean ignoring rational choice, but it does require a balance of intuition and analysis. Moreover, because most people have a preference for an intuitive or analytical mode of reasoning, becoming intuitively intelligent also means stepping out of our cognitive comfort zone into the unfamiliar world of the analytical or the intuitive mind. For example, how comfortable a person feels with the rational choice model depends on their preferred mode of thinking, it's likely to appeal to analytically-minded people who in general like to approach decision making and problem solving in a way which is deliberate, detached and detail conscious.

🔑 Key Facts No. 6: The Analytical Manager

Deliberative	Do things step-by-step.
Detached	Feelings have much less of a priority than being cool, calm and rational.
Detail conscious	Focus on the 'nitty-gritty' of a problem, see the trees rather than the wood.

But analysis alone can never be enough in the complex and dynamic world of business. If you're analytically-minded try stepping outside your analytical comfort zone and dipping your toe in the intuitive pool.

INTUITION WORKOUT No. 3: OUTSIDE YOUR ANALYTICAL COMFORT ZONE

If you're analytically-minded, how does it feel to step outside of the analysis comfort zone and give your intuitive mind a 'work-out'? (If your preferred mode is intuitive skip this workout.)

Imagine that an intuitive friend or partner comes up with what she or he thinks is a 'great idea', she says: 'Let's take a completely unplanned, last-minute holiday on the other side of the world'. Your analytical mind's default setting is to approach this decision in a deliberative, detached and detail-conscious way. How would you take this particular decision if your analytical mind was, as usual, in the driving seat; what things might come to mind?

1. Being detached about the idea of taking a completely unplanned, last-minute holiday on the other side of the world would mean that I'd ...

2. Being deliberative about this decision would mean that I'd ...

---

3. Being detail-focused about taking this decision would mean that I'd ...

Now try switching mental gears. *Think differently.*

If your intuitive mind were in the driving seat for this decision you'd be more affective, spontaneous and holistic. Try being intuitively-minded just for a moment; what would you do differently?

1. Being affective about the idea of a completely unplanned, last-minute holiday on the other side of the world means that I'd ...
2. Being spontaneous about this decision means that I'd ...
3. Being holistic about this decision means that I'd ...

Are there any threats in being outside your analytical comfort zone? What are they?

Are there any opportunities in being outside your analytical comfort zone? What are they?[10]

For many analytically-minded people exploring the unfamiliar territory of the intuitive mind can feel uncomfortable and create uncertainties. But on the other hand being in an unfamiliar place can create exciting new possibilities in one's personal and professional life.

The Intuitive Manager

Whilst analytical management enjoyed its heyday in the middle decades of the 20th century, there were dissenting voices almost from the start. For example, in 1938 Chester Barnard (1886–1961) an AT&T Executive and author of one of the first management 'best sellers' *The Functions of the Executive* (1938) acknowledged the existence of the 'logical mental processes' that go on inside the head of every manager and leader; but he also knew that there was something more: 'the handling of a mass of experience or a complex of abstractions in a flash' which Barnard described as a 'feeling in our marrow' the vagueness of which shields it from the scrutiny of the analytical mind. This feeling is intuition, referred to by Barnard as 'non-logical mental' processes – inexpressible in words and unanalysable by the thinker.

A decade later Nobel Prize winner Herbert Simon (1916–2001) of Carnegie Mellon University in his seminal book *Administrative Behavior* (first published in 1945) proposed the notion of bounded rationality – the notion that managers 'satisfice' rather than maximise (meaning that managers search for a solution that they're satisfied will do the job, and then terminate the search rather than maximise the search by endlessly looking for the best solution). Simon recognised that every manager needs to analyse and plan, but he or she also needs to be able to respond to situations quickly through intuitive judgement cultivated over many years of training and experience.[11]

Harold G. Leavitt (1922–2007) of Stanford University commented in 1975 on a disenchantment with the 'hard-nosed, number oriented emphasis' and the intellectual snobbishness that had become associated with analytical management which resulted in non-users of the rational method often being pigeonholed as 'second-class thinkers'. Allied to this was the unfortunate consequence of an analytically-biased management education system that produced fledgling managers who left business school under the misguided apprehension that they could conquer the world equipped with an armoury of the latest analytical tools and techniques (but perhaps lacking the judgement that comes with experience).

By the 1980s more managers and researchers started to take intuition seriously. A survey of several hundred top executives in the US confirmed what was long-suspected: they used intuition to guide many of their most important decisions, but on the other hand they didn't rely exclusively on intuition or analysis. In the 1990s a major international survey of over 1000 managers found that intuition was perceived to add most value to management decision making in the areas of corporate strategy, human resources and marketing. Later in the same decade in-depth interviews with managers scratched beneath the surface of the sketchy picture that survey data had produced to reveal that managers had their own 'folk theory' of intuition: they saw it as enabling experience-based decisions but that these involved feelings that welled up from subconscious mental processes which occurred automatically 'in the background' of conscious awareness as hunch or gut feeling. Finally, intuition came of age in 2006 which saw the publication of a major best international seller on the subject of 'thin slices' by the *New Yorker* columnist Malcolm Gladwell – *Blink: the power of thinking without thinking*.[12] By the beginning of the 21st century the intuitive manager had finally emerged from the closet where he or she was hiding (or being hidden) to reveal him or herself.

⌘━◑ Key Facts No. 7: The Intuitive Manager

Spontaneous	Has the experience, expertise and confidence to trust intuition and go with gut feeling.
Holistic	Can stand back and look at the 'big picture' without succumbing to analysis paralysis.
Affective	Pays attention to feelings and acknowledges that the soft data of 'feeling' can be as important as the 'hard' facts.

Fallible	The intuitive mind isn't right 100 % of the time, but intuitive managers tend to have more 'hits' than 'misses'.
Informed	Over many years of learning, experience and feedback intuitive managers instinctively know what to do without being able to explain why.

Attributes such as these are invaluable in entrepreneurship, HR, strategy, leadership and many other aspects of management, but intuition alone can never be enough in the complex and dynamic world of business. If you're intuitively-minded you'll always need to be able to step outside your intuitive comfort zone and dip your toe in the analytical pool.

INTUITION WORKOUT No. 4: OUTSIDE YOUR INTUITIVE COMFORT ZONE

If you're intuitively-minded, how does it feel to step outside of the intuitive comfort zone and give your analytical mind a work-out? (If your preferred mode is analytic skip this workout.)

Imagine that an analytical friend or partner comes up with what she or he thinks is 'quite a nice idea', he says: 'Let's take a two-week holiday somewhere near to home in about twelve months' time'. Your intuitive mind's default setting is to approach this decision in an affective, spontaneous and holistic way. How would you take this particular decision if your intuitive mind was, as usual, in the driving seat?

1. Being affective about the idea of taking a two-week holiday in your home country in about twelve months' time would mean that I'd ...

2. Being spontaneous about this decision would mean that I'd …

3. Being holistic about this decision would mean that I'd …

Now try switching mental gears. *Think differently.*

If your analytical mind were in the driving seat for this decision you'd probably be more detached and deliberative, with an eye for the detail. Try being analytically-minded just for a moment; what would you do differently?

1. Being detached about the idea of taking a two-week holiday in your home country in about twelve months' time means that I'd …;

2. Being deliberative about this decision means that I'd …;

3. Being detail-focused about this decision means that I'd …

Are there any threats in being outside your intuitive comfort zone? What are they?

Are there any opportunities in being outside your intuitive comfort zone? What are they?

For many intuitively-minded people exploring the unfamiliar territory of the analytical mind can feel uncomfortable and create uncertainties. But on the other hand being in an unfamiliar place can create exciting new possibilities in one's personal and professional life. Even for the most intuitively-minded manager developing intuition is a life-long project because attaining any kind of wisdom, and 'intuitive wisdom' is no exception, is a journey, not a destination. The cognitive (mental) versatility that is the hallmark of intuitive intelligence can help one along the path to becoming a wiser leader or manager.

Cognitive Ambidexterity

As we've seen analytically-minded managers are more likely to be concerned with 'hard' facts and figures, computations, business processes and points of detail. On the other hand, intuitively-minded managers are more likely to be concerned with 'softer' data (such as feelings), the bigger picture and the world of poss-ibilities and the imagination. Mindedness, analogous to 'handed-ness', is important in personal and professional life because it can sometimes be helpful to think not only in our habitual way, but in ways that fit the situation. One area in which a manager's or leader's preferred mode of thinking is crucially important is in business venturing, and the skill of thinking divergently and 'outside the box' is a crucial attribute for entrepreneurial success. We might expect entrepreneurs to be off-the-scale intuitives – but does this stereotype match the reality?

THE SCIENCE OF THE INTUITIVE MIND – THINKING LIKE AN ENTREPRENEUR?

Researchers in the USA compared the thinking styles of entre-preneurs with those of two other very different and contrasting groups, actors and accountants. The entrepreneurs weren't novices, on average they had around thirteen years of experi-ence as founders or co-founders of businesses. The researchers looked at how the three groups compared in terms of their scores on a creative/intuitive thinking versus linear/analytical thinking test (shown here as score out of 100).

	Linear/Analytical	Creative/Intuitive	Difference
Accountants	82	54	–28
Actors	51	80	+29
Entrepreneurs	72	67	–5

The cognitive profiles of the entrepreneurs were more balanced (the difference was minus five) than the accountants who were highly analytical (minus twenty eight) or the actors (plus twenty nine) who were highly intuitive. The entrepreneurs in this study had seemingly balanced the intuitive and the analytical modes. These results don't support the popular stereotype of the off-the-scale intuitive entrepreneur whose only concern is creativity and novelty – instead the entrepreneurs who took part in this research preferred to rely on their intuitive and analytical minds in roughly equal measure.

Sources: Groves, K.S., Vance, C.M., Choi, D.Y. and Mendez, J.L. (2008) An examination of the non-linear thinking style profile stereotype of successful entrepreneurs, *Journal of Enterprising Culture*, **16**(2): 133–59.

Personality, background and education are important formative influences on managers' thinking, but there are also important factors in the work environment that affect whether or not the intuitive or analytical mind is in the driving seat. For example, is the stereotype of the executive who 'manages from the gut' accurate, and is it related to how high-up in a business somebody is? The data is pretty unequivocal in showing that senior managers are definitely more inclined to 'go with their gut' than managers lower down the hierarchy – executives and senior managers are more intuitive than middle managers, who in turn are more intuitive than junior managers.[13] But whether this is down to personality, education and training or context is an open question. The fact that senior managers are more intuitive could be for a number of reasons:

1. Being more intuitive gives people the 'right stuff' to succeed and be promoted.
2. Being in a more senior role means that managers have to be more intuitive.
3. Being in a position of power allows executives to wield their intuition (sometimes with abandon) and be seen to be 'managing from the gut'.

The chances are that all three factors have some role to play in making senior managers more intuitively-minded. One consequence of this is that if a manager isn't particularly intuitive but aspires to a more senior role he or she may need to take steps to develop better intuitive judgement skills. At higher levels in organisations the decisions and problems managers and leaders face are often more complex, big-picture and future-oriented. To deal with these types of decisions and operate successfully at senior levels on the corporate ladder managers and leaders need to be intuitively-minded. An interview in *Harvard Business Review* with a senior executive of one of the world's largest pharmaceutical companies showed just how important intuitive judgement can be for corporate climbers:

> Very often people will do a brilliant job up through the middle management levels where it's heavily quantitative, in terms of the decision-making. But then they reach senior management, where the problems get more complex and ambiguous, and we discover that their judgement or intuition is not what it should be. And when that happens it's a big problem.[14]

The balance between intuition and analysis is also important in different jobs and types of tasks. Certain tasks and specialised jobs are more suited to the analytical mind (for example, where dealing with hard data is more important) whilst others are more suited to the intuitive mind (for example, where dealing with people is more important). For this reason it's important for managers and leaders to be able to match their mode of thinking to suit the task (Figure 2.3).

Tasks that require the analytical mind tend to be well-structured, objective, quantitative and computationally complex (and often are performed better by a machine than a person, especially in situations where fatigue and human error can creep in – for example manually checking reams of financial data). These are 'computational' tasks.

Tasks in other aspects of work ranging from ethical and moral choices through to business venturing decisions require an intuitive judgement that's informed by learning and experience and instinct. These are 'judgemental' tasks and have one or more of a number of distinctive characteristics.

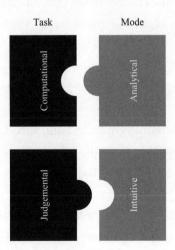

FIGURE 2.3 Use the mode of thinking, problem solving and deciding that fits the task

---

🔧 Application No. 3: How to Identify Judgemental Tasks

Dynamic	The situation is so fluid that it's hard to pin down.
Poorly structured	All the facts aren't known or can't be known.
Subjective	There's no purely right or wrong answer, but nevertheless a judgement call has to be made.
Novel	A solution's required that isn't already known about by someone somewhere.
People related	Human beings, with all their foibles, idiosyncrasies and complexities, are involved.
Time pressured	Waiting around to gather more data or do a detailed analysis isn't an option.

If you're inclined to be intuitively-minded and happen to be faced with a task where the issues of dynamism, poor structure, subjectivity, novelty, time pressure and people-relatedness figure prominently you've already engaged the right mental gear – so the advice would be to 'stay in gear'. Equally, if you're inclined to be analytically-minded and find yourself dealing with tasks that are computational, again the message is 'stay in gear'.

On the other hand, if you're intuitively-minded and faced with a computational-type task and don't seem to be making progress try 'switching gear', or team up with an analytically-minded colleague. If you're analytically-minded and faced with a judgemental task you might consider switching gear or teaming up with an intuitively-minded colleague (Figure 2.4).

If you currently have a strong preference for intuition or analysis you can develop the skill of being able to switch modes with sufficient practice and feedback, and with extended practice and feedback you're even likely to get to the stage where you'll become

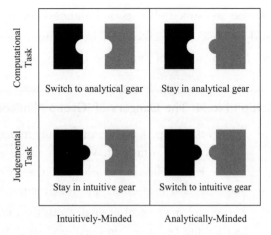

FIGURE 2.4 To 'switch' or 'not to switch' gear (task in black, gear in grey)

cognitively ambidextrous (this book will help you). It's worth re-emphasising: knowing when to change gear and being able to flip between your analytical and intuitive mind is one of the key attributes of intuitive intelligence. There are very few jobs that are exclusively data-driven or people-driven, or can be performed successfully by being exclusively analytically-minded or intuitively-minded – in most jobs it's essential to be able to combine the two.

The Ambidextrous Team

In business organisations people work together in groups to accomplish things collectively that they couldn't accomplish as individuals. In the changed and ever-changing world of work in the 21st century many jobs, as well as requiring intuitive and analytical mental gears, require interaction, collaboration and team-working. 'Group mindedness', the mix of thinking preferences within the group, can be a crucial factor that can either make or break team working. A football team full of great goal scorers but no defenders when averaged out over the long run is unlikely to be as successful as a balanced team with good defenders and goal scorers. Likewise, in business there are four main dangers of too much of one type of thinking:

✎ Application No. 4: The Dangers of 'Group Mindedness'

Imbalance	If a work group is highly analytically-minded it's likely to excel at tasks that require attention to detail but be less proficient in tasks where a more holistic and less hard data-driven approach is necessary.
Collective 'planning paralysis'	The group may excel at analysis to the extent that its thinking becomes 'grooved' and stuck in an analytical rut. Where the problems and decisions require intuitive judgement the team may become paralysed by a collective cognitive short-sightedness, the result is that analysis paralysis can set in.
Group think	An overly-analytical mind-set can lead to an 'analytical group think' where analytical thinking is the accepted consensus irrespective of the task or the preferences of non-analytical group members – intuition may be seen as 'second class' thinking.
Alienation	Those who don't fit with analytical 'group think' may feel alienated, disenfranchised – second class minds in effect – and may end up withdrawing or exiting the organisation in the very circumstances where an alternative more intuitive perspective may be invaluable.

The reverse is true for an intuitively-minded group and the consequences are equally negative and undesirable. In the same way that businesses need cognitively ambidextrous leaders and managers, modern business organisations also need ambidextrous teams. Most work tasks need intuition and analysis. The message is clear: groups, like individuals, need to be able to switch mental gears.

An advantage that a group has over an individual is that even if the group is made up of a mix of highly intuitive and highly analytical individuals who are hard to shift out of their cognitive comfort zone, both mental gears can be engaged by the group so long as communication between the two mind sets can be developed and maintained. One way this exchange of ideas can be achieved is by having an intermediary who can see both points of view, speak both languages, provide 'translation', diplomacy and mediation – in other words the facilitation skills of a team member who can be a 'mindedness mediator'. Such a person needs to be able to understand the intuitive and analytical languages, value both approaches, have the interpersonal skills to bridge the gap between extremes and blend the unique and invaluable contributions of each.

INTUITION WORKOUT No. 5: MIND THE GAP

If you're a member of any kind of group (work, friendship or family) can you think of any occasions in which you've seen extreme 'mindedness' at work, and have its effects helped or hindered the group in its processes or relationships?

1. Who are the intuitively-minded and who are the analytically-minded people in the group?
2. In which type of tasks does their contribution tend to be most valuable and least valuable?
3. How could these differences be addressed so that, overall, the group is able to get the most out of the mental gears that it has at its disposal?
4. Is there a 'mindedness mediator' who can help members of the group to bridge the gap?
5. How will you know you're part of a fully-functioning ambidextrous team?

With group ambidexterity there comes diversity – a collective of mixed minds is likely to perceive situations in a variety of ways and exhibit markedly divergent approaches to solving problems and making decisions. In the right combination, under the right circumstances and managed and led in the right way this cognitive diversity can be a distinctive and difficult-to-copy asset which is so rare and valuable as to set apart a team or a business from the competition – a vital synergy can occur. A group of mixed minds also has to be handled skilfully and sensitively, and a key leadership skill is to be able to tolerate ambiguity, invite opinions, explore options and propose ideas that take people outside of their cognitive comfort zones in secure and safe ways without feeling that integrity of their personal preference is being challenged or devalued.[15]

For a work group to function effectively it's important that analytically-minded members can communicate with intuitively-minded members, and vice versa. And it's not only about communication: the view can look very different depending on whether you're looking through an analytical or an intuitive lens – the picture of the world shifts from mind to mind – and we have to take each other's word for that. Even if it's impossible to see the world in the same way as someone else does, we can acknowledge that there are different and complementary ways of thinking, judging and deciding. Developing the skills to be able to switch cognitive gears and work constructively with people whose 'mindedness' isn't the same as ours can not only make for better personal, inter-personal and business effectiveness, it can also be the basis of a unique asset which can't be copied or taken away from us.

INTUITIVE INTELLIGENCE PRINCIPLE No. 2: SWITCH
MENTAL GEARS

With practice it's possible to become more analytically-minded
or intuitively-minded. The potential benefits of becoming 'cognitively ambidextrous' are significant, but to do so requires:

1. Self awareness – instinctively you probably have a pretty
   good idea what your thinking preference is. To move out
   of your comfort zone you need to know whether you're
   analytically-minded or intuitively-minded.
   • Which one are you?
2. Practice – to move out of your comfort zone you need to
   be able to try a different approach in a safe situation. Practising your intuition in real-life situations can be risky to
   you and others; it can also induce fear which is one of the
   biggest barriers to any kind of learning.
   • What kinds of situations would make good 'practice
     grounds' for you?
3. Feedback – you need feedback on how well your intuition
   or analysis is performing if it's unfamiliar territory for you.
   • Who's there to give you trustworthy feedback that will
     be candid but constructive?

NOTES

[1] 'The Nobel Prize in Literature 1953' retrieved on 13th September 2008
from http://www.nobelprize.org/ and 'Brian May Official Biography'
retrieved on 13th September 2008 from http://www.brianmay.com/
brian/biog.html.

[2] Isenberg, D.J. (1984) How senior managers think, *Harvard Business
Review* November/December: 81–90.

[3] Decision researcher Gary Klein discusses the ways in which experienced decision makers deal with violations of their expectations in his
two path-breaking books on the subject of intuition in professional
practice *Sources of Power* (1998) and *Intuition at Work* (2003).

[4]Goldberg, E. (2005) *The Wisdom Paradox: how your mind can grow stronger as your brain grows older*. London: Free Press.

[5]The image of the balance or 'see saw' is used in order to convey the idea of the thinking preferences that most people exhibit. The notion of two minds interacting in parallel suggests that human beings do in fact use both styles and that some individuals are mentally ambidextrous to the extent that they can be simultaneously high both on analysis and intuition but this is a situation that's impossible to represent using the see saw image. The fact that correlations between intuition and analysis are of the order of $r = 0.50$ indicate the extent to which individuals express a thinking style preference. For further discussions see: Allinson, C.W. and Hayes, J. (1996) The cognitive style index: A measure of intuition-analysis for organizational research. *Journal of Management Studies*, **33**, 119–35; Hodgkinson, G.P. and Sadler-Smith, E. (2003) Complex or unitary? A critique and empirical reassessment of the Allinson-Hayes Cognitive Style Index. *Journal of Occupational and Organizational Psychology*, **76**: 243–268. Hodgkinson, G.P., Sadler-Smith, E., Sinclair, M. and Ashkanasy, N. (2009) More than meets the eye? Intuition and analysis revisited, *Personality and Individual Differences*, **47**(4): 342–6.

[6]Agor, W.A. (1986) The logic of intuition: how top executives make important decisions, *Organizational Dynamics*, **13**(4), 5–18; Burke, L.A. and Miller, M.K. (1999) Taking the mystery out of intuitive decision-making, *Academy of Management Executive*, **13**:, 91–9; Clarke, I. and Mackaness, W. (2001) Management 'intuition': An interpretative account of structure and content of decision schemas using cognitive maps. *Journal of Management Studies*, **38**(2): 147–72; Hayashi, A.M. (2001) When to trust your gut, *Harvard Business Review*, February: 59–65; Isenberg, D.J. (1984) How senior managers think, *Harvard Business Review*, November/December: 81–90; Parikh, J. (1994) *Intuition: the new frontier of management*. Oxford: Blackwell Business.

[7]Pondy, L.R. (1983) Union of Rationality and Intuition in Management Action. Chapter 7 in Part 2 Processes of Experiencing and Sense Making in: *The Executive Mind: new insights on managerial thought and action*. Edited by Srivastva, Suresh ed. San Francisco: Jossey-Bass, 169–91.

[8]Leavitt, H.J. (1975) Beyond the analytic manager, *California Management Review*, **XVII**(3): 5–12.

[9]Klein, G. (2003) *Intuition at Work: why developing your gut instincts will make you better at what you do*. New York: Doubleday: 67–8.

[10]Adapted from the 'forced fit' exercise developed by Prof. Dr Karlien Vanderheyden, Vlerick Leuven Gent Management School, Competence Centre People & Organisation, Belgium.

[11]Simon, H.A. (1987) Making management decisions: the role of intuition and emotion, *Academy of Management Executive*, **1**(1): 57–64.

[12]Agor, W.H. (1986) The Logic of Intuition: How Top Executives Make Important Decisions, *Organizational Dynamics*, **14**(3): 5–18; Burke, L.A. and Miller, M.K. (1999) Taking the Mystery Out of Intuitive Decision Making, *Academy of Management Executive*, **13**(4): 91–9; Parikh, J. (1994) *Intuition: the new frontier of management*. Oxford: Blackwell Business.

[13]Allinson, C.W. and Hayes, J. (1996) The Cognitive Style Index: a measure of intuition-analysis for organizational research, *Journal of Management Studies*, **33**: 119–35; Hodgkinson, G.P. and Sadler-Smith, E. (2003) Complex or unitary? A critique and empirical reassessment of the Allinson-Hayes Cognitive Style Index, *Journal of Occupational and Organizational Psychology*, **76**: 243–68; Sadler-Smith, E., Spicer D. and Tsang, F. (2000) The Cognitive Style Index: a replication and extension, *British Journal of Management*, **11**: 175–81.

[14]Hayashi, A.M. (2001) When to trust your gut, *Harvard Business Review*, February: 59–65.

[15]Dotlich, D.L., Cairo, P.C. and Rhinesmith, S.H. (2006) *Head, Heart and Guts: how the world's best companies develop complete leaders*. San Francisco: Jossey-Bass.

Chapter 3

INSIGHTS, INTUITIONS AND THE MORAL INSTINCT

Insight enables the mind to make connections which haven't been made before and enables people to see the world anew. Insights are the engine room of invention and innovation; moreover it's possible to create the conditions for such insights to arise. Insight is about 'seeing' new connections, intuition is about 'sensing' new connections. Human beings' intuitive sense of right, which manifests as a moral instinct, enables managers and leaders to know intuitively whether a decision or behaviour fits with a set of core values and whether it's intrinsically right.

Petrol and diesel fuels have been the mainstays of internal combustion engines since the development of the modern automobile by Karl Benz in 1885. However, in a world of highly unstable oil prices and ever-declining reserves of fossil fuels car manufacturers are ever vigilant for new ways of providing more environmentally sustainable innovations. This is especially pressing given the burgeoning demand in a world in which more and more people expect the kind of personalised transport that the West has been used to for decades. Many automotive companies have spent vast sums of money on trying to produce power plants for vehicles that give sustainability into the 21st century and beyond.

A creative breakthrough in this area came as far back as the 1970s when electrical engineer David Arthur, in the small town of

Springdale, Arkansas, built a 75-mile per gallon hybrid gasoline/ electric vehicle using off-the-shelf and military surplus parts.[1] This invention broke the mould of single-fuel source vehicle engines and introduced the world to the hybrid-powered vehicle. Arthur's new vision provided an insight that ushered in a previously unimagined world of powered transport.

Over a quarter of a century later Toyota and Honda are amongst the world's leading manufacturers of hybrids, vehicles that have a gasoline engine as the main power source and an electric motor that kicks in when extra power is needed in start-up, acceleration and overtaking. The name *Insight* was chosen by Honda for its hybrid car because this was thought to be iconic of the company's vision of a new era in which attractive and affordable hybrid vehicles capable of seventy miles per gallon plus come within the reach of regular car buyers.[2]

The creative significance of the hybrid vehicle was that it took two ideas that had existed independently for decades – gasoline-powered and electrically-powered engines – but which hadn't been put together before into a new combined power plant. The inventors and designers of the hybrid saw the power plant for a car in a totally new way, they had the insight that a car didn't *have* to have only one source of power, and like many of the best inventions it seems obvious in retrospect. The hybrid gasoline/electric car, including Toyota's *Prius* (described by advertisers as 'mean but green') and Honda's aptly named *Insight*, is a prime example of an invention where a unique insight in the mind of the designer was the precursor to a commercially viable innovation that synergised already existing concepts in new and unexpected ways. The inventors 'joined up the dots' in ways that had never been done before.

Joining the Dots

Over the centuries insight has played a major role both in scientific discovery and business innovation. The most famous insight or 'Eureka!' moment in the world of science belongs to the Greek mathematician Archimedes of Syracuse. He lived in the third century BC and is alleged to have had his famous 'Eureka!' moment when solving an especially challenging problem. Archimedes needed to work out the volume of an elaborate crown ostensibly of pure gold but which was suspected being adulterated with silver. Easy enough if he'd have been allowed to pummel what was reputed to have been a remarkable work of craftsmanship into a rectangular lump and measure its length and breadth, but it had to be done without destroying the crown's shape. The problem was seemingly intractable.

After struggling with the problem Archimedes came to an impasse, but then – so the story goes – suddenly whilst climbing into his bath he saw the familiar sight of the rise in water level. 'Eureka!', the crucial connection was made, the rise in water level was proportionate to his body's own volume, so if he could use the displacement of water to measure the volume of his own body he could certainly do the same with the crown, calculate its volume, combine this with the figures for the densities of the two metals and confirm if it was pure gold. Archimedes was so pleased with his breakthrough that he's supposed to have leapt from his bath and run naked through the streets crying 'Eureka!' – literally 'I have found it!'. The impasse in Archimedes' thinking was broken when he was least expecting it, the parts of the problem suddenly came together, and he experienced insight.[3]

More recently and closer to home numerous inventors and entrepreneurs in the business world have reported similar experiences in developing products ranging from the trivial and ephemeral to the long-lasting and significant. For example, Edwin Land, inventor of the Polaroid instant camera, had his 'Eureka!' moment while holidaying with his young daughter – she asked the naïve but penetrating question of why she couldn't have their holiday snaps right away. The pieces of the jig saw came together for 3M's Spencer Silver, one of the inventors credited with the Post-It Note®, when his book marks fell out of his hymn book in a Sunday church service and he realised the potential applications for a non-sticky adhesive that he and his colleague Art Fry had developed but couldn't find a use for. And the 'million dollar mum' Sheri Schmelzer, inventor of 'Jibbitz' (gimmick stick-on buttons for children's 'croc' shoes), had her 'light bulb' moment one rainy afternoon when trying to keep her kids entertained by 'accessorizing' their footwear.[4]

Insight also played a crucial role in a chance observation made in 1916 by biologist Clarence Birdseye which ultimately revolutionised the world's eating habits. Up until Birdseye's discovery slow-freeze was the only available method for freezing fish. The problem was that the slowness of the process resulted in the formation of large ice crystals, which when defrosted robbed the fish meat of its 'just caught' quality. Birdseye was doing biological field research in northern Canada when he noticed that fish caught by the Inuit were flash-frozen by nature the instant they came out of the water. What surprised Birdseye was that Arctic quick-frozen fish tasted fresh and were of a much higher quality product than the slow-frozen fish that were being sold in American shops at the time. By 1924 Birdseye had patented a process that saw the launch of the frozen food industry and changed eating and cooking habits across the globe.[5]

The story of Birdseye and the other innovators prove that, contrary to what we may have been taught in school and college, it's possible to think *too* hard about a problem. Great ideas rarely arrive on demand, instead they tend to creep into a prepared mind at moments when the analytical mind's guard is down. In which case, it's often better to do the mental groundwork but then let go, slow down, open up to chance and playfulness, let random combinations happen and hand over the controls to the intuitive mind.

Let Yourself Go

Given what's just been said it may sound like a contradiction, but try your hand at having an insight with the ' Prisoner in the Tower' problem:

> A prisoner is trying to escape from a tower using a rope that was only half long enough to allow her to reach the ground safely. The prisoner divided the rope into two pieces, tied them together and was then able to escape successfully. How could this be?

Most people are initially perplexed by this problem. And whilst it's always possible to put in the extra muscle power in the hope that problem will yield to mental force, another approach to solving it might, paradoxically, be to think about it less. By taking a break from too much hard thinking solutions have the habit of emerging when they're least expected. It's as though intelligent, unconscious problem solving machinery is parallel processing backstage while our conscious mind 'puts its feet up' or gets on with other more mundane things, blithely unaware.

To put the theory to the test, absorb 'The Prisoner in the Tower' problem, make a mental note that you want to solve it, and then leave it alone. Read on, take a walk, read the paper, do a cross-word, watch TV, you could even sleep on it. You have all the knowledge and necessary information to come up with the right answer. And if the 'Prisoner in the Tower' problem succumbed immediately to your analytical mind here are some more puzzling scenarios all of which have a logical solution and for which you have all the necessary information and knowledge to be able to solve.[6]

INTUITION WORKOUT No. 6: 'EUREKA!' MOMENTS?

Murder in the Living Room? Jane comes home from work and finds Bill lying dead on the floor. Also on the floor are broken glass and some water. Tom is in the room as well. Jane takes one look around the room and immediately figures out how Bill died. How did Bill die?[a]

A Costly Error? A stranger approached the curator of Roman coins at my local museum and offered him an ancient silver coin. The coin had an authentic appearance and was clearly marked with the date, 54BC. The curator promptly called the police and had the stranger arrested for attempted fraud – but why?[b]

Death in the Desert? Two men were walking through a desert. They discovered on the sand the body of a man. The dead man had with him a small pack containing fresh food and water. He had a larger pack on his back and a large ring on the index finger of his right hand. The two men puzzled over the man's death but were unable to fathom what had happened. There was no obvious explanation for how the man had met his end. With nothing more they could do the travellers continued on

---

their way. Some miles further on one of the men accidentally dropped his handkerchief whilst mopping his brow and watched it float to earth. 'Eureka!' He suddenly realised how the man had died. Do you know how the man died?[c]

[a]Bill is a goldfish and Tom is a cat. Tom upset the goldfish bowl which smashed causing Bill to die.
[b]It would be impossible to date a coin 'BC' because the birth of Christ, in what we now call 54BC, was an unknown future event.
[c]His parachute failed to open, and the ring on his finger was attached to the rip cord that should have opened the parachute.

The process of 'joining up the dots' that leads to insight in minds that are prepared and receptive occurs as a result of:

1. Re-arrangement and re-combination: the necessary elements of the solution are available to the solver but they haven't yet come together in the right way or been seen from the right angle. Archimedes, for example, had all the scientific and mathematical knowledge needed to solve his crown conundrum; it just hadn't been 'packaged' in the right way.
2. Random inputs: a new and random piece of information provides the missing element that gives the mind the jolt that's needed and provides the link in the chain. Birdseye wasn't a fish novice, he was employed as a field naturalist working in the Canadian wilderness to pay his way through college as a biology major. But equally, Birdseye didn't set out for the Arctic to discover fish fingers, in his own words he was 'just a guy with a very large bump of curiosity and a gambling instinct'.[7]

Rearrangement, recombination and randomness can't be hurried; they're the products of slow thinking. The contrast between a mind unhurried and patiently waiting for connections to emerge with the harsh reality of business life couldn't be starker. In business organisations 'more and faster' are usually seen as preferable to 'less and slower'. But whether we like it or not, the generating of creative insights isn't something that comes about easily in high-energy or high-stress situations. One of the barriers to intuition and insight in the business world is that the creative connections made by the intuitive mind often get drowned out by what intuition pioneer and AT&T executive Chester Barnard, writing in 1938, called the 'incessant din of reasons' – the constant 'chatter' of the analytical mind.

The analytical mind is a cognitive heavyweight; it can take a firm grip on a problem, and is a consummate performer in logical, computational tasks. However, one of the analytical mind's failings is that it doesn't think all that effectively outside of the box and as a result often comes up with conservative and conventional solutions. Analytical thinking tends to be linear and convergent; creativity, on the other hand, is a product of lateral or divergent thinking – combining ideas or objects in previously unrecognised ways. For example, ten years ago who would have dreamt that phone, e-mail, music, video, maps and a camera could be combined together on a single platform – something we now know and almost take for granted in Apple's iPhone?

Once a problem is in the grip of the analytical mind, even if the intuitive mind does have a more creative and unconventional view to offer, it's hard for intuition to be 'heard' in conscious awareness. The intuitions and imaginations that lead to creative breakthroughs arise through the antithesis of convergent thinking, the condition of mental receptivity described in 1817 by the Romantic poet John Keats as 'negative capability': 'when man is capable of being in Mysteries, Doubts and Uncertainties, without any irritable reaching after fact and reason'. Keats' words advocate the suspension of the intellectualising of the analytical mind and the engagement of the intuitive mind.

THE SCIENCE OF THE INTUITIVE MIND – A FEELING OF KNOWING

A favourite technique of experimental psychologists employed to research the processes of insight is the so-called Remote Associate Tests (RAT). Here's an example: what word connects 'room', 'blood' and 'salts'?[8]

Unless you've come across the problem before it's quite unusual for the solution to leap out of the page, more usually it comes along as a flash in an unexpected moment. For many years psychologists speculated that insight occurs as a result of connections being made between previously learned concepts during an 'incubation period' in which we sometimes sense that a solution is 'brewing'.

Many people are familiar with the tip of the tongue phenomenon – we feel that we know we just can't put our finger on the answer. Intuitions about solutions, a 'feeling of knowing' (FOK), are often reported by problem solvers even though they don't yet know how or what the solution might be.

What is clear is that the journey towards the solution can be helped by temporarily distancing oneself from the problem and relaxing the analytical mind's stranglehold. Vague perceptions of coherence can't be described explicitly in words because the intuitive mind 'talks' in the language of gut feeling and hunch. Intuitions are signposts towards a problem solution. For example, Michael S. Brown, 1985 Nobel Prize winner in Medicine, said of his path to the discovery of the mechanism for the regulation of cholesterol in the human bloodstream: 'we almost felt at times that there was a hand guiding us. We would

---

go from one step to the next, and somehow we would know which was the right way to go. And I can't really tell how we know that'.[9]

The experiences of great scientists and inventors demonstrate unequivocally that the 'dots' that need to be joined in order to solve a problem have previously been uploaded into the problem solver's long-term memory – their intuitions aren't naïve, they're informed by in-depth knowledge and expertise. During an 'incubation' period there's an unconscious spread of neural activation between remotely related concepts (nodes). If the level of activation level between them reaches a threshold level the solution 'pops-out' fully-formed into conscious awareness. But whilst this is happening, informed intuition, in the form of a hunch, provides a reassuring and guiding hand through the pre-conscious phase of the discovery.

Source: Policastro, E. (1995) Creative intuition: an integrative review, *Creativity Research Journal,* **8**(2): 99–113.

The formalisation of the idea of 'incubation' in creativity and insight can be traced back to 1926 and the publication of *The Art of Thought* by the political theorist and psychologist Graham Wallas (1858–1932) of The London School of Economics.[10] Wallas proposed that creative solutions are incubated pre-consciously in an 'ante-room' of the mind. From a study of the lives and the writings of a number of famous scientists and mathematicians he discerned a series of events that's been witnessed many times in mathematical and scientific discovery as well as business management.

The bedrock of the process is the preparation stage – people who experience creative insights usually have an intimate familiarity with their topic of interest – they're deeply immersed in it. As Pasteur said, 'Chance only favours the prepared mind'. But the necessary preparation takes time; it takes at least ten years of learning, experience, practice and feedback to develop the relevant and sufficient expertise.[11] Even for experts the toughest problems don't yield very easily, for example the German chemist Kekulé worked at his structure of benzene problem for many years, and like many other scientists who made major breakthroughs, he eventually solved the problem only after coming to a mental impasse. The typical route map for the processes of invention via insight goes through five phases.

🔑 **Key Facts No. 8: The Process of Insight**

Preparation	Immersion and the development of expertise that gives creative intuition a substrate to work on.
Incubation	Retreat of the problem into the unconscious mind.
Intimation	Preconscious intuitive 'buzz' that a solution is about to emerge.
Illumination	'Eureka!' (literally 'I have found it!') moment.
Verification	Arduous process of proving the viability of the idea and commercially exploiting it.

The blockages and frustrations of a seeming dead end are a necessary precursor to the fulfilment of a creative breakthrough. Reaching a problem solving cul-de-sac is not a failure, and in the long run it may even be a good thing, it can signal that the mind is entering a quiet 'incubation' stage where images and intuitions have the space to surface. For example, Kekulé made his major breakthrough discovery of the structure of the benzene molecule while day dreaming, he saw a vision in his mind's eye of snakes swallowing their own tails which he took as an intuitive pointer that led to the discovery that the benzene molecule is a ring of carbon atoms joined together. Einstein, in developing his theory of relativity, is supposed to have experienced the mental image of riding on a street car at the speed of light and pondering how the world and the passage of time would look.

Illumination is the 'light bulb' moment, the sudden flash of insight, but as Wallas' theory and the experiences of many great inventors and innovators remind us, generating ideas is never enough, there's the equally important verification stage, the time-consuming process of proving and testing the new idea, and the final implementation and commercial exploitation. One of the world's most prolific inventors Thomas Edison, with over 1000 patents to his name, is reputed to have said: 'Genius is two per cent inspiration and 98 per cent perspiration'. Managers can learn invaluable lessons from inventors and scientists from Edison to Einstein about how to manage not only their personal creativity but that of the teams and organisations they lead.

🖋 Application No. 5: Preparing for Insight

Steep yourself in your subject	Insight and creative intuition really do favour the prepared mind, so learn your subject and show that you're passionate about it and enable others to do the same also.
Don't worry if you hit a brick wall	Many of the most famous scientists, technologists and inventors had the same experience, it's a natural part of the process.

Relax, let go and slow down	It's possible to think too hard, insights come when the analytical mind lets go, sometimes it can be smarter to think less.
Expect the unexpected	You can never know what new connections the intuitive mind will come up with. You have the power to create the conditions that make it more likely to happen.

The ideas and anecdotes from psychology and the history of science fit with managers' experiences of creativity. For example, a survey of 500 entrepreneurs in the UK found that only 29% said they had their most creative thoughts in the workplace, whilst a large proportion valued silence (40%) and solitude (27%) as the best stimulants for a 'Eureka!' moment. The findings also run counter to conventional wisdom on group brainstorming as a way of generating creative ideas – 90% of the entrepreneurs surveyed felt that other people's ideas restricted their own creativity.[12]

Even after the epiphany of a 'Eureka!' moment there may be years of wrong turns and frustrations between the insight and the reaping of any commercial reward, and for business venturers the risks are often high. For example, Clarence Birdseye first witnessed fish being flash frozen by Arctic winds in 1916, but Birdseye's first frozen food company went broke because shoppers were so sceptical. The world wasn't ready for him but, determined and undaunted, Birdseye worked on perfecting his freezing technology. He started the General Seafood Corporation and eventually sold out its assets and the patents in 1929 for a staggering $22 million. Birdseye is immortalised in the brand 'Birds Eye', a name synonymous with frozen food.

THE SCIENCE OF THE INTUITIVE MIND – THE NEUROSCIENCE OF INSIGHT

Modern cognitive neuroscience (the study of how complex mental functions occur within the brain) has begun to shed light on the interior workings of the mind in the lead-up to a 'Eureka!' moment.

The neuroscientist Mark Jung-Beeman and his colleagues used brain imaging techniques (functional Magnetic Resonance Imaging, fMRI) to study what goes on inside the brains of people when they solve insight problems. By using fMRI scans scientists are able to infer patterns of neural activity from observing changes of blood flow within the brain.

In their brain-scanning experiments Jung-Beeman and his colleagues observed two types of activation going on inside people's brains when they're solving insight problems (such as in 'remote associate tests' (RAT), e.g. 'room/blood/salts'):

1. a strong activation of information that's not relevant to the problem solution;
2. a weak activation of information that is problem-relevant.

The delayed problem solution came through the patterns of weak activation in the brain's right hemisphere which for a time were blocked by stronger more focused activation on problem-irrelevant associations in the left hemisphere. The left hemisphere activations produced strong but conventional associations which were blind alleys as far as solving the problem was concerned. Once these subsided the way was clear for the intuitive insights to emerge in the right hemisphere activations which produced weaker but more unusual and alternative associations that led to the solution of the problem.

> *Source:* Bowden, M., Jung-Beeman, M., Fleck, J. and Kounios, J. (2005) New approaches to de-mystifying insight, *Trends in Cognitive Sciences*, **9**(7): 322–8.

In many problem-solving situations analysis offers a quick and efficient way to get to a right answer, especially for 'computational problems'. But the analytical mind can't always provide the right answer, nonetheless in management rational analysis is often perceived as the 'best' and sometimes the only way to solve problems and take decisions. At least this is what students are taught in most business school programmes and is found in rule-bound bureaucratic business organisations. But many businesses in the 21st century need creative intuitions in order to survive, innovate and thrive in a globalised market place. For this reason organisations (including business schools) need to be able to create the conditions for creative intuitions and insights to flourish in the minds of managers and also the business students who provide the succession pool for the leaders and managers of the future. Businesses need creative and intuitive leaders.

Moreover, it's clear that hard, effortful thinking doesn't always lead to the type of solution needed for a creative breakthrough. So does that mean that it's okay to be a lazy thinker? Is it like losing weight without cutting down on calorie intake and not taking any exercise? Does it sound too good to be true?

If we're to believe the various apocryphal stories in the history of scientific discovery the Greek mathematician Archimedes had his 'Eureka!' moment whilst about to relax in a nice warm bath; for the English scientist Isaac Newton it was taking a break under an apple tree at Woolsthorpe Manor in the Lincolnshire countryside; whilst for the German scientist Kekulé it was while he was dozing on a London bus. We might infer from this that if you or I were to lie in the bath, sit under a tree or ride around on the bus, suddenly and unexpectedly we might be able to come up with an idea to solve business and management's most pressing problems. Unlikely – in fact not true. Whilst it's beyond doubt that the answers to many of science's intellectual conundrums emerged after a period of respite from hard mental work (bathing, resting and riding respectively), Archimedes, Newton and Kekulé had at least two very important things in common, they were:

1. experts, not to say geniuses, in their respective fields – geometry, mathematics and chemistry;
2. grappling with problems that for many years had eluded the greatest intellects of their age.

Far from being the outcome of lazy, effortless thinking most major insights are the fruit of many years of learning and hard work and are arrived at by people who are not only highly gifted but, equally importantly, also steeped in their subject. It's not easy to come up with a novel idea that's truly new to the world without the necessary expertise built up through years of training, practice and feedback. Even though the intuitive mind can deliver its insights in a flash, the processes going on 'backstage' not only need the necessary raw material to work with in the form of deep knowledge but also take time and undoubtedly benefit from a retreat from the hustle and bustle of professional life. Be it science or business, problem solvers and decision makers need to take opportunities for mental relaxation and contemplation in order to quiet their analytical minds.

Insight is not Intuition

The main focus of this book is intuition, but as far as this chapter is concerned so far the 'I' that's been discussed is 'insight'. Even though people often use 'insight' and 'intuition' as though they mean the same thing there's a subtle and important difference. When insight occurs the logic of the solution that's been arrived at suddenly becomes crystal clear and can be explained, in words, numbers, or an image. Intuition, on the other hand, creates a sense (as gut feeling or hunch) of a direction to be followed (a signpost) or of an impending solution (a feeling of knowing). An intuition is more subtle than an insight; it's a subjective private feeling of conviction, a cognitive nudge, a sneaking suspicion – but one which is hard to explain. The major differences between intuition and insight are outlined below.

🔑 Key Facts No. 9: Insight versus Intuition

Insight is objective	Intuition is subjective
Insight is clear	Intuition is 'fuzzy'
Insight is easy to articulate	Intuition is hard to articulate
Insight can be for public consumption	Intuition is a more private matter

---

Even if intuition is subjective, fuzzy and hard to articulate it's by no means weak, it can be utterly compelling and dumbfounding – we know but can't say how or why we know. One way in which psychologists have researched human beings' ability to sense whether or not things 'fit' has been to use a test known as a 'closure task'. Take a look at the two pictures below (Figure 3.1). Do the elements of one picture seem to be more coherent than those of the other?

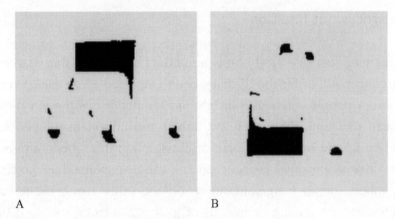

A   B

FIGURE 3.1 Which has more coherence, A or B?
Source: Bolte, A. and Goschke, T. (2008) Intuition in the context of object perception, *Cognition*, **108**: 608–16. Reproduced by kind permission of Elsevier Science.

Participants in laboratory experiments often judge the group of shapes like those on the left to be more coherent than those on the right. But actually both pictures are made up of exactly the same elements, but on the left they're in a meaningful arrangement whilst on the right they're randomly arranged and therefore don't form any meaningful pattern. The fact that people can judge the potentially meaningful arrangement as coherent is based on an intuitive judgement – if quizzed before insight strikes they're unable to say why the elements fit together, but nonetheless they're convinced that somehow they do. Insight often occurs when the problem solver is told that the pattern on the left is a truck. Once the connection is made they're unable to see the shapes and the pattern they form in any other way – the perception and interpretation of the image become 'sticky'.

THE SCIENCE OF INTUITION – THE GIST EXTRACTOR

The sense of coherence that's sometimes experienced when solving a problem is thought to involve the spread of neural activation between concepts in memory. But it's only a *sense* of coherence because the activation isn't strong enough to support any conscious retrieval of what the actual connection is. In this situation, thinking is beneath the level of conscious awareness; it's 'covert cognition'. Our brains extract the gist of a pattern which gives rise to an intuitive impression of coherence which often, but not always, leads to insight. The intuitive sense of coherence can influence judgement, and is similar to the 'tip of the tongue' experience. Cognitive neuroscientists working in this field distinguish between:

1. Intuition: 'implicit processing of unconsciously-activated material'.
2. Insight: the sudden realisation of a solution originating from covert cognitive processes.

It appears that the brain quickly transfers a perception such as a visual image to a relevant brain area where the intuitive mind makes an 'initial guess' about what the object being perceived is. The output of this mental process is felt as a 'preliminary perception of coherence'.

The human brain is very efficient in extracting the gist from a stimulus and making an approximation at what it means. This makes good sense from an evolutionary point of view – potential threats in the environment had to be quickly interpreted and evaluated. Where in the brain these perceptions of coherence emanate from depends upon the stimulus, for example words versus pictures. Particular stimuli (such as visual patterns) activate the visual areas of the brain which means that intuition in general can't be localised to any intuitive 'hot spot' in the brain.

Source: Ilg, R., Vogeley, K., Goschke, T., Bolte, A., Shah, J.N., Pöppel, E. and Fink, G.R. (2007) Neural processes underlying intuitive coherence judgements as revealed by fMRI on a semantic judgment task, *NeuroImage*, **38**: 228–38.

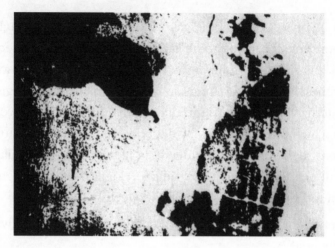

FIGURE 3.2   Patterned perception persist

The phenomenon of extracting and interpreting the 'gist' of a pattern highlights one of the dangers of perception: if the human brain can take a short cut it will, as a result we tend to look for patterns, and once one is found it takes a firm hold, so much so that it becomes almost impossible to see things in any other way again. One of the downsides of this is that our perception and thinking can become stuck. Take a look at the picture above (Figure 3.2). If you haven't seen it before it can look like a meaningless bunch of blobs. But then if I tell you that it's a cow's face looking out of the picture at you it's unlikely that you'll ever be able to see this pattern in any other way again. The up side of seeing the image as a cow makes it possible to make sense of it and discuss it; the downside can be mental 'stuckness'.

Patterned thinking can help managers and leaders to respond quickly and efficiently because it takes up fewer precious cognitive resources. But there's a potential downside – the patterns that we base our perceptions on can result in a mental 'stuckness', a cognitive inertia hitched to an outmoded business model, which can become deeply entrenched, taking on a life of its own, irrespective of what's actually happening in the business world and thus expose whole industries to significant threats to their survival. For example, in the 1990s UK real estate managers' perceptions of their industry remained largely unchanged over a twelve to eighteen month period during which time there was a significant and widely reported downturn in the UK property market. When this happens the risks may range from the traumatic (the demise of individual firms) to the titanic (the decline of entire industries).[13] The billionaire financier George Soros blamed the credit crunch of 2008 at least in part on a cognitive inertia inherent in the mental models of market participants which assumed that financial markets would always be self correcting and that house prices would always be on the rise. Instead Soros argues that managers and leaders should frequently re-examine their assumptions about the world and be primed and ready to sense and exploit moments of cataclysmic change.[14] The rational model in management adopts an outwardly-focused perception, sometimes resulting in a failure to direct attention to the most important place, inside ourself, where our intuitions maybe quietly voicing their concerns or sensing viable opportunities to be taken.

INTUITION WORKOUT No. 7: DROP IN ON THE MOMENT

Mindfulness is about paying attention, and developing mindfulness is about refining our capacity for paying attention. John Kabat-Zinn, founder of the Stress Reduction Clinic and Center for Mindfulness in Medicine at the University of Massachusetts Medical School, offers the simplest and perhaps the most powerful illustration of mindfulness: the perception of our breath. Breath is something that's always there, we take it for granted and don't intentionally observe it. One of the exercises that Kabat-Zinn uses in his mindfulness training is focusing attention on the feeling of breathing. In Kabat-Zinn's words:

Let's see if we can feel our breath moving in and out of our bodies and keep our minds focused on it. Don't breathe deeply. Just let the breath happen. Although we could focus on a million different things, let's just feature the direct, sense-based experiencing of the breath centre-stage in the field of our awareness moment by moment for a period of time, and let everything else be in the wings.

This exercise can last as little as five minutes or as long as an hour and sitting still and quietly with nothing but one's own breath is a surprisingly difficult thing to do. The analytical mind wants to take attention away from any single object of attention (in this case the breath but an external object, such as a candle flame, could equally be the focus) and grab other things that happen to be around, or draw up thoughts and memories to work on. The discipline of focus and practice, the freedom to see thoughts as transitory events and let them go, and the curiosity of where mindfulness may lead brings about calmness and stability of perception – a 'one-pointed stillness of mind'. Through non-activity, doing-without-doing, the space is created for insightful connections to occur and for the voice of the intuitive mind to be heard. The solutions to 'out there' problems can come from 'in here'.

Source: Kabat-Zinn, J. (2002) Meditation is about paying attention, *Reflections*, **3**(3): 68–9.

Creativity involves putting together things that weren't previously connected into a pattern that's coherent. For example, self service-shopping viewed through 21st century eyes seems obvious and natural, but when it was invented in the USA in the 1930s, when empty warehouses were converted into supermarkets and customers served themselves, it was a radical recombination of things that were already available – space, customers, shop-workers, goods and money. These elements were re-configured not only in a highly original way, but also in a way that completely revolutionised the retail business.

In any aspect of human endeavour from relativity to retailing, a creative person is someone who's demonstrated the ability to produce novel ideas and inventions which are useful and valuable. To produce novelty, original and unexpected connections are made between objects and ideas, which even though they're out there in the world, no one else thought to connect them before.[15] Creative intuition is one of the most precious but under exploited assets that many employees, managers and business organisations have in abundance. The conscious hard work of uploading the relevant knowledge and skill is necessary but insufficient for insight, intuition, creativity and innovation. Some of the most insightful and creative ideas come in states of relaxation, reverie or dreaming, when the analytical mind is in neutral gear and the intuitive mind has more freedom to roam and make novel connections. Intuitions can be intimations of an impending insight, signals from the intuitive mind that a solution is in the pipeline. When intuition becomes insight the solution emerges into the spotlight of conscious awareness and it's possible to 'join the dots'. On the one hand, intuitive judgements are compelling and persuasive, but on the other they're difficult to put into words. Moreover, the jury's out until, with the passage of time, the intuition is proven to be a right decision or a wrong decision, or a good judgement or a bad judgement. There aren't any guarantees with gut feeling, but as far as the two minds are concerned it's a level playing field because there aren't any guarantees with rational analysis either. Nonetheless there are several sure-fire ways to kill-off creative intuitions in business organisations.

> ✐ **Application No. 6: How to Kill Off Creative Intuitions**
>
> 1. Assume faster thinking is better thinking.
> 2. Never be in uncertainty and doubt.
> 3. Act like you know the answer in advance.
> 4. Let the analytical mind call the shots.
> 5. Yield to pressure to conform.
> 6. Suppress your own and other people's intuitions.
> 7. Expect analysis to be right 100% of the time.

Moral Instincts

We usually associate 'instinct' with animal behaviour, for example birds have homing instincts that enable them to navigate hundreds of miles back to their nests, newly-hatched turtles on a beach automatically head for the ocean. But test out your human moral 'instinct' by considering this hypothetical scenario used by the social psychologist Jonathan Haidt in his research into our own species' moral judgement.

> A family's pet dog, which was healthy and well-cared for, was killed by a car on the road outside their house. The house owners had heard that some people have been known to enjoy eating dog meat, and so being willing to experiment, they decided to try it out for themselves. They cooked their dog in a stew and ate it.[16]

Many people, especially in the West, respond to this scenario with disgust and condemn it as morally wrong, but when asked to justify why it's wrong, people begin to flounder. On objective grounds eating the dog doesn't seem to be all that problematic – it was well looked after, it died instantly, it's a source of protein, moreover people in other parts of the world routinely eat dog meat. Following this style of reasoning it's not easy to condemn the family's actions. But reasoning why the family's actions should be judged morally wrong is more difficult, so much so that many people end up being 'morally dumbfounded', unable to give good reasons for why they think it's wrong – 'it just is!'. The conviction that eating the dog is wrong is as strongly felt as it is unreasonable and illogical.

Haidt explained people's dumbfounding by turning the conventional idea about moral judgement on its head. From an intuitionist perspective moral judgement isn't so much the result of reasoning and logic, it's more instinctive – the outcome of a quick intuitive response based on a feeling (in the case of dog eating, a disgust which is culture specific). It's only after the fact that reasons are constructed that fit with the instinctive unreasoned moral judgement. Our default setting may be for an instinctive moral reasoning that isn't rational, instead it's intuitive, based on feeling with rationalisation deployed after the fact in order to justify an affectively driven intuitive moral reasoning process.

But the emotions that are set off by this vignette are likely to vary depending on the cultural context – in other words the (emotional) moral reaction depends on the conditions in which the action is situated. The question remains therefore: is there a more fundamental mechanism that forms the substrate for human beings' moral judgement upon which culture superimposes variations within biologically circumscribed limits? Do human beings possess a universal sense of right and wrong based on a set of guiding principles which are analogous to the language faculty that gives every human society the capacity to form and use a language of their own?

According to Marc D. Hauser, Harvard evolutionary psychologist and biologist and author of *Moral Minds* (2006), the answer is 'yes': the roots of human morality are more in nature than they are in nurture, and there half a dozen or so innate moral principles that:

1. guide moral judgement, but don't determine how we act;
2. generate automatic and rapid judgements;
3. aren't accessible to conscious awareness;
4. operate on real and imagined experiences;
5. require little or no instruction;
6. can be impaired by damage to the neural circuitry which 'hard wires' moral instinct (more on this in Chapter 7).[17]

Fairness is an example of a moral principle and to illustrate the point Hauser used the example of a simple game favoured by economists – the 'Ultimatum Game'. The Ultimatum Game is played between pairs of participants, with one of the pair acting as the 'Proposer' and the other as 'Responder', and a $10 pot of money. The Proposer starts off by announcing an offer to the Responder to give him or her some portion of the $10 (which can range from a substantial amount to nothing at all). The Responder either accepts or rejects the Proposer's offer. If the Responder accepts he or she gets to keep the offered amount, the Proposer gets to keep what's left. If the Responder rejects the Proposer's offer they both get nothing at all.

In the Ultimatum Game a greedy (or rational money-maximising) Proposer should offer a small amount (for example a dollar), and a rational Responder should take whatever is offered since one dollar is better than zero dollars by anyone's reckoning. But of course the Responder can reject the offer leaving both of them with zero dollars. But when the Ultimatum Game is played something seemingly quite irrational happens: Proposers usually offer in the range of $5 (arguably a quite generous act), and Responders reject offers of less than $2 (arguably a foolish act). The explanation is that as a species we have evolved a deep sense of fairness which translates into a compassion and concern for the welfare of others. But if genes are 'selfish', why should we care for the welfare of genetically unrelated others?

Hauser takes this one step further by considering the 'Dictator Game'. It's even simpler: the Proposer starts off with $10 and can give the Responder some portion or nothing at all of the $10 pot. The game is very short: once the Proposer announces the offer the game ends, and the Responder takes what is offered (which may be something or it can be nothing). When the game is played some Proposers offer nothing, whilst others engage in the seemingly irrational act of offering half the pot. The explanation that's offered for the altruism of the generous Proposers is, once again, the sense of fairness argument – human beings' tendency towards generosity, even when such actions may reduce personal gain.

But a moment's thought reveals an added twist to the Dictator Game: in human society, especially those involving relatively close-knit groups – tribes of all sorts, including business organisations – interactions aren't one-offs, they're usually repeated events. If the Dictator Game is played with three people: B proposing to A and then C proposing to A, and B offers A zero dollars and C offers A $5, and then another round is played with A as the Proposer and B and C as receivers, what's likely to happen? Knowing the past behaviour of B and C it's unlikely that A will make the same offer to B as to C; it's more likely that B will be offered zero and C something around $5.

Is this something that's culture specific and to be found only in the psychology labs of universities in Westernised countries? Hauser describes research by anthropologists using bargaining games in remote communities where the fairness principle is also witnessed, albeit varying within certain parameters. For example, in the Ache tribe of Paraguay Responders accept low offers and Proposers typically offer more than 40%, whilst in the Au and Gnau tribes of Papua New Guinea Proposers offer around 40% of the 'pot', but Responders reject at rates of between 50 and 100%. What counts as a fair and permissible transaction varies between cultures, there's no set point for fairness, but in each society the principle of fairness is always expressed (in the case of bargaining games offers are rarely made of less than 15% or more than 50%).

The Ultimatum Game and the Dictator Game are (ultimately) games of cooperation that tend towards stability if the participants have information about past behaviours. In cooperative activity reputation is crucial; in Hauser's words it 'fuels cooperation and provides a shield against defection' and he offers an evolutionary explanation for the importance of reputation which came about as *Homo sapiens* shifted from small groups of hunter-gatherers (where chance encounters with other groups occurred) to a more sedentary existence with the rudiments of agriculture and animal husbandry:

... two features of our environment changed, which would forever alter the problem of cooperation: group size increased, and we started to rely on shared resources, locally available through the development of agriculture and farming. With an increase in the number of people [in a group], opportunities to interact and cooperate increased, especially with genetically unrelated individuals.

In such situations a key to success, and therefore survival, would have been to remember 'who did what to whom and when'. There are clear implications for management and leadership. For example, in geographical concentrations of inter-connected small and medium enterprises (clusters) trust and collaboration are vital in fighting off shared threats and for the competitiveness of the cluster as a whole. The potential that clusters have for the competitiveness of a region is clearly demonstrated in regions like Silicon Valley and Boston's Route 128. The cooperation between firms in clusters allows for joint action, coordination, heightened group responsiveness in globalised markets and sharing of technologies.[18] Any transgression of the cluster norms which results in the breaking of trust within such tightly coupled groups of firms can quickly damage a firm's reputation. Firms which don't cooperate are the losers – they end up limiting their own knowledge base and inhibiting their innovative capacity.[19]

Neither the moral instinct nor economic rationality determines how we act. The intuitive and the analytical minds interact and sometimes conflict. Rationality (the norm in many organisations), brain biology (we instinctively recoil with disgust from certain stimuli), hard wired moral principles (we have an innate sense of justice and fairness) and cultural norms (in some cultures dog eating would not elicit the same reaction as it does in pet-loving nations) often push and pull us in opposing directions. However, it seems that as far as moral judgement goes, the intuitive mind is in the driving seat more often than some have been prepared to admit: it seems we intuit first, rationalise later. The mechanism which triggers our 'gut felt' moral instincts may have evolved in our ancestors to promote bonding, cohesiveness, trust and coop-eration within the comparatively large social groups they lived in once hunting and gathering gave way to agriculture. The moral instinct gives us a calibrated sense towards others that manifests as fairness, loyalty, respect, empathy (a fundamental deficit in psychopaths) and altruism towards others.[20] The moral instinct endows us with an innate sense of what is 'right'[21] within the permitted variations that exist across different cultural contexts. It is a sobering thought that when we experience an immediate and unreasoned conviction of whether something is intuitively right or wrong it's the invisible hand of our ancestors and forbears, via our evolutionary and socio-cultural inheritances, who are helping whether we like it or not to shape our thoughts, decisions and actions.[22]

INTUITIVE INTELLIGENCE PRINCIPLE No. 3: DON'T MIX UP YOUR I'S

- Intuition is not the same as insight.
- Insight allows us to see new connections.
- Creative intuition enables us to sense new connections.
- Analysis, if adhered to mindlessly, can blind us to making new connections and seeing the world in different ways.
- Moral instinct enables us to sense intuitively the rightness or wrongness of our thoughts or actions.

NOTES

[1] 'Update: David Arthurs' Hybrid Electric Car' retrieved on 13th September 2008 from http://www.motherearthnews.com/Green-Transportation/1980-01-01/Update-David-Arthurs-Hybrid-Electric-car.aspx.

[2] 'Honda to display concept Model of All-New Insight' retrieved on 13th September 2008 from http://world.honda.com/news/2008/4080904All-New-Insight and http://www.channel4.com/4car/news/news-story.jsp. Accessed 13th September 2008.

[3] Adapted from: A. Koestler (1964) *The Act of Creation*, London: Pan Books, p. 105.

[4] Rose, H. (2008) Million dollar mum, *The Sunday Times Magazine*, 19th July 2008: 26–9.

[5] Lukas, P. (2003) Mr. Freeze Clarence Birdseye's flash of inspiration won him a place in your icebox. *Fortune Small Business*. Retrieved on 2nd February 2009 from http://money.cnn.com/magazines/fsb/fsb_archive/2003/03/01/338758/index.htm.

[6] Adapted from: G. Mosler. (1977) *The Puzzle School*, New York: Abelard-Schuma. Cited in Seifert, C.M., Meyer, D.E., Davidson, N., Patalano, A.L. and Yaniv, I. (1996) 'Demystification of cognitive insight: Opportunistic assimilation and the prepared-mind perspective', In Sternberg, R.J. and Davidson, J.E. (Eds), *The Nature of Insight*, Cambridge, MA.: The MIT Press, pp. 65–124.

[7] Clarence Birdseye: a chilling discovery, retrieved on 2nd February 2009 from: http://www.entrepreneur.com/growyourbusiness/radicalsandvisionaries/article197546.html.

[8] The answer is 'bath'.

[9] Press Release: Nobel Prize in Physiology or Medicine 1985, retrieved on 2nd February 2008 from http://nobelprize.org/nobel_prizes/medicine/laureates/1985/press.html.

[10] Graham Wallas (1858–1932), retrieved on 2nd February 2009 from http://www.lse.ac.uk/resources/LSEHistory/wallas.htm.

[11] See: Ericsson K.A. and Charness, N. (1994) Expert performance: Its structure and acquisition, *American Psychologist*, **49**: 725–47.

[12] How do entrepreneurs get their 'eureka' moments? Research finds out how. Retrieved on 17th April 2009 from http://www.publictechnology.net/.

[13] Hodgkinson, G.P. (1997) Cognitive inertia in a turbulent market: the case of UK residential estate agents, *Journal of Management Studies*, **34**(6): 921–45.

[14] 'The credit crunch according to Soros' by Chrystia Freeland (*Financial Times*). Retrieved on 14th April 2009 from: http://www.ft.com/cms/s/2/9553cce2-eb65-11dd-8838-0000779fd2ac.html.

[15] Boden, M. (2003) *The Creative Mind: Myths and Mechanisms*. Oxford: Routledge; Sternberg, R.J. 1999. *Handbook of Creativity*. Cambridge: Cambridge University Press.

[16] This is an adaptation of the dog-eating vignette to be found in: Haidt, J., Koller, S. and Dias, M. (1993) 'Affect morality and culture, or is it wrong to eat your dog?' *Journal of Personality and Social Psychology*, **65**: 613–28.

[17] Hauser, M.D. (2006) *Moral Minds*. London: Abacus.

[18] Mesquita, L.F. (2007) Starting over when the bickering never ends: rebuilding aggregate trust amongst clustered firms through trust facilitators, *Academy of Management Review*, **32**(1): 72–91.

[19] Pittaway, L., Robertson, M., Munir, K., Denyer, D. and Neely, A. (2004). Networking and innovation: a systematic review of the evidence, *International Journal of Management Reviews*, **5–6**: 3–4, 137–68.

[20] Hauser, M.D. (2006) *Moral Minds*. London: Abacus.

[21] Miller, G. (2008) The roots of morality, *Science* **320**: 734–7.

[22] Wild, K.W. (1938) *Intuition*. Cambridge: Cambridge University Press.

Chapter 4

INTUITIVE MIND READING

In this chapter I'll introduce the idea of 'thin slices' – brief glimpses into someone else's mind and personal qualities – and explore the role they play in social intuitions. The intuitive mind can be an effective decoder of the non-verbal signals that we all give out unwittingly in any social interaction, but it's not a magical mind-reading machine, and we need to use both our intuitive and analytical minds to guard against our own biases and the deceptive behaviours that human beings sometimes engage in. The chapter concludes by exploring the neural mechanisms – so-called 'mirror neurons' – that lie behind our instinctive ability to infer other people's thoughts, feelings and intentions.

Finding a mate is one of the most important decisions anyone can face. In the past it tended to be a leisurely, if not long and drawn out, process with all the rituals and romance of the pursuit, courtship and marriage. It needn't be any more, thanks to the inventors of speed-dating who have supercharged the efficiency of finding a romantic partner by capitalising on one of the most remarkable things about the intuitive mind: its ability to make on-the-spot people-related judgements.[1]

Speed dating is thought to have been invented by Rabbi Yaacov Deyo in Los Angeles in the 1990s to help single Jewish people meet each other. It relies on the principle that on a brief 'date' – typically four minutes – people communicate enough about their personality, motives and intentions through their face, body and voice that they can arrive at a decision about whether they'd like to see each other again.[2] Researchers call these compressed brief glimpses into someone else's mind and personal qualities a 'thin-slice'.

In a speed date or any other social interaction it's possible to consciously manipulate certain types of information we wish to communicate about ourselves, for example by employing good manners and engaging in polite conversation, as well as in more superficial signals such as trendy hairstyles, luxury brands and expensive jewellery. Whilst a well-schooled greeting, name dropping or a conspicuous designer wrist watch might impress superficially, the intuitive mind is more attuned to biology and body language than boasting or accoutrements. In a social encounter the most important information we send out is communicated unwittingly and involuntarily by micro movements in facial muscles, telltale body postures and movements and the subtleties of speech and tone of voice usually in the first few seconds of an encounter.

It's Not *What* You Say ...

Intuitions begin with perceptions, be they of persons, objects or places. In social settings non-verbal cues (those of voice, facial expression, posture and movement) are outwardly visible signs of a person's internal mental state. Perceptions of these non-verbal behaviours, whilst they don't provide a basis for mind reading, may be used to intuit a person's feelings, motives and intentions. The vast majority of non-verbal signals are exceedingly difficult to control, for example consciously manipulating blink rate, facial expression, posture and tone of voice simultaneously whilst holding a conversation is virtually impossible. Mental labour is divided and much of it is automated; it has to be simply in order to get by in most real world situations, and social interactions, including conversations, are no exception. That said, some people, such as skilled liars, are able to train themselves to self monitor and regulate their non-verbal behaviours in attempts to confound the receiver.

🗝️ Key Facts No. 10: Mental Labour is Divided

Analytical Mind	The analytical mind focuses its attention on the demanding task of interpreting the content of what's being said by both parties, consequently there isn't very much thinking resource left over.
Intuitive Mind	The intuitive mind deals with 'non-verbals', these are automated to the extent that the sender isn't even aware of them even though they may be all too obvious to the receiver.[3]

Any form of interaction is a two-way street, for example, speed daters aren't only opening themselves up to be interrogated by the other person's intuitive mind, they're also trusting their own intuitive mind to make a snap judgement of whether or not a romantic, and perhaps lifelong, relationship might be on the cards. The same applies in many other social interactions that are the stuff of personal and professional life – we send out, process and receive a vast amount of information rapidly and non-consciously in very thin slices of information based on signals given out by our voice, facial expressions and body language. Managers and leaders are no exception, and Robert Dilts, one of the leading authorities in the field of neuro-linguistic programming (NLP), and his consulting colleagues Ann Deering and Julian Russell, suggest that leaders can heighten their awareness by reading behind the words that people utter:

✐ Application No. 7: Reading Behind the Words

Body language that supports verbal messages	Word/body congruence: the speaker smiles when talking about positive things; frowns about negative things. Speaker's body posture is symmetrical. Regular tempo in the voice.
Body language that contradicts verbal messages	Speaker seems hesitant or lacking confidence in the message and conveyed emotion seems to deny the words. Speaker's body posture is asymmetrical. Movements are jerky.

Non-verbal information and the way it's perceived, processed and interpreted is one of the most important influences on the way we judge people and the way we respond to them. The part of the human body that we rely on more than any other as a source of information about another person's competence, ability, motivations and intentions is the face. It's the face that is used to communicate not only our inner emotional state but also our reactions to what other people do or say.

THE SCIENCE OF THE INTUITIVE MIND – JUST SMILE!

The 'Smiley face' is a symbol of happiness and is ubiquitous in modern culture. But has it become so universal as to be meaningless? Is the over-used smile a facial expression that can be used to infer how someone genuinely feels? The psychologist Paul Ekman and his colleagues attempted to unravel the smile conundrum by cataloguing different types of smile:

1. 'False smiles' are made to convince someone else that you're having fun when actually you're not.
2. 'Masking smiles' conceal a negative emotion.

---

3. 'Miserable smiles' say 'okay this situation is pretty bad but I'm going to put up with it'.

Sitting alongside these in the smile catalogue is the genuine enjoyment, or Duchenne, smile.

Duchenne de Boulogne was a 19th century French anatomist who identified the distinctive features of the smile of spontaneous enjoyment, and which was named subsequently in his honour. The 'Duchenne smile' involves the contraction of a very specific set of facial muscles (the obicularis oculi, and the pars lateralis and zygomatic major muscles) and it cannot lie – it's a true sign of enjoyment. For example:

1. Depressed patients did more Duchenne smiling in their hospital discharge interview than in their admission interview.
2. Psychotherapy patients who improved did more Duchenne smiling during their treatment.
3. And perhaps unsurprisingly, people did more Duchenne smiling when they watched nice films of puppies playing and gorillas in the zoo bathing than they did when watching gruesome films of leg amputations and third degree burns.

The Duchenne smile is an automatic signifier of enjoyment, happiness, amusement, relief, contentment, satisfaction, achievement and sensory pleasure. The muscles around the eye that control the Duchenne smile can't be activated at will, they are in Duchenne's words 'only brought into play by a true feeling' whilst their refusal to budge unmasks a false smile. In common with other facial expressions, the thin-slice perception of a false smile is easily unmasked by the intuitive mind without any explicit knowledge of facial anatomy.

Source: Ekman, P., Davidson, R.J. and Friesen, W.V. (1990) The Duchenne smile: Emotional expression and brain physiology II, *Journal of Personality and Social Psychology,* **58**(2): 342–53.

The face is so important in social interaction that we use it to make judgements beyond what might reasonably be inferred from a person's face alone. The psychologist Alexander Todorov and his colleagues looked at the extent to which quick, unreflective judgements based on facial appearance predicted the outcomes of US congressional elections. They presented people with pairs of head shot photos of winners and runners-up in the elections for the US Senate (2000, 2002 and 2004) and House (2002 and 2004) (a photo was excluded if a participant recognised the candidate) and asked to judge which one of the pair looked more competent. The candidate who was perceived as more competent from nothing more than a black and white head shot was the actual winner in 72% of the Senate elections and 67% of the House races.

In a refinement of their experiment they cut the exposure to the photos down to one second – the accuracy remained high at 68% and even when they used sophisticated statistical techniques to partial-out the age and attractiveness of the candidates so that the judgement was purely on the perception of competence the effect remained. It seems that voters' decisions are anchored to the intuitive mind's initial inferences of competence from facial appearance information. Subsequent corrections by the analytical mind based on a candidate's values and beliefs may not have sufficient strength to overcome the initial intuitive judgement which acts as a strong, if not immovable, anchor.

Similar results were observed by researchers in Europe in an experiment in which children had to choose a captain for a fictional computer-based perilous Homeric voyage. The photographs were of candidates in French parliamentary elections of 2002. The children chose the successful parliamentary candidate as the captain for their voyage with 71% accuracy. Adults and children alike make similar snap visual judgements about who to trust and follow based on facial appearance even though it's not necessarily related to competence or intelligence.[4]

Judging a Book by Its Cover

One of the world's leading 'thin-slice' researchers is the Harvard-educated psychologist Nalini Ambady. In the 1990s she and her colleague Robert Rosenthal did a series of experiments in which they compared the ratings given to college professors by classes at the end of semester with ratings that another group of students gave the same professors based only on three ten-second video clips with the sound turned off.

Can a ten-second thin-slice yield any meaningful information which could be used to give a valid and reliable rating of a professor? Surely any student rating based on a silent video clip couldn't be much better than a guess? And how could it be anything like as accurate as the ratings of students who endured a professor's classes for a whole semester.

The results were astonishing. When the data were analysed the semester-long and the ten-second groups basically agreed about how good or bad the professors were. As far as professors' performance ratings go ten-seconds' worth of silent video clip information counted for almost as much as a whole semester's worth of interaction.

Not to be deterred, the researchers pushed their idea a little further. They tried compressing the thin slice – maybe ten seconds was too much time? What happens if the slice of the professors' behaviour is made even thinner? Surely students couldn't make any meaningful judgement on anything less than ten seconds? Wrong. The ratings given by students who watched three six-second video clips were essentially the same as the ten-second clip and the end of semester ratings. Maybe college students are smart judges of professors' behaviour – after all they have virtually a life-time's experience of teachers of one sort or another? Does thin-slicing work in other situations? The answer from the research is 'yes' across a variety of professional contexts, for example:

1. Surgeons rated as domineering on twenty-second audio thin-slices were more likely to have been sued for malpractice in the past.
2. Physical therapists who were rated on twenty-second video thin-slices as distancing themselves from patients (for example by not smiling or by looking away) were more likely to have clients whose physical and mental functioning showed long-term decline.
3. Judgements based on the first ten seconds of a mock employment interview with time for no more than a handshake, sit down and brief introduction predicted the same outcome as a full interview with a skilled interviewer.
4. Thin-slices of sales managers' speech predicted accurately how effective they were in their job as measured by not only supervisors' ratings but also actual sales performance.[5]

The intuitive mind quickly forms an impression of a person, and whilst the non-conscious processes behind it cannot be easily put into words, they result nonetheless in a judgement: for example, 'is this person going to be a good professor?', 'can he be trusted?' or 'will she be a good hire?' these are all questions with *uncertain* outcomes. In an ideal world certainty might be preferable, but whether a person turns out to be a good teacher, honest or a good hire can only be known *after* the fact. Social intuitions are hypotheses about people. But we need them to help us decide what to do, whether it's cutting classes or offering someone a job – we often have to decide with incomplete information. Thin-slicing can help. The evidence suggests that the inter-personal qualities and skills needed to be effective in a variety of people-related jobs may be apparent to the intuitive mind on the basis of thin slices of behaviour.

But perhaps the intuitive mind judges people who are physically attractive as competent, confident, likeable, trustworthy and warm? For example, do we have a natural eye for body symmetry (people do have preferences for symmetrical faces), 'averageness' (computer-generated average faces are rated as more attractive than the individual faces they're constructed from), and so-called 'hormone markers' (prominent cheek bones, good skin condition, amount and location of face or body hair)[6] and mix these up with personal and job-related attributes? Does beauty get in the way of the intuitive mind? When asked to judge such attributes on the basis of photographs physical attractiveness can influence people's opinions – a photograph, perhaps because it's not the real thing, can fool the intuitive mind. However, when we actually meet someone in the flesh the intuitive mind becomes much more discerning. An attractive person with an unattractive voice gets a lower rating, and a video in which the person speaks is a much better basis for a thin-slice judgement than a photo.[7] More-over, recall from the US election research by Todorov and his colleagues that they filtered out the effect of attractiveness from their results and even then found that people's judgement of competence from a photo agreed with voters' reactions in actual elections to the tune of 60 to 70%. Clearly something is going on the backstage of the mind.

THE SCIENCE OF THE INTUITIVE MIND – 'MIND BLINDNESS'

Most of us have a 'theory of mind' – we intuitively know that other people have minds and that their experiences of having a mind are probably quite like what we ourselves experience.[8] Human beings normally develop a 'theory of mind' at around four years of age. It allows us to infer other people's emotional states, motivations and intentions, and explain and predict their behaviour in terms of their presumed thoughts and feelings. Without a theory of mind, as is the case with severe autism, people have extreme difficulty in appreciating another person's mental state; as a result their ability to relate and cooperate breaks down. 'Mind blindness'[9] – a lack of intuitions into the minds of others – can be socially debilitating, for example whilst it is possible for such individuals to learn the rules of social behaviour they often lack the intuitive judgement of where and when to apply them. Things that are routinely used to spice-up social interactions, like irony and playfulness, throw them completely.

Autism is a strongly heritable condition suffered by four times more males than females and characterised by abnormal social and communicative development. It's been suggested that a possible mechanism behind autism – related to mind-blindness – is a malfunction in a group of brain cells called mirror neurons. Mirror neurons were discovered in the early 1990s in research on monkey brains, they fire not only when an action is per-formed (for example a gesture) but also when the gesture is observed in others (hence they're sometimes called 'monkey see, monkey do' neurons). In research with people with autism their mirror neurons only responded to their own movement and not that of others. This malfunction in the mirror neuron mechanism may contribute to the impairments in comprehending and responding appropriately to other's behaviour that characterise autism – referred to by some as 'an extreme form of male brain'.

Sources: Frith, U. (2001) Mind blindness and the brain in autism, *Neuron*, **32**: 969–79.; Oberman, L.M., Hubbard, E.M., McCleery, J.P., Altschuler, E.L., Ramachandran, V.S. and Pineda, J.A. (2005) EEG evidence for mirror neuron dysfunction in autism spectrum disorders. *Cognitive Brain Research*, **24**: 190–8.

Our intuitive mind tends to look beyond physical attractiveness when forming an impression of another person. Moreover, a smile in isolation isn't enough to win someone over since it's hard to fake and can be interpreted in a variety of ways depending on the context. The intuitive mind is attuned to the processes of perception and interpretation by picking-up signals from a number of different channels (for example, the intuitive mind can simultaneously decode facial expressions, body movements and postures, and tone of voice) and interpreting these signals in relation to the context we observe them in (for example, in the thin-slice college research students' intuitive minds weren't strongly biased in their judgements of how good a teacher is by the teacher's physical attractiveness).

Non-verbal decoding isn't totally innate – we get better at it as we get older, more experienced and wiser.[10] Moreover, our intuitive decoder focuses on non-verbal facial expressions and bodily movements which, unlike verbal expressions, are:

1. easily noticed by the receiver;
2. harder for the sender to control and suppress;
3. 'leaky' – they give away a great deal of valuable information.[11]

The intuitive mind does the decoding of non-verbal behaviour automatically, rapidly and effortlessly, communicating its views not as words but as gut feelings.[12] It's also quite impervious to fatigue, boredom or financial incentive – thin-slice researchers who offered participants rewards for improved accuracy didn't see any significant gain.

On the basis of an extensive programme of studies in a wide variety of professional contexts the thin slice researchers have identified a range of positive and negative personal attributes in which intuitive impressions count. Many of these attributes are vitally important for leading and managing teams of employees, dealing with customers and clients and a wide variety of social interactions in the workplace.

Application No. 8: Where First Impressions Count[13]

Ambition	Anxiety	Competence
Confidence	Distancing	Dominance
Employability	Enthusiasm	Expressiveness
Influence	Likeability	Nervousness
Optimism	Persuasiveness	Politeness
Trustworthiness	Warmth	Willingness

It seems that the intuitive mind not only automatically decodes many of the facial expressions, gestures, vocal and bodily signals that we unintentionally give out, it also makes an assessment of the attitudes, feelings, intentions, motivations, personalities and even perceived skill levels of others. But making a judgement of another person, especially in business and management contexts, often involves a process of categorisation. The social psychologist Susan T. Fiske proposed that we perceive and judge other people by putting them into a category based on some obvious attribute, for example gender, and then making either a:

1. quick, low-effort, category-based 'top-down' approach (intuitive) that relies heavily on the knowledge we already have about the category we've assigned the person to and the stereotypes of it that we hold, or;
2. high-effort more piecemeal 'bottom-up' approach in which we piece together the available information (analytical) to arrive at a more discerning and considered judgement.

Which approach is adopted is likely to depend on the decision maker's preferred thinking style (for example, analytical or intuitive) and whether circumstances or personal motivations require us to make the more high effort 'individuated' rather than stereotyped impressions (depending on whether the decision is high or low stakes for us personally). In the bottom-up approach we tend to not rely solely on intuitive preconceptions but take the more effortful route – the person is seen as a unique individual and worthy of careful scrutiny. Nonetheless, as with many other decisions, feeling *does* play an important role. Even though the intuitive mind has the power to make fast accurate judgements in some of the most crucial aspects of inter-personal relations, the analytical mind need not be an impotent bystander. In high stakes situations (such as making job offers or business partnering) it's better to get as much information about a person as possible in the time available or if necessary defer making a decision until a clearer picture has emerged, in order to be as confident as you can be that you're balancing analysis with genuine intuitive judgement and not categorising a person unfairly on the basis of a negative stereotype. Since it's under conscious control the analytical mind has the power to be engaged and step in as a check-and-balance and guard against some of the enemies of good intuitive judgement – bias, prejudice, stereotyping and wishful thinking (I'll look in more detail at the effects of these four things in the next chapter).

Smarter by Thinking Less?

The intuitive mind and the analytical mind evolved as a partnership. However, there can be a down side to enlisting the help of the analytical mind. A radical model of the way the mind works has been put forward by the Dutch psychologist Ap Dijksterhuis and his colleagues. They proposed their 'Unconscious Thought Theory' based on the counter-intuitive notion that deliberately engaging in 'not thinking' about certain types of problems can lead to a better solution than by thinking about them. In their experiments they investigated how satisfied buyers of a number of consumer items of varying degrees of complexity, including shampoo, CDs, shoes, and video cameras, were after they'd made their choices:

1. People who didn't think hard about their choices were more satisfied with their selection of a complex item such as a video camera, but less satisfied with their choice of a simple item such as a bottle of shampoo.
2. On the other hand the people who thought hard reported being more satisfied with their shampoo choice (low complexity item) than with their video camera choice (high complexity item).

In another experiment Dijksterhuis and his colleagues also found that people who consciously worked hard on problem-related thinking produced less original ideas than people who were distracted into an unconscious thought mode.[14] If the Unconscious Thought Theory is valid – and it's a controversial idea[15] – it seems that when choosing a complex (and therefore expensive) consumer item, or aiming to be creative and original it might be better to let the intuitive mind do at least some if not most of the hard work for you.[16]

Other researchers over the past decade and a half have found that thinking too much can interfere with and be detrimental to intuitive judgements. Psychologists Timothy Wilson and Jonathan Schooler conducted an experiment in which they compared college students' preferences for different brands of strawberry jam preserves with jam experts' ratings. The students who didn't analyse why they felt the way they did about the jams agreed more with the experts' jam ratings than did the students who analysed their feelings about the jams. In another experiment Wilson and his colleagues had two groups of students choose art posters. One group was asked to engage their analytical mind and list their reasons for liking or disliking each poster ('conscious thinkers'). The other group didn't have the opportunity to think consciously about which poster and had to choose intuitively ('non-conscious thinkers'). Conscious and non-conscious thinkers expressed strong preferences and were given their favourite poster to take home. They were phoned a few weeks later to see how they felt about their choices. The conscious thinkers who used their analytical mind were less satisfied with their posters than the non-conscious thinkers who chose intuitively.[17] How happy or sad we are is also important. When people are in a sad mood they rely on a more analytical and less intuitive approach to decoding non-verbal behaviours. The result is that the accuracy of their thin-slices judgement suffers.

The intuitive mind is adept at dealing with slices of behaviour that are several seconds in length. But this can seem like an age in some life-threatening situations. People who've been through shootings and muggings, and lived to tell the tale, report that time seems to almost stand still – seconds can seem like hours. Police officers dealing with potential armed threats sometimes have to decide to shoot or hold back in space of one or two seconds. In biological terms instinctive responses to a threat travel along a short, very fast route in which information is transmitted almost instantaneously to a part of the brain – the amygdala – which induces a 'flight-or-fight' reaction. When the slice gets too thin intuition breaks down and biological reflexes and the survival instinct can take over. The speed of the response is so fast that neither the analytical nor the intuitive mind has a chance to react. These lightning fast responses can be an advantage in life-threatening situations as they put us ahead of the game. But these kinds of instinctive responses can also 'hi-jack' our decision making and behaviour in situations where they've outlived their original biological function and aren't necessary.[18]

In many emotionally charged situations in the workplace it's best if at all possible to avoid knee-jerk instinctive reactions because they often turn out to be a mindless form of rage or passion that have the habit of subsiding as quickly as they arose. Nonetheless, controlling emotions such as fear and anger can be difficult and it's not something we're normally trained or educated to be able to do. But being aware of your bodily state, for example how tense or relaxed your body feels, is a first step. Responding to flight or fight reactions by techniques as simple as slower breathing or slow counting can help to cool things down. In the heat of an emotionally charged moment the cool of the analytical mind can help to quell a potentially destructive knee-jerk reaction that in the long term may only lead to a 'lose-lose' situation.

A surprising – and perhaps counter-intuitive – implication from the scientific research on quick, intuitive judgement is that the more introspective and diligent we are, the worse our thin-slice social judgement can become. Perhaps in becoming diligent we ignore feelings (affect) and instead focus on finding the right (analytical) words to express our views, and adopt a cooler, calm, emotionally detached approach when in fact it might be better to go with gut feeling?[19] The problem with introspecting – in effect analysing – is that it can cause people to focus on those attributes of a product or person that can be put into words. The words that exist in our verbal language or that we have in our personal vocabulary aren't necessarily the best reason for making the choice – feelings can sometimes be a better guide. One of the paradoxes of intuition is that it's easier to respond to a gut feeling than to describe it. By introspecting too much people may end up moderating their initial and more accurate feelings-based intuitive judgement.[20] So whether its preserves, posters or people we're judging, we may ignore intuition sometimes at our peril.

Deceiving the Intuitive Mind

Give it a thin-slice and your intuitive mind automatically makes fast, people-related judgements. In a longer-term working relationship can the intuitive mind be manipulated and outwitted? Is it possible for an unscrupulous employee to gain advantage by managing the impression they make on a colleague or boss by consciously manipulating on an on-going basis the signals they give out? The answer is 'sometimes'. Human beings can be devious and engage in deception in social situations to try and win friends and resources, but on the other hand in social groupings that are glued together by cooperation and trust this has to be balanced with not making too many enemies.

Often it isn't so much what two people say when they are conversing that intuitively signals how well a conversation's going, as the way that they say it, and some aspects of communication have the potential to be deliberately manipulated. Emphasising pitch and volume can convey emotionality, and how active we are in the conversation can signal our engagement with the other person. Other aspects of speech are less easily controlled. Non-conscious mimicry – 'mirroring' – of the other person's body movements, facial expressions or speech signals empathy. Utterances like 'uh-huh', 'yup', 'OK?' and 'OK!' can improve the outcome of a conversation. We tend to mimic when we want to affiliate with or get the approval of the other person. For example, when waitresses mimicked the speech of their customers they received higher tips than when they didn't. Skilled liars tend to smile less and engage in more self-manipulations (for example scratching the hand, touching one's hair and adjustment of clothing) when lying. Some experienced criminal offenders are aware that smiling and laughing reduces their credibility in the eyes of the listener; they also use self manipulations to try to distract listeners from the content of their lies. Experienced or gifted criminal offenders may have a sophisticated knowledge of how to appear credible and become intuitive liars. On the other hand some people are so attuned to body language and emotional expressions that it's almost as though they have a built-in lie detector.[21]

THE SCIENCE OF THE INTUITIVE MIND – LYING IN ORDER TO LOOK GOOD

Although it is seen as morally wrong and frowned upon it's been estimated that on average people in general tell lies two or three times a day. Moreover, across hundreds of experiments the rates of lie-truth discrimination is around 54%, in other words the average person can tell lies from truths at a level slightly better than can be achieved by tossing a coin. This has encouraged researchers to speculate that this is a natural equilibrium – if lies were very effective truth telling would be less common; whereas if lie detection was very effective fewer lies would be told.

A job interview is a high stakes situation for all parties – the outcome can be a costly decision for an employer and it can make or break a person's career and change their life course. Even given the fact that 'half the truth is a whole lie' in a job interview, many people do nonetheless succumb to the temptation to manage the impression that they want to create by embellishing on the truth. For example, it's been estimated that 44% of CVs contain 'misrepresentations'. In the UK one of the contestants on the BBC TV prime time reality TV show 'The Apprentice' apparently pretended to have spent two years at university when he only stayed there four months – he faced a barrage of criticism but nonetheless went on to win the contest.[22]

Research in the USA with psychology undergraduates investigated lying in job selection by using a simulated interview for a tutor position which the students actually believed they were applying for. After the interview the students were told that they were only participating in an experiment – there was no tutor job – and were shown a videotape of their interview. In reviewing the tape they admitted to:

1. lying on application forms and in interviews and lying two or three times per 15-minute interview;
2. being especially boastful about their statistical and organisational capabilities for technical job requirements (in an attempt to compensate for lack of job-relevant skills) – and, perhaps unsurprisingly, extraverts were especially prone to self-promotion.

Lying and deception isn't confined only to employees. As cases of corporate corruption and scandal testify, if the process of deception in an organisation goes unchecked it can take-on a life of its own, escalate and consume the whole organisation and eventually kill off a business.

Sources: Bond, C.F. and DePaulo, B.M. (2006) Accuracy of deception judgements, *Personality and Social Psychology Review*, **10**(3): 214–34; Fleming, P. and Zygliopoulos, S.C. (2008) The escalation of deception in organizations, *Journal of Business Ethics*, **81**: 837–50; Weiss, B. and Feldman, R.S. (2006) Looking good and lying to do it: deception as an impression management strategy in job interviews, *Journal of Applied Social Psychology*, **36**(4): 1070–86.

In the workplace there's a variety of 'impression management' tactics that people use, some are aimed directly at the supervisor, whilst others are focused on the job itself:

1. Ingratiation: supervisor-focused tactics often use ingratiation, for example praising and complementing the boss, agreeing with their ideas and doing favours for them. Such tactics seem to pay off: ingratiators are seen by bosses as good 'organisational citizens' and get better performance ratings and judgements of interpersonal attraction from their bosses.

2. Self-promotion: job-related impression management tactics are used to try to make an impact on others by self-promotion, taking responsibility for good outcomes, making a bad outcome you're responsible for seem not quite so bad, and 'bigging-up' one's own achievements and credentials. Job-related impression management tactics don't seem to pay off: self-promoters are less successful in their careers and get lower supervisor ratings of their performance.

It seems that bosses are only human after all – they like it when people appear to like them, but on the other hand they, and co-workers, seem to take exception to braggarts and charlatans.[23] Finally, it's salutary to note that some scientists believe that our great ape cousins are also capable of certain more primitive types of deceptions in their social interactions. For example, female gorillas have been observed deceiving the dominant male in the troupe by engineering a situation in which they and a younger male become separate from the rest of the group in order to copulate. Male chimps in the presence of the dominant male have been observed to strategically place a hand over their erect genitals so that they're visible to potential female mate, but hidden from the view of the dominant male. Whether apes are Machiavellian to the extent that they are able to infer the mental states of the other members of their troupe is a fascinating and controversial question.[24] The question remains open as to whether *Homo sapiens* is not only hard-wired for engaging in deception but also for the interpretation of the cheating behaviours of others?[25]

See, Do, Empathise

In the 1990s in the lab of the Italian neurophysiologist Giacomo Rizzolatti at the University of Parma a remarkable discovery was made during a series of experiments into the firing of neurons in the pre-motor cortex of macaque monkeys. The findings have profound implications for understanding human intuition.

Neurons are the cells that create brain activity by carrying an electrical signal from one to another through a vast network of interconnections. In a piece of brain tissue the size of grain of sand there would be 100,000 neurons, there are billions of connections between them and they create the physiological basis of our mental lives.[26] Amongst the functions of the brain's pre-motor cortex are guidance of movement, coding of space, interpretation of the properties of objects and, crucially from the point of view of understanding intuition, learning by association.[27] The thing that astounded Rizzolatti and his colleagues was that they observed neurons firing in the brains of monkeys not only when a monkey grasped a piece of food such as a grape with its own hand, but also when it watched a human experimenter or other monkey doing the same action. Rizzolatti named these structures 'mirror neurons' because they switch on not only in the process of performing an action (such as a gesture) but also in response to seeing an action being performed. Some people have called them 'monkey see, monkey do neurons'. The activation of mirror neurons 'reflects' the actions in the brain of another monkey or the experimenter – in the 'receiver' of the visual stimulus the receiver's hand does not move but the neurons fire, nonetheless. A similar general mirror neuron system has been found in humans also, but the human system has been found not only to respond to seeing an action such as a hand movement, but also when an action is imagined.

One of Rizzolatti's colleagues at the University of Parma, Vittorio Gallese, described the neural mechanism as 'involuntary and automatic', and with it we don't have to *think* about what other people are doing or feeling, we simply *know*.[28] The potential of the mirror neuron concept for understanding our intuitions is that mirror neurons may not merely be concerned with imitation learning and the creation of neural pathways to imitate an action, they may also transform visual information relating to an act (such as a gesture) into an intuitive knowledge and understanding of the act and *what it means*. An action done by another individual may be understood by the receiver's intuitive mind without the analytical mind having much of a say in the matter. Mirror neurons may enable us to 'get inside someone else's head'.

The researchers have also proposed the existence of 'echo-neurons' which are activated in response to verbal information which opens up the possibility for an intuitive component to listening to what someone is saying as well as in watching what someone else does.[29] Rizzolatti has suggested that in humans, one of the few species that learns by looking and then copying,[30] the neuro-physiological mechanism of the mirror neuron is the basis of much of our learning. Mirror neuron research has gone beyond the study of simple grasping movements and hand gestures and looked at quite complex motor behaviours. Scientists in Rizzolatti's lab have investigated the ways in which novice guitarists learn guitar chords through observation and imitation of expert guitarists. Using functional magnetic resonance imaging (fMRI) brain imaging techniques they found that:

1. mirror neurons were activated in novices' brains when they were asked to observe experts' hand movements in forming guitar chords;
2. new neural patterns were formed for the actual playing of the chord which corresponded to the mirror neurons being activated merely by observing the action of someone else who could play.

The evidence from the mirror neuron research is that much non-verbal communication (a vital aspect in any social relationship including those in the workplace) occurs without conscious effort, is under the control of the intuitive mind rather than the analytical mind and can be understood without conscious awareness of *how* we know. As Harvard social cognitive neuroscientist Matt Lieberman has argued, mirror neurons may play a particularly important role in the process of 'a complex reciprocal non-verbal "dance" that occurs between interaction partners' the dynamics of which provide each of the players with a basis for their interpretation of human social interaction.[31]

Since Rizzolatti's ground-breaking research mirror neuron research has continued apace. For example, brain scanning research with dancers at London's Royal Ballet by Daniel Glaser of University College London has found that dancers' mirror neuron systems show more activity when dancers watched movements they'd been trained to perform than when they watched movements they hadn't been trained to perform. By contrast the mirror system in non-dancers showed less activity in response to watching any type of dancing. One implication of this may be that it's possible to maintain our levels of the skills that we've already acquired through practice by imagining the relevant action sequence in a mental simulation.

The mirror neuron research suggests that intuitive mind has evolved in humans to such an extent as to endow us with the capacity to 'read' (in a non-psychic sense) someone else's state of mind. The mirror neuron system may allow us to infer another person's motivations and intentions and to rehearse a sequence of actions virtually in anticipation of the actual performance.[32] In business management the interactions between leaders and followers are based, at least in part, on a reciprocal intuitive understanding of each others' actions, an implication being that leaders have the capacity to empathise with what a follower may feel by a reading of their facial and body movements and vice versa. Mirror neurons may have evolved to enable us to get inside someone else's skin and walk in their shoes. The mirror neuron system may also be the neural circuitry that's behind our empathetic sense of justice and fairness towards other human beings – the feeling of their predicament – that we experience on the basis of nothing more or less than a gut perception of someone else's emotional state.[33]

The final and perhaps most profound implication of the mirror neuron research has been proposed by the neuroscientist V.S. Ramachandran. He suggested that at some point in human evolution, say 40–50,000 years ago, our mirror neuron system took a quantum leap forward. This enabled us, as one of the most social of all animal species, to learn quickly through imitation and therefore adapt to environmental changes. Human learning became more efficient and effective as a result of social interactions ('human see, human do') rather than through millions of years of evolution (which is the way many other organisms have to adapt to environmental change). For example, rather than evolving a thicker coat human beings were able to learn by watching others of our species that an animal could be killed and skinned and its fur used to ward off the effects of a colder environment. The same might be said of the mirror neuron systems of leaders and managers in the 21st century – it's perhaps the basis of our most important mental asset, the capacity to learn how to deal with complex, dynamic and uncertain situations as they arise by rapid adaptation rather than slow evolution. Ramachandran has gone as far as to say that mirror neurons was one of the most underpublicised stories of the decade and that the implication of mirror neurons will do for psychology what DNA did for biology.[34]

The trust that is placed in intuition should be tempered with the knowledge that intuitions, like any other human judgement, are fallible. For all the potential power of the mirror neuron system in understanding our social intuitions, the intuitive mind shouldn't be thought of as a 'mind reading' machine, mystical or otherwise. It evolved to alert us to the *possibility* of lies and deception as well as how trustworthy and effective somebody might be. At the end of the day intuitive judgements aren't cast iron certainties. Intuitions are hypotheses and judgements which can be compelling but are also fallible, and the intuitive mind can be all too easily fooled when circumstances conspire to lure it into taking certain types of mental shortcuts for which it is ill-equipped.

INTUITIVE INTELLIGENCE PRINCIPLE No. 4: COUNT ON FIRST IMPRESSIONS, MAKE FIRST IMPRESSIONS COUNT

A little goes a very long way as far as the intuitive mind is concerned. It's capable of making accurate inferences and judgements about others on very thin slices of their behaviour. We convey through our words and actions a great deal about ourselves in the first few seconds of meeting somebody and the initial impressions that we create and the initial judgements that the intuitive mind makes are 'sticky'. Thin slices speak volumes about another person's emotional state, and our gut reactions determine the extent to which we are able to empathise with them, and their situation.

NOTES

[1] Finkel, E.J. and Eastwick, P.W. (2008) Speed-dating, *Current Directions in Psychological Science*, **17**(3): 193–7; Fisman, R.F., Iyengar, S.S., Kamenica, E. and Simonson, I. (2006) Gender differences in mate selection: Evidence from a speed-dating experiment, *The Quarterly Journal of Economics*, May: 673–9.

[2] Finkel, E.J. and Eastwick, P.W. (2008) Speed-dating, *Current Directions in Psychological Science*, **17**(3): 193–7.

[3] Lieberman, M.D. (2000) Intuition: A social cognitive neuroscience approach. *Psychological Bulletin*, **126**, 109–37.

[4] Todorov, A., Mandisodza, A.N., Goren, A. and Hall, C.C. (2005) Inferences of competence from faces predict election outcomes, *Science*, **308**: 1623–6; Antonakis, J. and Dalgas, O. (2009) Predicting elections: Child's play, *Science*, **323**: 1183; Henderson, M. (2009) Let's face it, looks win votes, *The Times* 7 March 2009.

[5] Ambady, N., Koo, J.J., Rosenthal, R. and Winograd, C. (2002) Physical therapists' non-verbal communication predicts geriatric patients' health

outcomes, *Psychology and Aging*, **17**: 443–52; Ambady, N. and Krab-benhoft, M.A. (2006) The 30-sec sale: Using thin slice judgements to evaluate sales effectiveness, *Journal of Consumer Psychology*, **16**(1): 4–13; Ambady, N., La Plante D., Nguen, T., Rosenthal, R. and Levinson, W. (2002) Surgeon's tone of voice: A clue to malpractice history, *Surgery*, **132**: 5–9; Prickett, T., Gada-Jain, N. and Bernieri, F.J. (1999) *First impression formation in a job interview: The first 20 seconds.* Unpublished manuscript.

[6]Fink, B. and Penton-Oak, I. (2002) Evolutionary psychology of facial attractiveness, *Current Directions in Psychological Science*, **11**(5): 154–8; Weeden, J. and Sabini, J. (2005) Physical attractiveness and health in Western societies: A review, *Psychological Bulletin*, **131**(5): 635–53.

[7]Ambady, N. and Rosenthal, R. (1993) Half a minute: Predicting teacher evaluations from thin-slices of behaviour and physical attractiveness, *Journal of Personality and Social Psychology*, **64**(3): 431–41.

[8]Dunbar, R. (2004) *The human story*, London: Faber.

[9]Baron-Cohen, S. (1995) *Mind blindness: an essay on autism and theory of mind*, Cambridge, MA: MIT Press.

[10]Lieberman op cit.

[11]Ambady and Krabbenhoft op cit.

[12]Perrachio, L.A. and Luna, D. (2006) The role of thin-slice judgements in consumer psychology, *Journal of Consumer Psychology*, **16**(1): 25–32.

[13]Sources: Ambady et al. (2002) op cit., Ambady and Krabbenhoft, (2006) op cit.; Prickett et al., op cit., (1999).

[14]Dijksterhuis A., Bos, M.W., Nordgren, L.F. and van Baaren, R.B. (2006) On Making the Right Choice: The Deliberation-Without-Attention Effect, *Science*, **311**: 1005–7; Dijksterhuis, A. and Meurs, T. (2006) Where creativity resides: the generative power of unconscious thought, *Consciousness and Cognition*, **15**: 135–46.

[15]Newell, B.R., Wong, K.Y., Cheung, H. and Rakow, T. (2008) Think, blink or sleep on it, *The Quarterly Journal of Experimental Psychology* (in press). As the lead researcher in this project commented: 'Going with your gut may be right when you're an expert. For example, maybe choosing lunch every day is easy because we do it every

day. But we don't move [house] every day, so when making a choice about where to live, we have no expertise.' http://www.time.com/time/health/article/0,8599,1835431,00.html. Accessed 7th September 2008.

[16] Gladwell, M. (2005) *Blink: the power of thinking without thinking*, London: Allen Lane/Penguin; Goleman, D. (1997) *Emotional Intelligence*, London: Bloomsbury; Le Doux, J.E. (1996) *The Emotional Brain*, New York: Simon and Schuster.

[17] Dijksterhuis, A. and van Olden, Z. (2005) On the benefits of thinking unconsciously: unconscious thought can increase post choice satisfaction, *Journal of Experimental Social Psychology*, **42**(5) 627–31; Wilson, T.D., Lisle, D., Schooler, J.W., Hodges, S.D., Klaaren K.J. and LaFleur S.J. (1993) Introspecting about reasons can reduce post-choice satisfaction, *Personality and Social Psychology Bulletin*, **19**: 331–9.

[18] Gladwell, op cit.; Goleman, op cit.; Le Doux, op cit.

[19] Ambady, N. and Gray, H.M. (2002) On being sad and mistaken: Mood effects on the accuracy of thin-slice judgements, *Journal of Personality and Social Psychology*, **83**(4): 947–61.

[20] Wilson, T.D. (2002) *Strangers to Ourselves: Discovering the adaptive unconscious*, Cambridge, MA: Belknap/Harvard University Press.

[21] Curhan, J.R. and Pentland, A. (2007) Thin-slices of negotiation: Predicting outcomes from conversational dynamics within the first five minutes, *Journal of Applied Psychology*, **92**(3): 802–11; Porter, S., Doucette, N.L., Woodworth, M., Earle, J. and MacNeil, B. (2008) Halfe the world knowes not how the other halfe lies: investigation of verbal and non-verbal signs of deception exhibited by criminal offenders and non-offenders, *Legal and Criminal Psychology*, **13**: 27–38; Carter, R. (1998) *Mapping the Mind*. London: Orion Books.

[22] The Apprentice: top five CV liars' retrieved on 27th August 2008 from http://www.telegraph.co.uk/arts/main.jhtml?xml=/arts/2008/06/11.

[23] Bolino, M.C., Varela, J.A., Bande, B. and Turnley, W.H. (2006) The impact of impression management tactics on supervisor ratings of organizational citizenship behaviour, *Journal of Organizational*

Behavior, **27**: 281–97; Gordon, R.A. (1996) Impact of ingratiation on judgments and evaluations: A meta-analytic investigation, *Journal of Personality and Social Psychology*, **71**: 54–70; Judge, T.A. and Bretz, R.D. (1994) Political influence and career success, *Journal of Management*, **20**: 43–65; Wayne, S.J. and Ferris, G.R. (1990) Influence tactics, affect, and exchange quality in supervisor-subordinate interactions: a laboratory experiment and field study, *Journal of Applied Psychology*, **75**: 487–99.

[24] Byrne, R.W. and Whiten, A. (Eds). (1988) *Machiavellian Intelligence: social expertise and the evolution of intellect in monkeys, apes and humans*. Oxford: Clarendon Press; Corballis, M.C. (2001) Evolution of the generative mind. In Sternberg, R.J. and Kaufman, J.C. (Eds). *The Evolution of Intelligence*. Hillsdale, N.J.: Lawrence Erlbaum Associates, 117–44. Mithen, S. (1996) *The Prehistory of the Mind: a search for the origins of art, religion and science*. London: Thames and Hudson.

[25] Spinney, L. (1998) Liar! Liar! *New Scientist*, **2121**: 22.

[26] Carter, R. (1998) *Mapping the Mind*. London: Orion Books; Ramachandran, V.S. and Blakeslee, S. (1998) *Phantoms in the Brain*. London: Fourth Estate.

[27] Gallese, V., Fadiga, L., Fogassi, L. and Rizzolatti, G. (1996) Action recognition in the pre-motor cortex, *Brain*, **119**: 593–609.

[28] 'The mind's mirror' by Lea Winerman. Retrieved from http://www.apa.org/monitor/oct05/mirror.html on 15th April 2009.

[29] Rizzolatti, G. and Craighero, L. (2004) The mirror neuron system, *Annual Review of Neuroscience*, **27**: 169–92.

[30] There are controversies about the extent to which other great apes (for example chimps and gorillas) can exhibit true imitation. See: Chiappe, D. and MacDonald, K. (2005) 'The evolution of domain general mechanisms in intelligence and learning', *The Journal of General Psychology*, **132**(1): 5–40.

[31] Lieberman, M.D. (2007) 'Social cognitive neuroscience: a review of core processes', *Annual Review of Psychology*, 259–89 (p. 271).

[32] 'Daniel Glaser's latest study with ballet and capoeira dancers' retrieved from http://www.pbs.org/wgbh/nova/sciencenow/3204/01-resup.html on 15th April 2009.

[33] Hauser, M.D. (2006) *Moral Minds: how nature designed our universal sense of right and wrong.* London: Abacus

[34] 'Mirror neurons and imitation learning and the driving force behind the "great leap forward" in human evolution' by V.S. Ramachandran retrieved from http://www.edge.org/3rd_culture/ramachandran/ramachandran_p1.html on 15th April 2009.

Chapter 5

INTUITIVE SHORTCUTS

In this chapter the four enemies of good intuition – logical errors, biased judgement, stereotyping and wishful thinking – which come about when we take mental shortcuts will be outlined. I'll explain how the intuitive mind can tempt us into taking these shortcuts, how they can lead us badly astray, and also offer some suggestions for avoiding the feeble intuitions that accrue from errors, biases, stereotyping and wishful thinking.

When confronted with choices many people tend to go for the option that offers least resistance and requires least energy. This 'least effort principle' applies in many different walks of life: many people tend to buy what's handy, cook what's convenient and watch what happens to be on TV at the time. It's not so different when we use our brains to make judgements and take decisions; even though we have an analytical mind at our disposal we often behave like 'cognitive misers' who look for the easy option – the mental 'quick fix'.

Whilst the analytical mind is a heavy consumer of cognitive calories, the lightweight intuitive mind operates deftly with minimal effort. So the natural choice for a life of low mental strain is to engage the intuitive mind and let the analytical mind coast along. In the right hands and under the right conditions the intuitive mind can be a powerful and indispensable decision-making tool. The downside is that in the wrong hands and under the wrong conditions intuitive shortcuts can be an open invitation to the four enemies of good judgement: logical errors, biased judgement, stereotyping and wishful thinking:[1] feeble intuitions are the result.

Downside of the Intuitive Mind No. 1: Logical Errors

One of the downsides of the intuitive mind is that it's especially fallible when it comes to logic. By jumping the gun and intervening in judgements that are better left to its analytical counterpart the intuitive mind opens the way for some quite basic errors of logic. One vivid illustration of this is the famous 'Linda Problem' developed by the psychologists Daniel Kahneman and Amos Tversky in the 1970s:

> Linda is a 31-year old who's outspoken and very bright. Her university degree was in philosophy and whilst at university she was deeply concerned with issues of discrimination and social justice, she also participated in anti-nuclear demonstrations.

If you had to make a judgement about Linda which one of the following do you think would be more likely?

1. Linda is a bank teller.
2. Linda is a bank teller and is active in the feminist movement.

If you're anything like the majority of participants in the Linda Problem experiments conducted by psychologists Kahneman and Tversky[2] you'll have chosen (2) 'Linda is a bank teller and is active in the feminist movement'. If you made this choice why did you do so? One of the most common arguments people gave for their choice was that 'Linda is more likely to be a feminist bank teller than she is likely to be a bank teller because she resembles an active feminist more than she resembles a bank teller'. If you chose (2) pause and reflect for a moment – is (2) really *more* probable than (1)?

By now you may be suspecting that in choosing (2) you, or more correctly your intuitive mind, made a logical error. But that's nothing to be ashamed of, you're in good company. In Kahneman and Tversky's experiments with undergraduates at one of North America's top universities 85 % chose (2), and 65 % made this choice on the basis of the argument that the picture presented of Linda represents the prototype of 'an active feminist'.

But recall that you were being asked to judge which of the two statements (1) or (2) was more likely, which one was the more *probable* occurrence. Think about all bank tellers. Some of them are active in the feminist movement, others may be active in the Green movement, some have brown hair and some of them prefer ketchup rather than mayonnaise on their fries. Can it be more likely that a person (of any description) is more likely to be a bank teller who prefers ketchup than merely a bank teller? No. Why not? Because 'bank tellers who prefer ketchup', just like 'bank tellers with brown hair' or 'bank tellers who are active in the feminist movement', is a subset of 'bank tellers'. The probability of a person being in the smaller category 'ketchup-preferring bank tellers' can't be greater than the probability that they are a member of the larger category 'bank tellers'. In spite of the picture your intuitive mind constructed, the same I'm afraid is true of Linda – the probability of her being a member of subset (2) can't be greater than the probability of her being a member of set (1). (2) is a subset of (1). If you made this error blame your intuitive mind, it caused you to fall foul of what Kahneman and Tversky called the 'conjunction fallacy' – you mixed up how the image presented of Linda was representative of a particular type of bank teller (a feminist one) with the probability of her being in a larger set (bank teller).

Is it possible to avoid making such errors of logic (whether they matter all that much in daily life is a different question)? Well, yes but not easily or routinely. Statistical knowledge and IQ can help guard against these kinds of intuitive mistakes:

1. People with knowledge of statistics are more able and likely to follow the laws of logic rather than their intuition when doing the Linda Problem – being well versed in the laws of probability and statistics helps, whereas being statistically naïve is a distinct disadvantage.
2. People with high IQs are able to understand and can apply the necessary logic: in the language of the analytical mind 'if P is the probability of an event, then P (bank teller and active feminist) ≤ P (bank teller)', armed with this knowledge the analytical mind can step-in and over-ride the intuitive mind's erroneous judgement.[3]

The Linda Problem is one of the most insightful and informative experiments in the psychology of intuition. People have tried to dismiss the findings, and have nit-picked over almost every word of it including the exact meaning of 'and'.[4] Debates have gone on since the 1970s trying to unravel or take issue with exactly what's going on.

THE SCIENCE OF THE INTUITIVE MIND – TRYING TO UNRAVEL THE CONJUNCTION FALLACY

Seymour Epstein and his colleagues attempted to get at what the intuitive mind was up to by using a different test called 'The Lottery Vignette':

> Tom buys two lottery tickets, one from the state lottery and
> one from the local fire department. The chances of winning

---

the state lottery are one in a million. The chances of winning the fire department lottery are one in a thousand.

Which of the following is most likely: (1) Tom wins the state lottery; (2) Tom wins the fire department lottery; (3) Tom wins the state lottery and the fire department lottery?

In The Lottery Vignette only 6.5 % of people made a 'conjunction error' (that the probability is higher that Tom would win both lotteries, i.e. option (3). This is a complete reversal of what's typically observed in The Linda Problem – around 80 % make the conjunction error. So what's happening here?

Epstein's explanation was that the intuitive mind does in fact 'know' the conjunction rule but only in context through exposure to concrete, natural problems in everyday life in which thinking about probabilities is common, such as lotteries, raffles and gambling. The intuitive mind knows the rule and can apply it to certain types of problem. He acknowledged that The Linda Problem is concrete (rather than abstract) but took the view that, unlike the lottery problem, it's un-natural (have you ever had to make a Linda Problem-type probability judgement?).

Source: Epstein, S., Denes-Raj, V. and Pacini, R. (1995) The Linda Problem revisited from the perspective of Cognitive-Experiential Self-Theory, *Personality and Social Psychology Bulletin,* **21**(11): 1124–38.

In an interesting aside Epstein and his co-researchers found that performance on The Linda Problem is improved if it comes after The Lottery Problem, maybe because doing it this way around alerts the intuitive mind to any latent understanding it has of the conjunction rule.

In spite of the logical argument and irrespective of the evidence that option (1) in The Linda Problem is more likely, the intuitive mind can adopt a state of denial – 'go on, read it, she's got to be more than a bank teller',[5] nonetheless the analysis is correct: (1) is more likely than (2). So, if you chose (2) what went 'wrong'?

Your intuitive mind judged the relative probability of (1) or (2) using a prototype it constructed of Linda according to an image conjured up on the basis of a description of a single, bright, socially concerned female activist. On this basis that she couldn't just be a bank teller she just had to be something more. The conjunction error is one of the errors of logic that our intuitive mind commits if left to its own devices. It's difficult to guard against conjunction errors for several reasons.

🔑 Key Facts No. 11: Why the Intuitive Mind Makes Conjunction Errors

Inclination	We're naturally 'cognitive misers', and let the intuitive mind engage in its speciality – low effort thinking.
Introspection	It's hard to get to the root of the logical fallacy: we find if difficult to introspect on the reasoning behind our choice.[6]
Functionality	The intuitive mind works on the basis of similarity to prototypes, not on the laws of probability: our minds evolved to function in the everyday world in which *prototypes* matter more than *probabilities*.[7]

In a couple of twists to this story researchers looked at the effect that a person's mood and the time of day can have on their responses to The Linda Problem: happier people have greater confidence in their initial intuitive, but as it turns out incorrect, judgement; sadder people doubted their initial impressions and this tended to push them towards the right answer;[8] 'morning people' are more susceptible to conjunction errors in the evening, and 'evening people' are more likely to commit the conjunction errors in the morning.[9]

Downside of the Intuitive Mind No. 2: Biased Judgement

As well as committing errors of logic, your intuitive mind is often prone to bias when it takes a mental shortcut.[10] For example, MIT Professor Dan Ariely looked at how the intuitive mind can be tricked into capricious spending. He asked a group of students to write down the last two digits of their social security number (for example 'two' and 'five'). Ariely then asked whether or not they'd be willing to pay more or less than that number in dollars ($ 25) for four different items – a nice bottle of wine, an average bottle of wine, a book, and a box of chocolates. He then asked them to write down the maximum price they'd be willing to pay for each item (which could be more, the same or less than their two digit number, in this case $ 25). When the prices they were willing to pay for all the items were totalled the results were astonishing, he found that students with social security numbers between:

1. 00 and 19 were willing to pay a mere $ 67 for the items;
2. 20 and 39 were willing to pay $ 102;
3. 80 and 99 were willing to pay an exorbitant $ 198.

When asked whether or not they thought that their price estimates were affected by their social security numbers the students dismissed the idea as preposterous. But they were undoubtedly influenced into making biased assessments by Ariely's clever trick – they fixated on the social security number, irrespective of what it was, and intuitively priced the goods upwards or downwards with estimates that were anchored to the initial and completely arbitrary value. The prices that students unfortunate enough to have high social security numbers were willing to pay were almost three times greater than those with low social security numbers.

This bias is called 'anchoring and adjustment'. Intuitive estimates can be strongly influenced by the starting value that's given, even if the starting value is totally arbitrary or utterly implausible. For example, people who were first asked to decide 'yes or no' as to whether Ghandi died before or after the age of 140 years (which would make him the oldest man who ever lived) estimated his age to be around sixty-seven; people who were asked first to decide if Ghandi died before or after the age of nine (a fact which might be difficult to explain to his children) estimated that he lived to be around fifty (he actually died in his late seventies in 1948).

Anchors are 'sticky', and an upward or downward adjustment from the anchor can be costly in personal as well as professional life. For example, if an employee's performance appraisal starts with current performance as an explicit anchoring value adjusting from this to future performance targets may mean they end up too close to the anchor.[11] Anchoring and adjustment can also lead to the price we finally agree to pay for something being over-influenced by a completely irrelevant starting value.[12]

So beware of salespeople who show you the most expensive house, car or computer first – the other items, which they may actually *want* to sell more, are going to seem better value by comparison. Anchoring and adjustment is important for buyers and sellers because it can have a significant impact on purchasing decisions and the final price that's paid for a product or service. Sellers sometimes try, albeit not deliberately, to sell their products and services to us via our intuitive mind and exploit the errors and biases that it's prone to.

THE SCIENCE OF THE INTUITIVE MIND – ANCHORING AND ADJUSTMENT – BUYERS (AND SELLERS) BEWARE

A common tactic is for sellers to bundle products together in order that consumers will buy more than they need (or buy a more comprehensive and 'better value' package, depending on your viewpoint). But the evaluation of bundles of products – for example computer with a stand and a printer, a bed with a chest of drawers, or a flight with hotel and car hire – is a sensitive and complex matter. In their overall evaluation of a bundle consumers examine items in descending order of perceived importance (you look at the computer first if that's the item you need – it's the anchor). Researchers have found that when evaluating the bundle of products:

1. Faced with an excellent anchor but only moderate add-ons consumers' overall evaluation of the bundle is downwards (the add-on is seen as a loss).
2. However, moderate add-ons have a worse effect on excellent anchors than they do on poor anchors (in this latter case the consumer tends to see the add-on as a real gain).

The choice of add-on is crucial: it's much easier to hurt an anchor than to help it. The lesson is 'sellers beware' – overall the level of quality across bundle is an important factor in influencing consumer choice.

eBay, the online auction house, is one of the great consumer successes of the information age. On eBay sellers set shipping

145

prices which can be the minimum postage value but sometimes they're several times higher than this. Details about shipping prices are not presented overtly on the web page. Consumers tend to anchor their assessment of the value of the deal to the agreed bidding price and overlook rolling the shipping price into the equation. Consumers' perceptions of the price they are paying are biased downwards towards the anchor, thereby fuelling the profit of the seller; bargain-hunters end up paying more than they bargained for. Similarly, the price we see on Amazon Market place (a 10 cent 'used but as new' book) anchors our judgement of the cost downwards and we tend to ignore the postage and packing price which could be 30 times the price of the item itself ($ 3.00).

Sources: Yadav, M.S. (1994) How buyers evaluate product bundles: A model of anchoring and adjustment, *Journal of Consumer Research*, **21** (September): 342–53; Nelson, L.D. and Simmons, J.P. (2005) Favored favorites: inequalities in equivalence outcomes, *Advances in Consumer Research*, **32**(1): 125–8; Clark, J.M. and Sinde, G.W. (2008) Consumer behaviour in online auctions: an examination of partitioned prices on eBay, *Journal of Marketing Theory and Practice*, **16**(1): 57–66.

Many consumer decisions boil down to a choice between two alternative items which differ in quality and price. Research has found that people first identify with the higher quality item – it becomes the anchor – they then adjust for the price difference in trying to equate the items. But often the higher quality item tends to get selected anyway. Why? Psychologists think this may be because the intuitive mind provides a quick but imperfect anchor of the high quality item and the analytical mind under-corrects – the result is a decision that's biased towards the intuitive and higher priced item. The reason the intuitive mind prevails is because it sends out two signals – one is how much the item is valued (this is the anchor value) but it supplements this with another signal in the form of a feeling of confidence in the initial preference. If the feeling of confidence is high it's hard for the analytical mind to argue – the intuitive mind wins out because of the power of affect (our feelings about the product). The message to shoppers of luxury goods is clear: beware of the gullibility and impulsivity of the intuitive mind; it can sometimes be a feeble judge, take your time, walk away, calm down and let the analytical mind examine the deal coldly and calmly.

Another way in which intuitive estimates can be biased is according to how easily an event or an image comes to mind. Which of the following do you think is most common as a cause of death in the USA in 2005?

1. diabetes;
2. homicide;
3. septicemia (blood poisoning);
4. suicide.

The death rates from homicide and suicide in the USA in 2005 were roughly half those of septicemia and diabetes respectively, and septicemia is the most common out of the four.[13] People in general are medically naïve and therefore tend to underestimate death rates from relatively common diseases such as septicemia and diabetes, and over-estimate death rates from relatively uncommon but more widely reported events such as homicide and suicide. Homicide and suicide are intuitively rated as more common than they actually are. Why? If relevant, and preferably vivid, examples of an event (from TV or newspapers where 'if it bleeds it leads') can be called to mind the event is intuitively judged as more probable. Homicides make dramatic news, septicaemia doesn't. Similarly, the probability of being killed in a plane crash is often felt to be much greater than the probability of being killed in a road traffic accident simply because instances of plane crashes are vivid and come more readily to mind. The influence exerted by readily available vivid images over our intuitive mind is yet another example of the negative consequences that occur if we allow the intuitive mind to make judgements for which it's ill suited.

Intuition is fuelled by images, and as far as the intuitive mind is concerned the more vivid the better. The power of vivid images in biasing intuitive judgement was demonstrated by psychologists when they compared people's judgement of the likelihood of contracting an easy-to-imagine disease with the likelihood of a hard-to-imagine disease. The easy-to-imagine disease symptoms described were quite specific: low energy level, muscle aches and severe headaches. The hard-to-imagine symptoms were a vague sense of disorientation, a malfunctioning nervous system and an inflamed liver. An easy-to-imagine disease was judged as more likely to be contracted than was a hard-to-imagine disease.

But the power that images have to fuel intuitions also has an upside and applies to gut feeling judgements in fields as disparate as health, sport and – most crucially for organisations in times of crisis and change – visionary leadership.

INTUITION WORKOUT No. 8: JUST IMAGINE ...

The fact that the intuitive mind can be beguiled by images can be a positive thing. As many sports people know, imagining oneself making the winning shot can be an important factor in bringing about success. One of the greatest golfers of all time Jack Nicklaus said: 'I never hit a shot, not even in practice, without having a very sharp in-focus picture of it in my head. It's like a colour movie'.[14] The technique of visualisation is routinely used by coaches and sports psychologists to enhance performance.

Whilst we can't will something into being (that would be pure wishful thinking), the imaginability of an event is an important factor in the judgement we make of the likelihood of the event coming about. Like the golfer rehearsing his swing, it can help leaders and followers to achieve a goal if they can visualise the steps involved and imagine themselves in the vision:

1. Effective leaders are those who articulate clearly and share their vision widely.
2. A poorly communicated vision produces an over-active rumour mill, and followers grope in the dark for scraps of information.
3. Without a vision employees end up creating their own images of what they hope or fear might be going on.
4. A clearly articulated and feasible vision should be scrutinised for any trace of purely wishful thinking or delusion.

The clear message for leaders who feel they have a vision is that it's not enough to personally hold the vision. It must be communicated vividly to other members of the organisation for them to not only buy into the vision, but also believe in its likelihood of coming about, and so not concoct their own potentially negative and damaging images of the future.

Homicides and airline crashes are vivid and striking events which spring easily to mind and bias the intuitive mind's estimates of their likelihood of occurrence.[15] This aspect of the intuitive 'least effort principle' has a negative consequence: it means that people tend when confronted by a difficult or abstract question to answer the easier one which springs to mind (often recalled as a highly vivid real-life scenario). For example, a person who's asked 'What proportion of small business start-ups fail within a year?' may answer the much easier question of 'Do any examples of early, and perhaps dramatic, failure of small business start-ups come easily to mind?'[16] Their response might be based on a vivid and dramatic story such as the tale of a friend of a friend who lost it all in a capricious business venture but which may nonetheless be a picture that owes more to melodrama than realism. Once again the analytical mind can be deployed to challenge intuitions which have little basis in facts.

Downside of the Intuitive Mind No. 3: Stereotyping

Stereotyping is a commonly used intuitive reaction in judging or responding to people. The origins of the term go back to the late 18th century and methods used by typesetters to reproduce an image 'perpetuated without change' from a printing plate.[17] With the passage of time it's come to refer to the use of broad social categories, such as nationality, race, gender, social class, religion, age or appearance to make what are often negative evaluations and pejorative inferences. For example: engineers are supposedly 'conservative and careful' and librarians are 'helpful but shy'; the English are 'reserved and conservative'; Germans are 'efficient and practical'; Americans are 'materialistic and ambitious'; and Italians are 'passionate and pleasure loving';[18] and of course 'women are more intuitive than men'. Other stereotypes can be less innocent and are a potent means of controlling other people and exercising power over them.[19] Stereotyping is low on mental effort – it's another type of mental shortcut. People can be classified automatically merely on the basis of their appearance, they then get associated with the stereotypical, and perhaps negative, attributes of a group.

✐ Application No. 9: Negative Effects of Stereotypes

Stickiness	Initial perceptions become 'sticky' and it's possible to end up reacting in uncontrolled, inappropriate and often negative ways towards people.
Group Effects	Groups play an important role in stereotyping: people are generally biased towards their in-group and biased against the out-group.

Stereotypes of an out-group are often a mixture of negatives and positives, for example 'respecting but disliking'. Stereotypes of out-groups tend to be more negative and more extreme, and can be used to reinforce the control exercised by the dominant group.[20]

Is your intuitive mind prone to stereotyping? Consider the following scenario:

A panel of psychologists once interviewed and administered personality tests to a sample of 100 people, consisting of seventy engineers and thirty lawyers, all successful in their respective fields. On the basis of this information thumbnail sketches were written.

Meet one of the people they interviewed, Jack: he's a forty-five year old man. He's married and has four children. He is generally conservative, careful, and ambitious. He shows no interest in political and social issues and spends most of his free time on his many hobbies, which include home carpentry, sailing and mathematical puzzles.

(A) What do you think the chance is, as a percentage, that Jack is one of the engineers in the sample?
(B) What do you think the chance as a percent would be if the make-up of the sample were reversed to thirty engineers and seventy lawyers?

When psychologists Amos Tversky and Daniel Kahneman used this problem in one of their ingenious experiments they found that people intuitively judged the chance of Jack being an engineer the same in (A) and (B). But to do so, in terms of the laws of probability, is quite wrong.

How did your response compare, did you rate the probability of Jack being an engineer the same in both cases?

If you did you may have ignored the fact that the odds of Jack being an engineer should be judged higher in (A) (the chance is 70%) than in (B) (the chance is 30%). In Tversky and Kahneman's experiments the subjects' intuitive minds were impervious to the different proportions of engineers and lawyers in (A) and (B); they simply went with the stereotype of Jack and ignored the make-up of the sample.

A moment's reflection on what the response might be if no personality sketch were provided (therefore depriving the intuitive mind of the stereotype) illustrates the point.

What do you think the chance is of an unknown individual 'Mr X' being an engineer in a sample in which there are seventy engineers and thirty lawyers?

What's the chance of an unknown individual 'Mr X' being an engineer in a sample in which there are thirty engineers and seventy lawyers?

In the first case the chance of Mr X being and engineer is 70%, in the second case it's 30%. Most people get it right this time. In this version of the problem there's no description that the intuitive mind can latch on to and use to make its erroneous inferences, and in this case the intuitive mind is left high and dry as the analytical mind steps in and makes the correct inference.

The intuitive mind relies on the similarity of Jack to its stereotype of an engineer. If a different description and occupation had been used, for example 'Lucy is very shy and withdrawn, invariably helpful, but with little interest in people, or in the world of reality. A meek and tidy soul, she has a need for order and structure, and a passion for detail' as the stereotype of a librarian, the same effect would be observed. The intuitive mind is nothing if not consistent in its misuse of the laws of probability and its determination to stick to stereotypes. Curiously though, base rates as illustrated by the example of Mr X (the proportion of a group of interest in the population as a whole) *are* taken into account when there is no description of the person, it seems that when it's deprived of vivid, concrete information the intuitive mind defers to the analytical mind.

THE SCIENCE OF THE INTUITIVE MIND – BRAND PERSONALITY

The marketers of consumer products have seized upon the fact that the intuitive impressions that we form of people can be determined quickly and effortlessly from the attributes we associate with the person including the clothes they wear, the cars they drive and so forth. For example, compare the impressions that you might form of a middle-aged man driving a Porsche 911 along The Strip in Las Vegas with the impression you'd form if you saw the same middle-aged man driving a Fiat Punto along the same stretch of road.

In each case what do we infer automatically about the man, his lifestyle, personality, occupation and income? Are our perceptions likely to be fair and justified?

It's a fact of life that we have lived through an age of media celebrities and luxury brands in which as far as some people were concerned, 'you are what you wear'.

Marketing and advertising uses the relationship that we create in our minds between a brand's 'personality' and the personality of its owner. Brand personality dimensions such as 'sincerity', 'excitement', 'competence', 'sophistication' and 'ruggedness' affect our perceptions of personality traits of the owner of the brand. For example, a man driving the latest 4 × 4 Sports Utility Vehicle might be judged as 'rugged' (an impression he may be seeking to create). The processes of stereotyping and impression formation in the intuitive mind automatically transfer the brand's personality traits to the consumer's personality.

Sources: Fennis, B.M. and Pruyn, A.T.H. (2006) You are what you wear. Brand personality influences consumer impression formation,

Journal of Business Research, **60**: 634–9; Fiske, S.T. (1993) Controlling other people, *American Psychologist*, **48**(6): 621–8; Nelson, T.E., Acker, M. and Manis, M. (1996) Irrepressible stereotypes, *Journal of Experimental and Social Psychology*, **32**: 13–38.

The intuitive mind is a potent stereotyping system for two reasons:

1. It can assign a person to a social category and judges them very quickly on the basis of very thin slices of information, including things that are irrelevant (for example, physical attributes irrelevant to job performance) or can be manipulated (for example, through purchasing power or skilfully managed media profiles).
2. Intuitions, as we know, are charged with feelings, this means they have power to influence different types of judgements and decisions, including those concerning people and social categories.

The second point is especially important if past encounters with members of certain social groups have been emotionally charged. The emotion is likely to be automatically re-activated, and the evidence suggests that the intuitive mind's decision-making mechanisms are especially attuned to negative affect (negative feelings). For these reasons guarding against the foibles of the intuitive mind that lead to bias, prejudice and discrimination is vitally important.

INTUITION WORKOUT No. 9: FIVE DO'S AND DON'TS OF GOOD INTUITIVE JUDGEMENT[21]

Don't intuitively generalise about an individual, even when a stereotype contains a 'kernel of truth' (for example, men do favour engineering as a major at college).

Do be wary of self-fulfilling prophecies – stereotypical beliefs may lead people to behave in ways consistent with the stereotype (employees may perform badly simply because their boss's stereotype leads him to expect them to do so).

Don't intuitively assume that just because a person is a member of a group that they share the features of that group (try to find out more about them as a person).

Do be especially wary of stereotypes that contain evaluative ('positive' or 'negative') elements (cultural stereotypes based on religion, gender, or race often contain potentially harmful negative evaluations).

Do judge a person by the content of their character,[22] not by one's own preconceptions or primitive perceptions.

Downside of the Intuitive Mind No. 4: Wishful Thinking

The intuitive mind is capable of selecting and using evidence automatically simply because it's consistent with our wishes, cravings and desires. An untamed intuitive mind is consummate in building one-sided cases, but pretty poor at disregarding inconsistent evidence.

In the 1960s the psychologist Peter Wason investigated something he called 'confirmation bias'. If I give you the sequence 2–4–6 what's your guess about the rule I'm following to create my sequence of numbers? Can you read my mind? Here's another one, 8–10–12, does it follow your hypothesised rule? How about 22–24–26? Or 246–248–250? It's intuitively obvious what the rule is, isn't it? It must be 'successive even numbers' – how can it be anything else?

Here's another sequence that follows the rule I have in my mind 2–4–8. And another one 1–2–3, and another 124–365–948. The rule is 'any ascending sequence of numbers'. When Wason tried this idea in the psychology lab he found that subjects came up with a hypothesis and then looked for evidence to confirm their hypothesis. To avoid this error they might have looked for evidence to disconfirm their 'successive even numbers' hypothesis (for example, offering the sequence 1–2–3 back to the experimenter and asking if this is the rule would immediately disconfirm the even numbers hypothesis and an alternative explanation would have to be found) but they tended not to do so.[23]

The students in Wason's experiment sought, unconsciously, to confirm the hypothesis that they'd formed. They didn't consciously seek to falsify it, presumably because they hoped they were right. Outside of the psychology lab this tendency to confirm or act in ways that fit with our hopes and aspirations or cravings and desires can affect judgement in one's personal and professional life:[24]

1. In criminal cases the confirmation bias could lead investigators to disregard evidence that challenged their personal theory of a case or a suspect; one result might be a false conviction. In the UK there are several notable examples of cases where the courts of appeal have eventually overturned the over-zealous pursuit of an individual who happened to fit with law enforcement officers' preconceptions.

2. Physicians estimating the probability of patients contracting a bacterial infection in the blood stream gave lower estimates in high-risk patients compared with low-risk patients, possibly because they sincerely hoped for the patients' sake that it wouldn't happen because the consequences could be much more severe.

3. Chartered Financial Analysts in the USA and Investment Managers in Taiwan rated events that they felt were desirable (for example, 'portfolios will become more international' or 'passing of legislation permitting trade with China') as more likely to occur.

4. People over-estimate the likelihood of their favourite candidate winning an election, their favourite team winning a sports contest, and rate the chances of positive events happening to them as higher (having a happy marriage, not losing their jobs, not contracting serious illness).

Entrepreneurs' passion for their business venture can be a double-edged sword. Without doubt entrepreneurs need the passion for their vision in order to energise themselves and maintain momentum through what is often a long, arduous and risky journey. On the other hand passion, of any kind, can also be blind. For example, in business venturing if the passion isn't based on the right blend of determination, expert knowledge, a workable idea, a track record, interpersonal skills and professional networks but instead is purely a desire rooted in wishful thinking or a craving for wealth, it can end up being a costly failure.

THE SCIENCE OF THE INTUITIVE MIND – ANATOMY OF A COMPANY MELTDOWN

A company I'll refer to as HandyHome is a prime example of the ways in which wishful thinking and other biases can result in a business catastrophe.[25] HandyHome was the building materials division of a larger corporation. Its vision was for massive expansion by going for the novel approach of serving two markets simultaneously – professional home builders and amateur 'handymen'. The plan was that HandyHome would acquire existing scruffy building contractors' yards in out-of-town locations and refurbish them on a shoestring budget and make them into dual-purpose (trade and home) outlets. The whole scheme was a 'no brainer' – it couldn't fail.

Executives created a beguiling vision of the future which was embraced by managers who saw in it abundant career opportunities for themselves. Tentative assumptions became solid facts, loose predictions became hard and fast expectations, data were gathered if they confirmed these facts and expectations, and group-think took hold. How could the outcome be anything other than spectacular? HandyHome duly increased its number of building materials outlets by 500 % from twenty-four to 120. Unfortunately, the power of the vision meant that they lost sight of some brutal and quite basic business facts, including:

1. The locations they'd acquired were totally unsuited to DIY retailing (they were randomly distributed rather than located in prime metropolitan areas or thoroughfares).
2. Professional builders and handymen are very different animals (for example, handymen like nice see-through bubble packs, builders couldn't care less).
3. Chains headed by executives who really knew the retailing business were beginning to serve DIY customers in convenient locations (companies like Home Depot were setting up on main thoroughfares and in metropolitan areas).

This isn't an exhaustive list but it's clear with hindsight that HandyHome didn't stand a chance, within a few years the bright idea had become a nightmare: the mid-level managers who were going to build their careers on the expansion plans were out of work, all the stores had been sold or closed and the parent company abandoned HandyHome before it could bring down the whole business.

Source: Valentin, E.K. (1994) Anatomy of a fatal business strategy, *Journal of Management Studies*, **31**(3): 359–82.

It's one thing to have an inspiring vision and to imagine the steps involved in attaining it, but HandyHome was a prime example of a vision that was not only naïve and intuitively appealing to the uninformed mind but bought into by managers who disregarded disconfirming evidence and didn't have the necessary expertise firmly grounded in the retail business to see beyond the dream and judge its true viability. The only facts that mattered were those that fuelled and confirmed wishful thinking; the probability of the expected successes was grossly over estimated. The intuitive mind's wishful thinking ran haywire throughout the whole organisation. The HandyHome venture certainly was a 'no brainer' but of the wrong sort. The bosses at HandyHome weren't unique – we all form expectations easily and, like stereotypes, expectations tend to be 'sticky'. Our automatic reaction is to 'confirm' since it's only human to be a wishful thinker and biased towards things we see as desirable and which fulfil our emotional attachments and needs quickly and effortlessly.

The HandyHome debacle isn't a million miles from the vision of wealth creation sold to millions of ordinary people who invested in real estate and company shares pre-2008 credit crunch. They were beguiled by the images of low effort wealth creation sold to them by bankers and governments as part of the ideal of becoming part of a 'property-owning' largely middle class society.

Psychologists call this kind of wishful thinking the 'desirability bias'[26] – desires can and do influence our expectations about the future especially if those desires have an emotional component (for example, an affective attachment to a person, wealth, object or business venture). Wishful thinking works both ways – the undesirability of an outcome (the smoker who doubts they'll be the one to get lung cancer or the amateur investor who doubts their assets can be the ones that fall in price) can lead to a decrease in the expectation that it will occur ('it could never happen to me'). As far as confirmation and desirability biases are concerned the lessons both from the psychology lab and the real world point to a number of ways in which they can be combated.

🔧 **Application No. 10: Guarding Against Feeble Intuitions**

Seek disconfirming evidence	We should actively seek to disconfirm our hypotheses especially where we feel an emotional attachment to some desired future state and be open to evidence both for and against it no matter how desirable or beguiling the vision is.
Avoid stereotyping	We should avoid seeking out information that confirms our stereotypes, and be open to information that disconfirms a stereotype, especially where the stereotype can lead to a negative social judgement.
Interrogate intuitions	We should interrogate our intuitions – genuine intuitions will stand up to searching examination whereas biased, stereotyped and wishful thinking are likely to crumble under our own severe scrutiny and the critical gaze of others.
Beware of group think	We should be wary of the power of group-think, including the norms of a professional group or society as a whole: the majority in a group aren't *de facto* necessarily right; we should be prepared to be 'naysayers', the emperor may indeed be wearing no clothes.

If we mix up genuine intuitions with overly optimistic wishful thinking (how many failed entrepreneurs have proclaimed 'I just know "in my bones" that this business venture is a winner', not to mention home owners and amateur investors who've lost significant sums of money) we fool nobody but ourselves. We should have faith in genuine intuitions and in our vision of the future. By understanding your own intuitive mind you'll become better able to use the power of your intuition to sense and follow the authentic path towards a future that's right for you and not be side-tracked by biases and wishful thinking.

An Upside of Mental Shortcuts: Cheater Detection

Test your analytical and intuitive minds' powers of logical infer-ence task with the 'Wason selection task' outlined below (and named after the psychologist Peter Wason who developed it).

Each of these four cards has a letter on one side and a number on the other. Now consider the statement: 'If there is an A on one side of the card, then there is a 3 on the other side of the card'. Which of the four cards needs to be turned over to find out if this statement is true or false? The correct answer is A and 7 (and not 3). But this seemingly straightforward task is surprisingly difficult – only between 10 and 20 % of people get it right.

In the form shown in Figure 5.1 the task is abstract and bears little relation to the types of problems we're likely to meet in real life. However, consider the alternative and highly realistic form of the same logical inference task.

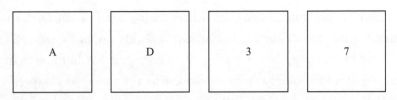

FIGURE 5.1   Wason selection task, abstract (logician's) form

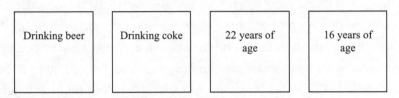

FIGURE 5.2   Wason selection task, concrete (bar tender's) form
Adapted from: Evans, J. St. B.T.   (2003) In two minds: dual process
accounts of reasoning, *Trends in Cognitive Sciences*, **7**(10): 454–9.
Reproduced by kind permission of Elsevier Science.

Imagine you work in a bar and you have to enforce the following
rule: 'to drink beer customers must be eighteen years or more of
age'. The cards shown in Figure 5.2 represent four different customers with their drink on one side and their age on the other. Which
of the cards do you turn over to check if the rule is being obeyed?

When confronted with this concrete version of the task most
people get it right – they choose the beer drinker and the sixteen
year old. The abstract form of the task is much harder than the concrete form. The reason that the concrete version is much easier is
that it's read as a form of social contract involving behaviour and
permissions and the human brain has evolved the ability to check
whether or not someone is complying with the rules of a social
contract and intuitively detect cheaters. In this case the cheater

(drinking beer under age) would be taking the benefit by transgressing the rules of group behaviour (nobody under the age of 18 should be drinking beer).[27] Marc D. Hauser, the evolutionary psychologist and biologist, whose work was discussed in Chapter 3, links the detection of cheaters to trust: 'our minds evolved a unique specialisation to both understand social contracts and detect violations' – such social contracts are commitments to the group and engage trust, and their violation 'engages distrust and a cascade of emotions designed to enhance vigilance and catalyse retribution'.[28] Even though the intuitive mind may be a lazy thinker under certain circumstances (for example, under situations of prejudice or wishful thinking) and be prone to making feeble intuitions when required to make logical inferences for which it wasn't designed (conjunction fallacies), in situations where logical inferences have to be made in circumstances similar to those for which nature designed it (such as violations of social contracts) it's a fast, automatic and potent computational system. Trust is a mutual bond between leaders and followers. The breaking of the leader-follower trust is something that can often be detected quickly and automatically by either party. It takes a great deal longer to re-build than it did to break once a party chooses to disengage their trust.

INTUITIVE INTELLIGENCE PRINCIPLE No. 5: BEWARE OF FEEBLE INTUITIONS

Human beings often tend towards being cognitive misers; the result is that we let the intuitive mind do certain tasks that it's not well suited to. The likely outcome is a feeble intuition based on logical errors, biased judgement, stereotyping and wishful thinking. Some of these errors and biases are hard to overcome because:

1. they occur automatically and outside of conscious awareness;

2. they're difficult to introspect about;
3. it's hard for an under-developed intuitive intelligence to disentangle them from genuine intuitions;
4. we're influenced by the larger social group of which we are a part and by patterns that we are a small player in – a 'Mexican wave' that intuitively and effortlessly passes through the crowd.

Nonetheless it is possible to be more aware of how intuitions can turn out to be fallible and be a hindrance in certain situations, for example when we stereotype others, or fool ourselves with overly optimistic wishful thinking and call it 'intuition'. If we're aware of these perils we can guard against them, this opens up the possibility for the analytical mind to do the things that it's good at in order to make up for the shortcomings of its intuitive counterpart. In this way we may get the 'best of both minds' and see our genuine intuitions in a clearer light, and not be fooled by feeble imitations of the real thing. The intuitive mind is able to make logical inferences in situations for which it was designed, such as the violation of social contracts and when this occurs one of the vital ingredients of group cohesion, trust, may be disengaged.

NOTES

[1]Another word for a 'mental shortcut' is a 'heuristic' – I'll use the former as it's a more user-friendly term. There is a vast literature on the subject of 'heuristics and biases', and for a technical overview of the subject see: Gilovich, T., Griffin D. and Kahneman D. (2002) *Heuristics and Biases: The psychology of intuitive judgement.* Cambridge: Cambridge University Press. For an appreciation of the seminal contribution of Amos Tversky and Daniel Kahneman see: Evans, J. St. B.T. and Over, D.E. (1997) The contribution of Amos Tversky, *Thinking and Reasoning,* **3**(1): 1–8.

[2]Tversky, A. and Kahneman, D. (2002) Extensional versus intuitive reasoning, In Gilovich, T., Griffin, D. and Kahneman, D. (Eds) *Heuristics and Biases: The psychology of intuitive judgement*, 19–48. Cambridge: Cambridge University Press.

[3]Kahneman, D. and Frederick, S. (2002) Representativeness re-visited: attribute substitution in intuitive judgment. In Gilovich, T., Griffin, D. and Kahneman, D. (Eds) *Heuristics and Biases: The psychology of intuitive judgement*, 49–81. Cambridge: Cambridge University Press.

[4]Kahneman and Frederick (2002) op cit.

[5]Hastie, R. and Dawes, R.M. (2001) *Rational Choice in an Uncertain World*. Thousand Oaks: Sage.

[6]Kahneman and Frederick (2002) op cit.

[7]Lakoff, G. and Johnson, M. (1999) *Philosophy in the Flesh*. New York: Basic Books.

[8]Clore, G.L. and Tamir, M. (2002) Affect as embodied information. *Psychological Inquiry*, **13**(1), 37–45.

[9]Bodenhausen, G.V. (1990) Stereotypes as judgmental heuristics: Evidence of circadian variations in discrimination, *Psychological Science*, **1**(5): 319–22.

[10]Manstead, S.R. and Hewstone, M. (1996) *The Blackwell Encyclopaedia of Social Psychology*. Oxford: Blackwell.

[11]Sjöberg, L. (1982) Aided and unaided decision-making: improving intuitive judgement, *Journal of Forecasting*, **1**: 349–63.

[12]Ariely, D. (2009) *Predictably Irrational*. New York: Harper Perrenial.

[13]Homicide(6.1/100000)orsepticemia(11.5/100000); suicide(11.0/100000) or diabetes (25.3/100000), retrieved on 7th August 2008 from http://www.cdc.gov/nchs/data/nvsr/nvsr56/nvsr56_10.pdf.

[14]Weinberg, R. (2008) Does imagery work? Effect on performance and mental skills, *Journal of Imagery Research in Sport and Physical Activity*, **3**(1): 1–21.

[15]Sherman, S.J., Cialdini, R.B., Schwartzman, D.F. and Reynolds, K.M. (2002) Imagining can heighten or lower the perceived likelihood of contracting a disease: The mediating effect of ease of imagery. In Gilovich, T., Griffin, D. and Kahneman, D. (Eds) *Heuristics and Biases: The psychology of intuitive judgement*, 98–102. Cambridge: Cambridge University Press.

[16]Tversky, A. and Kahneman, D. (1974) Judgment under uncertainty: Heuristics and biases, *Science*, **185**(4157): 1124–31.

[17]Online Etymology Dictionary retrieved on 7th September 2008 from http://www.etymonline.com/.

[18]Kreuger, J. (1996) Probabilistic national stereotypes, *European Journal of Social Psychology*, **26**: 961–80.

[19]Fiske, S.T. (1993) Controlling other people, *American Psychologist*, **48**(6): 621–8.

[20]Fiske, S.T., Cuddy, A.J., Glick, P. and Xu, J. (2002) A model of (often mixed) stereotype content: Competence and warmth respectively follow from perceived status and competition. *Journal of Personality and Social Psychology*, **82**, 878–902.

[21]Fiske, S.T. and Neuberg, S.L. (1990) A continuum of impression formation, from category-based to individuating processes: Influences of information and motivation on attention and interpretation. In M.P. Zanna (Ed.), *Advances in experimental social psychology*, **23**: 1–74. New York: Academic Press; Nelson, T.E. (1996) Irrepressible stereotypes, *Journal of Experimental and Social Psychology*, **32**: 13–38.

[22]'... will not be judged by the color of their skin but by the content of their character'. Martin Luther King, speech at a Civil Rights March in Washington 28th August 1963.

[23]Nickerson, R.S. (1998) Confirmation bias: A ubiquitous phenomenon in many guises, *Review of General Psychology*, **2**(2): 175–220; Wason, P. (1960) On the failure to eliminate a hypothesis in a conceptual task, *Quarterly Journal of Experimental Psychology*, **12**: 129–40.

[24]Budescu, D.V. and Bruderman, M. (1995) The relationship between illusion of control and the desirability bias, *Journal of Behavioral Decision-making*, **8**: 109–25; Hall, K. (2002) Reviewing intuitive decision-making and uncertainty: the implications for medical education, *Medical Education*, **36**: 216–24; O'Brien, B. and Ellsworth, P.C. (2006) Confirmation bias in criminal investigations. *1st Annual Conference on Empirical Legal Studies*, University of Texas at Austin, School of Law. Austin, Texas; Olsen, R.A. (1997) Desirability bias among professional investment managers: some evidence from experts, *Journal of Behavioral Decision-making*, **10**: 65–72.

[25] Based on: Valentin, E.K. (1994) Anatomy of a fatal business strategy, *Journal of Management Studies*, **31**(3): 359–82.

[26] Krizan, Z. and Windschitl, P.D. (2007) The influence of desirability of optimism, *Psychological Bulletin*, **133**(1): 95–121.

[27] Evans, J. St. B.T. (2003) In two minds: dual process accounts of reasoning, *Trends in Cognitive Sciences*, **7**(10): 454–9.

[28] Hauser, M.D. (2006) *Moral Minds*. London: Abacus.

Chapter 6

INTUITIVE ESP

In the previous chapter I drew attention to the downside of intuition, depicting gut feeling as something to be avoided in particular situations, and warned of the perils of feeble intuitions. But this is only half the story, there are other situations where informed intuition – what often looks and feels like a 'sixth sense' – can be the best and sometimes the only way to make important, time-pressured decisions. A quick and seemingly easy intuitive choice that's informed by expertise can result in judgements that have the power of economy of mental effort and accuracy of outcome.

The most exciting, glamorous and demanding class of automobile racing is Formula One (F1). The stakes for drivers are high – their lives are on the line every time they race, and for top performers salaries are counted in tens of millions of dollars. For automobile manufacturers the stakes are equally high – engines can cost in excess of $300000,[1] and to win the F1 World Championship is the pinnacle of technological achievement for leading engine manufacturers such as Ferrari, Mercedes, BMW, Toyota and Renault. F1 racing cars have to be driven at top speeds around sinuous circuits no two of which are the same. Drivers' minds and bodies need to be fully engaged during a race and at speeds of up to 200 miles per hour plus there's little room for error. It's only a select few drivers who possess the right combination of natural talent, courage, intelligence, athleticism and intuition to be able to win.[2]

The 2008 F1 World Champion Lewis Hamilton has all these qualities in abundance; as one commentator said of him: 'He is a bright boy, fit and fearless, and he has got that rare sixth sense for driving a Formula 1 car, knowing how much grip there is *before* he turns into a corner'.[3] Hamilton is not alone, top sportspeople develop an uncanny union with their performance which enables them to predict the movement of a ball, the handling of a car, or the intentions of the opposing team. It's been described by as a body-mind 'zone' in which supreme performers experience a profound joy, a feeling of effortlessness in the midst of intense exertion, a sense of the action taking place in slow motion and an acute intuition which at times feels like precognition.[4] When in this 'zone', peak performing sportspeople report feelings of effortlessness, immersion, lack of inhibition, a complete awareness in which body and mind are fused, joy and euphoria and even a sense of premonition.[5]

Like great sportspeople, many experienced and successful entrepreneurs know what it's like to be in the 'zone'. Researchers in the USA found that achieving success in business venturing often demands that an entrepreneur balances the inevitable and necessary stresses with the ability to cope with a multiplicity of obstacles and demands, all achieved in the face of great uncertainty; however the result can be peak performance in the 'zone'. Exceptional entrepreneurs find performing in the face of these demands rewarding and self-actualising, giving them a sense of meaningfulness, fulfilment, self-validation, richness and joy – a state referred to by the Hungarian psychologist Mihaly Csikszentmihalyi as 'flow'.[6] Other examples of flow can be found in the creative arts, for instance jazz musicians in the heat of a collective improvisation experience 'flow' and an intuitive 'sixth sense' for what's about to happen in the music before it actually does[7] – like other exceptional performers they have 'information from the future' which enables them to anticipate events.[8] When used in the right way the intuitive mind can give leaders and managers uncanny insights into the future and a vision of what might be possible.

The Sixth Sense?

Belief in supernatural agents and paranormal phenomena, and superstitious behaviour, are ubiquitous in human societies, for example people wear lucky charms, read horoscopes and pay significant sums of money to fortune tellers. One of the paradoxes of human nature is that the rational and the a-rational sides of our psyche coexist. It's natural for us to have different *types* of knowledge about the same thing, to be rational and superstitious at the same time.[9] Take performance in sport as an example: a professional sportsperson will know (rationally) that intense training, strict diet and high skill levels are important in the competitive arena, but this doesn't prevent people who have this knowledge from also subscribing to other more a-rational attitudes towards performance, and superstitious behaviours are important even for some of the top performers. For example, some top basketball players will bounce the ball in exactly the same way or the same number of times before every free throw, wear a lucky item of clothing or even wear socks inside out for luck. Superstitious soccer fans attributed France's success in the 1998 World Cup to the fact that team captain Laurent Blanc used to mark the start of each match by planting a kiss on the top of goalkeeper Fabien Barthez's bald head for good luck.[10]

THE 'SCIENCE' OF THE INTUITIVE MIND – A VIEW FROM AFAR

Without doubt intuition has for many people connotations of the paranormal. For example, mystics make claims for the intuitive powers of 'precognition' a form of Extra Sensory Perception (ESP) in which information received through paranormal channels allows certain people knowledge of events before they happen. Remote viewing is another type of ESP; it involves allegedly seeing things at a distance (usually spatial distance but also temporally distant – things in the future) beyond the range of the normal senses. In the 1970s Russell Targ and Harold (Hal) Puthoff at the Electronics and Bioengineering laboratory at the Stanford Research Institute (SRI) conducted remote viewing experiments in which they claimed to have found strong evidence that people could obtain information about remote or future events. The information usually came through visual images allegedly via an intuitive 'right-brain' intelligence.[11] Remote viewing experiments usually involve:

1. an 'out-bounder', the person who physically visits a target for the remote viewer – analogous to a 'transmitter' of signals;
2. a remote viewer or percipient, the person who is able to describe and experience objects, pictures and locations which are blocked from ordinary sensory perception – analogous to the receiver of the signals.

It's usually the case that the remote viewer enters a relaxed or meditative state in order to become dissociated from her or his immediate surroundings and to become more affiliated with the target and its surroundings. The percipient then makes note of information received in the form of drawings or verbal descriptions.

There've been numerous attempts to validate the phenomenon of remote viewing. For example, a series of remote viewing trials were carried out between locations in Wisconsin and Eastern Europe in which the percipient was asked to describe the location of an out-bounder who was 5000 miles away and twenty-four hours into the future. Judges' rating of the match between the photographs taken by the out-bounder of the target destination and the description provided by the remote viewer were said to be 'statistically significant'.

Sources and Further Reading: Lee. J.H. (2008) Remote viewing as applied to future studies, *Technological Forecasting and Social Change*, **75**(1): 142–53; Mack, J. and Powell, L. (2005) Perceptions of non-local communication: incidences associated with media consumption and individual differences, *North American Journal of Psychology*, **7**(2): 279–94; Sheldrake, R. (2003) *The Sense of Being Stared at and Other Aspects of the Extended Mind.* New York: Crown Publishers.

Intelligence and military organisations have shown an interest in the potential of remote viewing. But unfortunately for advocates of the technique a CIA report into military-based applications for remote viewing concluded that the information it provides is often vague and ambiguous and usually of insufficient quality and accuracy to be of any actionable value.

In spite of the criticisms and scientific evidence to the contrary, the proponents of remote viewing often appear utterly convinced of the reality of 'psi' abilities. Moreover in the populace at large many people have superstitious beliefs in the power of pre-cognition, for example in a random telephone survey in the USA over 50% of the 368 people surveyed reported they had experienced anticipated 'event precognition' and dream premonitions.[12]

A variant of 'remote viewing' that's less controversial and perhaps more accessible and more useful to the ordinary leaders and managers (rather being the exclusive preserve of gifted remote viewers or psychics) is Visionary/Virtual Time Travel (VVTT) developed by Oliver Markley.[13] Since in this technique the 'target' is the future there's nothing objective to be viewed (it hasn't happened yet), rather the 'travel' is a fictitious but informative journey into hypothetical futures. In VVTT a percipient is asked by a facilitator to put aside biasing beliefs and expectations and use the 'theatre of the imagination' to make a visioning-based intuitive projection into several alternative futures. The output from the exercise can be concrete (for example visioning a particular situation) or symbolic (the vision is a metaphor, for example a bright sunrise). A skilled facilitator plays a key role in deciphering the meaning of the symbolic data that arise by interpreting the 'guidance' that comes from within the individual – through the imaginative capability of the intuitive mind.[14] If they're based on previous experiences, especially if emotions were experienced and associated with the situation, imagined events have the power to evoke hunches and gut feelings and may simulate an 'as if' intuitive moment and evoke a sense of gut feeling.

INTUITION WORKOUT No. 10: 'AS IF' INTUITIVE MOMENTS

Next time you're faced with a decision that involves some form of risk, requires a judgement, cannot be solved by analysis alone, where feelings play a part and which is similar to situations you've faced in the past, imagine the scenario surrounding your choices by retreating, reflecting and rehearsing an 'as if' intuitive moment.

Retreat	Go to a quiet place away from interruptions by other people, cell phones, or e-mails. Form the decision in your mind as a question and be clear about the alternative choices available to you.
Reflect	Reflect on past action: remind yourself of similar situations that you've encountered in the past, run the past action sequence in your head (where was it, who was involved, what happened?). Be mindful of any changes you sense in your body as the past action unfolds.
Rehearse	Rehearse future action *as if* you'd been there before: run an 'as if' action sequence in your head (where will it be, who might be involved, what might happen if events unfold as they have done in the past?). Be mindful of the changes you sense in your body as the 'as if' action unfolds.

If there are other future action sequences (alternative choices) you can run them as 'as if' sequences in your head as well. What do the feelings you experience with each tell you about the different choices that you could make? Does 'retreat, reflect, rehearse' help you to narrow down the range of choices you could make? Does it tell you anything about the choice you feel you should make?

The biggest challenge that managers and leaders face is identifying and articulating a compelling and right vision of the future and leading and managing people and resources in pursuit of that vision. Managers and leaders live in the present, but the vision is part of a future which cannot be known in the present. Leaders and managers need a 'crystal ball' to guide them on their journey towards unknown futures. There's no doubt that a leadership and management sixth sense is required for doing business in the 21st century. But is intuitive ESP, or some other extraordinary phenomenon, a potential sixth sense within every leader and manager that they and their businesses can profit from?

The Fire-fighter, the Sailor and the Paramedic

Intuition can be a 'crystal ball', especially for experienced people whose jobs involve them in complex, time-pressured life-or-death decisions. One of the world's leading researchers in the psychology of intuition and its application to real-world decision making is Gary Klein. In over twenty years of research Klein and his team of scientists have found that intuition is important in 90% of the critical decisions taken by a wide range of professional groups including fire-fighters, emergency medical staff, military personnel and chief executives. Not only is intuition something vital which suffuses almost every aspect of their work, in some cases the intuitions they experience are so powerful as to convince responsible professionals such as fire fighters, medics and military personnel that they have ESP. Their stories are told in Klein's two ground-breaking intuition books *Sources of Power* (1998) and *Intuition at Work* (2003).[15]

The Fire-fighter's Story. A critical decision that fire-fighters face is when to break off or change tack in attempting to put out a fire and reduce the risk to themselves and their team. Just such a decision faced a young lieutenant interviewed by Klein. The lieutenant was in charge of a team called to a fire that was blazing in the kitchen area of a single-storey residential building. The team entered the building and made their way to the fire; and, as they were trained to do and had done so many times before, doused the fire with high pressure water jets. But something odd happened. The fire didn't behave as it ought to. Instead of succumbing to the water it simply roared back at them. The hose crew tried again. The same thing happened. Not just odd – weird. Even though the call was routine and on the face of it the building was a typical one-storey house, it started to give the lieutenant a 'bad vibe'. No clues as to why, it just didn't feel right. But one thing was for sure – it was time to make a hasty exit. No sooner had they exited the building than the floor where they'd been standing collapsed into an inferno underneath the floor. The seat of the fire was, unbeknownst to them, in the basement of the house. The lieutenant took a risk and trusted his intuitive ESP, the 'sixth sense' that, in his view, every fire-ground commander needs; and it saved his own and his team members' lives.

The Sailor's Story: One of the functions of Royal Navy destroyers during times of war is to protect a larger battle group from airborne attack, especially from missiles. In the first Gulf War in 1992 *HMS Gloucester* was protecting a group of ships including the *USS Missouri*. On board the *Gloucester* one of the critical roles of the anti-air warfare officers was to decide whether or not radar contacts were friend (a US plane) or foe (an Iraqi missile), and whether or not to shoot down the radar contact. The right decision can save the ship; the wrong decision can result in a dreaded, and inappropriately labelled, 'friendly fire' incident. In February 1992 the officer in charge of air defence on the *Gloucester* identified a blip on the screen and instantly believed it to be an attacking missile. He watched it for forty seconds to confirm his intuition, and then shot it down. In doing so he took a big risk because he didn't know for sure until confirmation came through later from the ground that he got it right (fortunately it was an Iraqi missile). Moreover he didn't know *why* he knew it was a foe and not a friend, and what's more important neither did the experts who looked at the recordings later – in their opinion there was no way to tell the blip from a friendly plane. When interviewed by Klein and his researchers the officer confessed to believing that it was his ESP that told him the instant he saw the object on the screen that it was a hostile missile.

The Paramedic's Story: Heart attack (myocardial infarction) is one of the most common causes of death in the Europe and North America. In research carried out by Klein and his colleague Beth Crandall a paramedic described a family gathering where she saw her father-in-law for the first time in many months. She instantly didn't like how he looked, something wasn't right; she told him so (much to his chagrin) and insisted that he go to the hospital. It was more than just lucky that she did, because the physician's examination revealed a blockage in a major artery which could have proved fatal. A day later the paramedic's father-in-law was in the operating theatre having major, potentially life-saving surgery to remove the blockage. Like the racing driver who knows how much grip he's got before he enters the corner of a wet racetrack, the paramedic that Klein and Crandall interviewed said she could tell when a person was going to have a heart attack, days or even months *before* it happened. Extra-sensory perception?

'ESP' doesn't happen only to the experienced, competent and highly trained professionals that Klein studied; it, or something like it, can happen to anyone. For example, have you ever been in the situation of thinking about a person when completely out of the blue you bump into them in the street, or have you ever been in the situation where the phone rings and you know who's calling even before you pick it up? It's not uncommon, in a telephone survey in the USA 67% of people said they'd experienced 'telephone source anticipation'.[16] But how much of this is just pure coincidence or is there something more going on? Can we, as many mystics have claimed, intuit the future and is this a source of power that leaders and managers can tap into?

THE SCIENCE OF INTUITION – CURIOUS COINCIDENCES?

In the practice sessions for the final F1 race of the 1997 season at Jerez in Spain three arch rivals for the championship were all vying for pole position on the grid. The three best drivers in the world, Jacques Villeneuve, Michael Schumacher and Heinz-Harold Frentzen all lapped in exactly one minute and 21.072 seconds – they couldn't be separated by even one thousandth of a second. Commentators and observers were astounded: how could three drivers lap in a time identical to within thousands of a second? Surely such a thing could never happen by pure chance. It was far too close to be merely a coincidence. Surely some great levelling power was at work? Perhaps an F1 deity was intervening to make sure that dedicated fans would see a heart-stopping race to end the season?

To see if this might be the case scientists Jack Cohen and Ian Stewart looked into the mathematical probabilities involved in this incident in terms of the 'sample space' – the event that we're interested in (the 'hits') and all possible alternatives (the 'misses'). The first thing is that as far as lap times go, barring mechanical failures or accident, the best drivers lap at roughly the same speed. This means that the three fastest times are likely to fall inside the same tenth-of-a-second period, which narrows it down considerably. Focusing in on intervals of a thousandth of a second there are 100 possible lap times for each, so there's a one in 100 chance that the second driver laps in the same time as the first, and a one in 100 chance that the third laps in the same time as the other two – which leads to an estimate of one in 10000 (100 × 100) as the probability of the coincidence happening. Cohen and Stewart describe this as low enough to be striking, but not so low as to be truly amazed by it. It's roughly as likely as a hole-in-one in golf; compare this with the chances of winning the UK's national lottery at around 14 million to one and where a 'hit' would be truly astounding. If the F1 example hadn't been reported there may have been some other amazing coincidence in golf, tennis or athletics that could draw the news media's thirst for a story and their need for an eye-catching headline. If there are ten major events in the list of 'would-be-worth-reporting' that would reduce the 1/10000 odds to 1/1000, the same as tossing a coin and turning up heads ten times in a row – something which is quite imaginable and well within the bounds of possibility and probability. So not such a curious coincidence after all?

Sources: Cohen, J. and Stewart, I. (1998) That's amazing isn't it – why intuition is worse than useless when it comes to spotting real coincidences, *New Scientist*, 17th January 1998.

Our intuitive fascination for coincidences is fed by the fact that 'hits' tend to get reported, whereas 'misses' aren't at all newsworthy (it wouldn't be worthy of news comment that the top three divers in the practice session all *didn't* lap in exactly the same time).

Like the news media with their choice of stories, some ESP researchers have been culpable of being selective in their sampling. For example, in a number of experiments ESP researchers asked thousands of subjects to guess cards from a special pack of five symbols. In the next phase of the experiment anyone whose success rate had been above average – and was thus potentially gifted with psychic intuition – was invited back and tested some more; these people seemed to have extraordinary powers and were worthy of more detailed investigation. But actually it turned out that these people were simply good (lucky) guessers in the early rounds, as time went on their success rates became average – their (non-existent) paranormal intuitive powers seemed to be running down – no doubt explicable as some form of draining of 'psychic energy'. When averaged out these gifted 'paranormals' were no better than you or I.

With any event (intuitive judgement calls included) if we only ever remember the successful predictions of the future – 'the hits' – they're bound, in retrospect, to seem astounding and amazing, even magical. Moreover, if we only ever remember our intuitive hits in personal and professional life and forget our intuitive misses we run the risk of putting more faith in our intuitive judgement than is warranted. So the next time the phone goes reflect on whether or not you were actually thinking of the person who turns out to be on the line before you picked it up. Also reflect on how many times you thought of that person and they didn't call and the events which became just another boring and forgettable miss.

Demystifying the Intuitive Mind

The intuitions of the fire-fighter, the sailor and the paramedic were certainly magical in the sense that they saved lives, but are they really paranormal events that are inexplicable by science? Outstanding performers in sports offer some clues as to whether intuition really is a supernatural sixth sense. The 2008 F1 World Champion Lewis Hamilton, after winning his first Grand Prix in Canada in June 2007, commented confidently: 'I felt that I have been ready for this win now for quite some time, and for me it was just a matter of when and where'. ESP perhaps, or even worse – misplaced over-confidence tinged with arrogance?

No, not when we realise that at the time he made this comment Hamilton had been a highly competitive driver from the age of six who could drive powerful go-karts better than most adults even as a small child. He won the UK 'Champions of the Future Event' aged ten, and the 'Go-Kart Kid' was offered his first contract by an F1 team three years later. By the time he won in Canada he had sixteen years of racing experience behind him. The reward was hard-won, and Hamilton's father paid tribute to the intense preparation that lay behind his son's first F1 victory: 'He puts a lot of work into his racing. Lewis has made a lot of sacrifices, apart from us as a family, and he's reaping the rewards now'. The social context that Hamilton was in was crucially important: his family gave him the encouragement and support needed right from the word go; for example he was named after the supreme American Olympic athlete Carl Lewis and his father took on extra part-time work on top of his regular railway job to pay for his son's racing passion.[17] Hamilton built his intuitive driving expertise by having the right:

1. individual attributes: motivation, personality, and hard-wired athleticism;
2. competencies: driving knowledge and skill honed by thousands of hours of practice and racing;
3. career experiences: being in the right place at the right time, for example meeting and impressing the head of the MacClaren F1 racing team aged ten and appearing on BBC children's' TV at the age of twelve;
4. environmental influences: resources and emotional support of friends and family in building driving expertise.[18]

We can't easily change the individual attributes that we're either born with or that get formed so early in our lives as to be quite fixed by the time we reach adulthood, but by the above reckoning they're only around one quarter of the recipe for developing intuitive expertise. Fortunately the other factors in the intuition recipe are things we can do something positive about. Here are some guidelines for developing intuitive ESP:

🔧 Application No. 11: Developing Intuitive ESP

Expertise	Acquire expertise. Develop your skill levels by identifying what the key competencies are that you need to develop, become highly-trained in these skills and acquire experience of using them in simulated and real environments. The benefits of intense practice, coaching and seeking feedback can't be overestimated. Intuitive ESP requires the highest levels of competence.
Support	Find support. Build an infrastructure of support around you in terms of people, resources and technology that will ease your path in developing the knowledge and skills and giving you the right feedback: there's an exceptional performer inside every one of us. Intuitive ESP is collaborative.
Proactivity	Be proactive. Manage your career experiences in order to give yourself the right exposure, get noticed, network and be in the right place at the right time: successful people create their own luck, and success breeds success. Intuitive ESP is controllable.

Although some people prefer magical explanations, it's not necessary to invoke magic and mystery in order to account for the intuitive 'ESP' that many experts display day in day out in their work. Seen in this light and when the bigger picture is taken into account it's perhaps unsurprising that outstanding sports people, like Hamilton, are able to perform effortlessly and intuitively and frequently be 'in the zone'. It might even be more surprising if they didn't achieve some degree of success. There's nothing 'magical' about it, and no supernatural sixth sense is at work that can predict the position of the ball, the feel of the race track, the nature of a blip on a radar screen, or the success of a business decision. Individual attributes, competencies and environmental influences combined with career experiences combine to create the ideal conditions for informed intuitive judgement to flourish in individuals who have by dint of determination and circumstance, as much as innate ability, become exceptional. And we can all do the same in our own particular ways through the right mix of opportunity recognition, encouragement, motivation and practice.

THE SCIENCE OF THE INTUITIVE MIND – EXPERT–NOVICE DIFFERENCES

The Dreyfus brothers, Hubert a philosopher and Stuart an engineer, wrote an influential, controversial and what was seen by some as an anti-artificial intelligence book entitled *Mind Over Machine: the power of human intuition and expertise in the age of the computer* (1988). They were interested in what it is that sets novices and experts apart, and whether or not a machine could possess the same level of intuitive expertise as a human (in their view it couldn't). In Klein's research many of the intuitive experts he studied didn't come up with a range of options from which to choose, they only came up with one. This was quite contrary to his initial expectations and very surprising – he thought they'd have a small number from which they'd then choose. Intuitive experts:

1. distinguish between situations that to the novice might seem similar – they perceive things that are important (salient) that novices overlook or ignore;
2. give an immediate response that is tailored specifically to the situation, rather than blindly following general rules;
3. intuitively do what they feel will work in a given, and often unique, situation but which they're able to make sense of on the basis of their experiences;
4. store tens of thousands of such situations and appropriate responses in an extended long-term memory bank which

184

form the basis for the generation of 'action scripts' for dealing with the problem at hand;

5. don't always know why or how they know what to do.

Experts develop a consummate command of a vast and subtle range of skills in their passage from being a novice, through competence to the peak of expert performance.

Sources: Dreyfus, H.L. and Dreyfus, S.E. (2005) Expertise in real world contexts, *Organization Studies,* **26**: 779–92; Klein, G. (2003) *Intuition at Work.* New York: Doubleday.

The skills that leaders and managers deploy can be divided into 'crude' skills (for example basic IT and word processing skills) and 'subtle' skills (for example, investment and business venturing decisions, hiring and firing, dealing with crises and emergencies). As far as a crude skill is concerned there's more margin for error as well as time available to make corrections. On the other hand, the decisions that require subtle skills often have to be taken quickly in complex and dynamic situations with a small margin for error (a small difference in what one does can have a huge impact on outcomes). Many leadership and management decisions fall into the subtle skills category (time pressured, complex and/ or narrow margin for error). Through their learning, exposure and experiences expert leaders and managers develop practical intuitions – what psychologist Robert J. Sternberg calls 'street smarts' – that enable them to weigh up the situation intuitively and do confidently what their intuitive judgement tells them is likely to work. Intuitive experts who back-track to calculated analysis may end-up thinking too much and questioning their intuitions. This can actually worsen their performance by losing the subtleties and nuances of their informed intuitive judgement; it may also be ill-advised to do so in a time-pressured situation.

Informed Intuition

Intuitive experts make use of *informed intuition* – Klein calls it 'intuitive muscle power'. Intuitive experts don't rely on magical ESP, luck or guesswork. In the same way that there's nothing 'magical' in the recipe for success of many intuitive sportspeople, equally the fire-fighter, the sailor and the paramedic in Klein's research can put their intuitive capabilities down to the fact that they're each, in their own way, exceptionally capable people able to weigh-up a situation and put all their hard-earned knowledge and skill into practice, even if they weren't fully aware at the time of exactly *what* they did or *how* they did it. But science can reveal the magic that lies behind experts' intuitions. For example, under detailed questioning the fire-fighter who thought he had ESP didn't realise there was a basement in the building, or that he and his team were standing directly over it, but he was able to recall that the:

1. flames didn't react as they were expected to when doused with water;
2. living room was hotter than would be expected in a small fire in a kitchen;
3. fire, which they expected to be noisy, was unusually quiet.

Klein sums this up as a 'violation of expectations' – many years of learning, practice, experience and feedback had created a set of expectations in the mind of the lieutenant which kicked in automatically for single storey house fires (he had a different set of expectations for other types of fires). What also kicked in automatically at the same time was the gut feeling that something was wrong when his expectations weren't met. It led to the identification not of a small number of options from which a choice could be made, but of one option only – evacuate. It was the same for the paramedic, her expectation of what her father-in-law *should* look like if he were as healthy as she remembered him was violated. The signs of an impending heart attack – pale greyish skin colouration, swelling of the wrists and ankles and a greenish tinge to the mouth – none of which on their own might amount to a cause for concern but when put together set off her intuitive alarm bell.

In areas where managers and leaders possess the necessary expertise the intuitive mind 'kicks in' with a solution based on what worked well in similar or related situations in the past. For example, when giving an important presentation to a tough-minded group of business executives a skilled public speaker might begin by using his or her experience to sense the atmosphere and tone in the room (for example, heavy or light) and establish an appropriate rapport (for example, sombre or cheerful) with the audience. Experts have been described as people who 'do what normally works' in complex situations, and expertise enables highly trained and experienced people to do demanding and complex things on 'autopilot' – or seemingly so. And it works at all levels, for example in the world of business an experienced customer contact employee, when confronted by an angry and an irate customer on the telephone, knows immediately and without applying a formula from a training course on how to calm the customer down, how to elicit the facts, and how to provide a satisfactory solution, in a way that proceeds with what, on the surface at least, appears to be effortless ease. But this is far from an automaton-like response; it's an intelligent and informed use of a deeply-embedded script chosen from a library of previous incidents in which rigorous training, practice, experience, coaching and feedback has built up levels of expert performance. Underneath the tip of the iceberg of smooth transactions, witnessed day in and day out in many aspects of personal and professional life, there's a vast body of learning, skill, knowledge hard-won through positive and negative experiences of dealing with similar situations in the past.

Managing with a 'Crystal Ball'

As we know only too well the world is uncertain and unpredictable, so what happens when a situation is encountered for which there isn't a single script that is *the* obvious choice to follow? Decision makers are sometimes confronted by an either-or question with two equally plausible choices: 'what would happen if I did that rather than this?' In these situations it's possible to combine the power of imagination and intuition to:

1. mentally fast forward how a possible future scenario might play-out in reality;
2. sense how we *feel* about the envisioned consequences.

Klein describes this approach as fast forwarding a 'DVD-in-the-head' – a mental simulation built up by specifying the building blocks of the scenario, putting them in a logical sequence, running the sequence and evaluating the outcome.

INTUITION WORKOUT No. 11: INTUITING FUTURES

Imagine the scenario of an important event, for example a house move and the choice between what seem to be on the face of it two equally plausible options (House A and House B). How to decide? One way would be to toss a coin. However, many people faced with a major life decision may feel uncomfortable with tossing a coin and might even see it as irresponsible. An alternative method might be to consult a variant of the crystal ball of Klein's mental simulation approach (the method can be adapted to any important decision in work or personal life, the difference between Klein's model and the version offered here is in the final stage 'Sense'). In the example

---

188

below the technique is applied to the complex, risky and uncertain events surrounding a house move, but it equally can be applied to other complex, risky and uncertain decisions in personal and professional life.

Specify	Identify the components of the image in the crystal ball, for example location, type of house, number of rooms, proximity to work, schools and family, aspect and size of garden, and so forth.
Assemble	Put the elements into a logical sequence for an everyday or important event such as the school run, shopping trips, getting to work, or visiting close family. Ask yourself: (1) What would the sequence of one of these events be like if you lived in House A? (2) What would the same sequence be like for House B?
Watch	Mentally observe the action in the crystal ball. You can run it forward, review, pause, replay, fast forward and rewind. For example, look into the crystal ball at a part of a typical day such as the school run for House A and for House B and watch the action unfold.
Sense	How does the action *feel* for you? Be mindful of the changes in your body landscape as the events in the crystal ball proceed. For example, can you imagine yourself doing the school run from House A and feeling good about it? How does it compare with the sequence in House B?

The final stage ('Sense') involves examining your gut feelings and is the crucial element of gazing into the crystal ball. Any bodily 'felt sense' that arises is invaluable as soft 'data'. It can be used just as much as hard data to guide judgement of how viable a particular option is.

There is of course an important caveat: gut feelings shouldn't be confused with the four enemies of good intuition (logical errors, bias, prejudice and wishful thinking) or with transient emotions and attachments that come with them. Weeding out these sources of feeble intuitions from genuine gut feeling is a vital intuitive competence that comes with practice.

By creating and accessing your own mental 'crystal ball' success is not guaranteed, but it does allow you to visit the future.

Application No. 12: Crystal Ball Gazing

Expose	Expose yourself to a virtual version of critical situations that you may meet in the real world.
Envision	Envision what might happen via your mental crystal ball.
Simulate	Control and manipulate events in a virtual environment that's low risk.
Judge	Judge the likelihood of success of an action sequence.
Sense	Ask yourself 'how do the events you're "observing" feel in your body?'
Anticipate	Anticipate problems and pitfalls.[19]

One of the down sides of mental simulation is that the intuitive mind has a preference for powerful stories, gripping narratives and vivid imagery; as a consequence it can take stories and scenarios too literally and latch on to what amounts to nothing more than the 'best story' as a cast-iron certainty, rather than as an open-to-question hypothesis.

THE SCIENCE OF THE INTUITIVE MIND – THE POWER OF STORY-TELLING

The decision researcher Reid Hastie has spent many years studying the complex judgements that take place in criminal trials. One of the striking things he found out about jurors is that they are quite capable of taking the evidence as presented to them and re-assembling it as a compelling narrative (lawyers often also attempt to influence jurors by presenting their case as a convincing story). There are a number of problems created by the power of stories and the strong appeal that they hold over our intuitive mind.

Different jurors tend to create different stories which can lead to different verdicts to convict or acquit. In everyday life people tend to stop after they have constructed one satisfactory story, but the legal system forces the construction of multiple scenarios. The more complete, detailed and unique a story is the greater the confidence jurors are likely to have in it.

From early childhood human beings are fascinated and beguiled by stories. They can exercise a compelling, but not always positive influence over the intuitive mind.

Source: Pennington, N. and Hastie, R. (1993) Reasoning in explanation-based decision making, *Cognition*, **49**: 123–63.

A distinctive feature of the stories that people construct is that the 'actors' in them tend to literally and definitely do things, for example they 'stab other people' rather than 'probably stab them', the vividness of a violent and dramatic image appeals to the narrative style that the intuitive mind is more comfortable with. To introduce the necessary degree of uncertainty or scepticism into our stories requires more analysis than people undertake spontaneously if the intuitive mind is in the driving seat.

Devil's Advocacy and Intuitive Judgement

The confabulations of the intuitive mind, and the confirmation biases that it's prone to, need to be tempered by the conservatism of a cautionary analytical mind. Mental simulation and intuitive judgement are invaluable in those areas where we have the expert knowledge to create valid narratives and the skills and experience to get a sense of their viability; however we should also be wary of being seduced by the drama of the narrative. Any potential excesses of the intuitive mind can be tempered by playing Devil's Advocate to our intuitions or conducting what decision researcher Gary Klein calls a *pre-mortem* of an intuitive decision.

The Devil's Advocate has its origins in the Roman Catholic Church in the Middle Ages where the Devil's Advocate (*advocatus diaboli*) was a formalised dissenting voice vital to the canonisation (saint declaration) process. The Devil's Advocate was required to take a sceptical position with the remit of finding holes in the qualities of a candidate being proposed for sainthood.[20] In the same way it's possible to consciously adopt a dissenting voice about our own or another person's intuitive judgement. Putting the negative side of the argument requires a Devil's Advocate to do three things:

✎ **Application No. 13: Being a Good Devil's Advocate**

Probe   Ask probing questions about biases, prejudices, wishful thinking.

Doubt   Cast doubts upon the experience and expertise behind the intuition.

Counter   Put the case for an alternative more analytical approach and see how this stacks up against an intuitive judgement.

The Devil's Advocate can be someone we know and trust (a critical friend) or we can be our own, sometimes severe, self-critic. If an intuition can stand up to the scrutiny of the Devil's Advocate and her or his arguments be rebutted this can dramatically increase levels of confidence in an intuitive judgement.

INTUITION WORKOUT No. 12: PLAY DEVIL'S ADVOCATE

An early proponent of the value of Devil's Advocacy in management was Charles Schwenk.[21] In his research Schwenk found that Devil's Advocates (DAs) can improve strategic decision making if certain rules are followed. To be effective a DA should play the role of objective critic of an intuitive judgement rather than a 'carping critic' of intuition in general, and in relation to a specific intuition the DA's role should be to point out:

1. weaknesses in the assumptions underlying the intuitive judgement (for example, are the assumptions biased or prejudiced?);
2. internal inconsistencies in the intuitive judgement (for example, does it make sense logically?);
3. long-term problems that might be encountered if the intuitive judgement is followed (for example, what hurdles along the way might lead to its failure?);
4. threats from feeble intuitions (for example, as a result of wishful thinking, emotional feelings and desires).

If an intuition fails to wilt under this level of scrutiny you can be more confident and assured about your intuitive judgement.

DA's enable critical flaws to be spotted and failures anticipated *before* they happen, but none of this is to say that the DA's views are necessarily correct – her or his role is merely to expose intuitive judgements to criticism. DAs can work one-on-one and in groups, however in group decision making DAs should only be used if all the decision makers in the group are genuinely open to having their intuitions questioned and willing to hear what the DA has to say. If they aren't the DAs' efforts will be a waste of time. In the longer term a failure to open up intuitions to criticism and feedback can only lead to the development of bad intuitive judgement and feeble intuitions. This is a perilous state of affairs for managers, leaders and followers and the business organisations of which they are a part.

INTUITIVE INTELLIGENCE PRINCIPLE No. 6:
DEVELOP EXPERTISE

Most managers don't view intuition as a paranormal power,[22] they're well aware that if intuitive judgement is a 'crystal ball' and intuition is any kind of 'sixth sense' these are only metaphors, and prediction on the basis of a hunch or a gut feeling is a perfectly normal function of the human mind.

But just because this and the other attributes of the intuitive mind are part of nature's design for an integrated body-mind system it doesn't mean that they're any less remarkable. Indeed your intuitive mind is all the more 'magical' because it's natural rather than supernatural.

Every one of us has it in some form or another and whether it manifests itself as social, creative, entrepreneurial, moral or expert intuition, it's possible for each of us to become better at using it by acquiring knowledge, developing skills, seeking honest and objective feedback, managing our experiences and making sense out of them. Building an infrastructure of support for the honing of our intuitive expertise lays the foundations for intuitive intelligence.

NOTES

[1] 'Sport sponsorship' retrieved on 8th September 2008 from http://www. rbssport.com/f1-numbers-game.html on 8th September 2008

[2] 'The Autoracing channel' retrieved on 8th September 2008 from http:// www.autoracing.com/formula-1/drivers/.

[3] 'Lewis Hamilton – the real deal' retrieved on 8th September 2008 from http://www.itv-f1.com/Feature.aspx?Type=Martin_Brundle&id=41531.

[4] Cooper, A. (1998) *Playing in the Zone: exploring the spiritual dimensions of sports*. Boston: Shambala Publications.

[5] Alessi, L.E. (1994) Breakaway into the zone: a phenomenological investigation from the athlete's perspective. *Dissertation Abstracts International*, 5602B (University Microfilms No. DAI9518256).

[6] Schindehutte, M., Morris, M. and Allen, J. (2006) Beyond achievement: entrepreneurship as extreme experience, *Small Business Economics*, **27**: 349–68.

[7] Hatch M.J. (1999) Exploring the empty spaces of organizing: how improvisational jazz helps re-describe organizational structure. *Organization Studies*, **20**(1): 75–100.

[8] For example, in *Star Wars* Jedi warriors could pre-cognize opponent's moves in combat through the power of 'the Force'.

[9] Lindeman, M. And Saher, M. (2007) Vitalism, purpose and superstition, *British Journal of Psychology*, **98**: 33–4; Vyse, S.A. (2000) *Believing in magic: the psychology of superstition*. Oxford: Oxford University Press, p. 28.

[10] 'Barthez's latest calamity threatens United career' retrieved on 24th December 2008 from http://sportsillustrated.cnn.com/soccer/news/ 2003/08/14/barthez_united/.

[11] Nadel, L. (1996) *Sixth Sense: how to unlock your intuitive brain*. London: Prion. In a more recent scientific publication James H. Lee of the University of Texas' Future Studies Program whilst acknowledging that the field is controversial claimed that '… precognition of the future has been widely experienced by the public. In a recent survey conducted at the University of Alabama, over half of the randomly selected participants have experienced a dream-based premonition. Fifty-three percent reported premonitions of future events that later happened. Forty-five-percent have changed travel plans as a result of an intuitive "sense", and subsequently have saved themselves effort or injury'. See:

Lee. J.H. (2008) Remote viewing as applied to futures studies, *Technological Forecasting and Social Change*, **75**(1): 142–53.

[12] 'Society for Scientific Exploration' retrieved on 24th September 2008 from http://www.scientificexploration.org/jse/abstracts/v10n1a4.php; + the psychology paper.

[13] 'Inward bound – the greatest journey we ever go on' retrieved on 24th September 2008 from http://www.inwardboundvisioning.com/. Accessed 24th September 2008

[14] Markely, O.W. (1988) Using depth intuition in creative problem solving and strategic innovation, *The Journal of Creative Behavior*, **22**(2): 65–100;

[15] Klein, G. (1998) *Sources of Power: how people make decisions*. Cambridge, MA.: The MIT Press; Klein, G. (2003) *Intuition at Work: why developing your gut instincts will make you better at what you do*. New York: Doubleday.

[16] Mack, J. and Powell, L. (2005) Perceptions of non-local communication: incidences associated with media consumption and individual differences, *North American Journal of Psychology*, **7**(2): 279–94.

[17] 'How a go kart kid took the fast track to £50m fortune' retrieved on 23rd September from http://www.journalisted.com/article?id=24411.

[18] Adapted from: Mumford, M.D., Zaccaro, S.J., Harding, F.D. and Jacobs, T.O. (2000) Leadership skills for a changing world: solving complex social problems, *Leadership Quarterly*, **11**(1): 11–35; Northouse, P.G. (2007) *Leadership: theory and practice*. Thousand Oaks, CA: Sage.

[19] Cannon-Bowers, J.A., and Bell, H.H. (1997) Training decision makers for complex environments: implications of the naturalistic decision making perspective, in Zsambok, C., and Klein, G. (Eds) *Naturalistic Decision Making*. Mahwah, NJ: Laurence Erlbaum Associates, pp. 99–110.

[20] Herbert, T.T. and Estes, R.W. (1977) Improving executive decisions by formalising dissent: the corporate Devil's Advocate, *Academy of Management Review*, **2**(4): 663–7.

[21] Schwenk, C.R. (1984) Devil's advocacy in managerial decision-making, *Journal of Management Studies*, **21**(2): 153–68.

[22] Burke, L.A. and Miller, M.M. (1999) Taking the mystery out of intuitive decision making, *Academy of Management Executive*, **13**(4): 91–9.

Chapter 7

THE INTUITIVE BRAIN

In the previous chapter the intuitive mind was depicted as a complex system able to perceive, make sense and decide what to do in complex situations quickly and effortlessly on the basis of learning and experience. As well as the view of 'intuition-as-expertise' there's another equally important aspect – 'intuition-as-feeling'. It's this side of the intuitive mind, and in particular its neural basis, that'll be explored in this chapter. Being able to distinguish between emotional feelings and intuitive (gut) feelings is a vital intuitive intelligence competence for leaders and managers.

In October 2001 the former American football star O.J. Simpson hit the media headlines again, this time over a supposed 'road rage' incident. *The New York Times* reported that motorist Jeffrey Pattinson testified in the Miami-Dade circuit court that Simpson ran a red light and nearly hit his car, forcing him to slam on his brakes. He said he honked at Simpson, who then stopped in front of him, walked angrily to his car and allegedly raged at Pattinson 'So I blew the stop sign, what are you going to do? Kill me and my kids?'. Simpson is then supposed to have reached into Pattinson's car, ripping off his glasses and allegedly inflicted a scratch on Pattinson's nose. In the end the charges of battery and burglarising a car, which can carry a jail sentence of up to sixteen years, were totally rejected by the six-person jury and Simpson was acquitted.[1]

Cases of road rage are by no means uncommon: a study by the UK's Automobile Association found that almost 90% of drivers had experienced road rage – an explosive form of aggression where a driver attempts to intimidate or injure another driver or pedestrian, or damage their vehicle.[2] In common with many other basic emotions the anger of road rage is 'hot'. The anger associated with road rage is a strong negative emotion that can lead to destructive patterns of behaviour, usually perpetrated by males on other males and sometimes resulting in injury and even death. Road rage researcher Leon James of the University of Hawaii sees it as an anger management issue – we switch from normal, rational human being 'to a mode of reptilian thinking' overwhelmed by the passions of the brain's limbic system.[3]

A Matter of Feeling

Perpetrating or being the victim of road rage is a matter of emotional feeling. Road rage, trolley rage, office rage, or any other kind of anger, occurs as an intense, short-lived burst of emotional energy in response to a situation in which we feel threatened, aggrieved or treated unfairly. As an instinctive emotional response anger can serve a useful function by equipping the organism for fighting. The emotion of anger (the distinctive feature of road rage) results in an outburst of aggression either verbal or physical which, in our evolutionary past, might have served the useful (adaptive) function of scaring away or even destroying a perceived enemy through violence.[4]

Like the other basic emotions fear also serves a potentially useful biological function – it equips the organism for flight. If we stumble across a gnarled stick on a forest path and mistake it for a poisonous snake our instantaneous reaction might be to recoil automatically. Hormonal messages are sent to the body from the hypothalamus (the part of the brain responsible for crucial metabolic functions) and these create physical changes (blood is pumped to the large muscles) the result of which is that we withdraw quickly out of range of the perceived threat. The emotional feeling that accompanies this response is fear – felt as quickened pulse rate, arousal and defensive behaviour. It's intense and shortlived. Fractions of a second later we may feel relieved and even foolish that we jumped at nothing more than a harmless piece of wood. But a moment's reflection tells us that actually this was a very smart thing to do: it's better to have a false alarm for something that looks like a poisonous snake than no alarm at all for things such as sticks that, on first glance, may be indistinguishable from poisonous snakes.

Any organism equipped to ignore snake-like objects on forest paths would be unlikely to survive for long; it would not find a mate, reproduce and pass on its genes to the next generation because it would be unfit for survival in hazardous forest habitats inhabited by snakes or other hard-to-spot potentially life-threatening creatures. The same wiring that enables us to have instinctive fear reactions can also flare up in *Homo sapiens'* modern habitat – at home or at work. In a civilised society the more extreme emotional responses that evolution has pre-programmed us with need to be managed intelligently. Elon Musk, founder and CEO of the Los Angeles-based space exploration technology company Spacex, has learned to be wary of emotion clouding the decision-making process or making an emotionally-charged decision that you'll later regret; in balancing control and passion, as he told *Fortune Magazine*: 'You have to be as clearheaded as possible. Of course it's a fine line, because you don't want to be completely dispassionate'.[5]

Managing anger, fear and other basic emotions begins with an understanding of their biological bases. So what's happening in the 'stick-or-snake' scenario? The answer to this question was provided by the neural scientist Joseph E. LeDoux, who discovered in experiments on rats that information passes to a small almond shaped structure in the brain – the amygdala (referred to in the singular, but there are two one on each side) – along two routes, a 'fast lane' and a 'slow(er) lane'.

🔑 Key Facts No. 12: The Highs and Lows of Emotion

Low Road	Initially the emotional stimulus travels along a 'quick and dirty' short circuit from the eye to the thalamus (the brain's relay station) to the amygdala (where fear is registered and generated). This emotional 'low road' produces an unconsciously determined withdrawal response and as a result we're able to recoil quickly to a safe distance.
High Road	A fraction of second later the visual information reaches the sensory cortex where it's analysed in more detail and interpreted. The information that travels via this 'high road' is subject to a more consciously controlled evaluation and results in a more considered response to the stimulus.

The amygdala is our 'fight or flight' organ. It produces emotional responses (especially where fear is involved) and is wired up to other parts of the brain. These circuits, which infuse feelings into the way we think and act, can by-pass higher brain centres and conscious awareness, as a result emotionally charged memories have an immense power to consciously and non consciously influence the way we evaluate objects, situations and people.

What can be done in the workplace situations where we're consciously aware that our emotional feelings are hijacking or about to hijack our analytical mind? Controlling anger in the office can come down to things as simple as: count to ten; take a few slow deep breaths; repeat to yourself a calming word or phrase (such as 'relax', 'let go' or 'calm down'); don't take things personally, they probably weren't meant that way; imagine how your role model would handle the situation; physically distance yourself from the source of the anger; don't say or do anything hurtful; lighten-up and try to see the not-so-serious, or even funny, side of it.[6]

THE SCIENCE OF THE INTUITIVE MIND – ON AN EMOTIONAL HIGH

Standing on a rickety suspension bridge can be an emotionally arousing experience giving rise to fear, exhilaration or 'high anxiety'. Sitting on a park bench, on the other hand, is emotionally relaxing rather than arousing. In the 1970s psychologists Donald Dutton and Arthur Aron explored whether being emotionally aroused by being on a 450-foot long wobbly wood-and-wire bridge suspended over a 230-foot drop to the rocks and shallow rapids of the Capilano Canyon in British Colombia could unconsciously affect men's levels of attraction to an unknown female and their degree of sexual arousal.

Men who were crossing the rickety bridge and therefore emotionally aroused by fear or excitement were approached by a female experimenter posing as psychology student. She asked them to fill out a bogus questionnaire on the 'effects of exposure to scenic attractions on creative expression', and also to write a brief dramatic story based on a picture of a young woman reaching out with one hand and covering her face with the other. When they'd done this the researcher offered to explain it all in detail when she had more time, and gave each interviewee her phone number with an invitation to call her up. The researcher followed exactly the same procedure with men who'd already crossed the bridge and were resting on a park bench and were no longer emotionally aroused or excited. Did the emotional state associated with being on the bridge unconsciously affect the men's level of attraction to the interviewer and their level of sexual arousal? How would their reactions to her compare with those of the unaroused men?

Of the men who were interviewed on the bridge 65% subsequently called up the experimenter; the comparable figure for the men who were interviewed on the park bench was only 30%. Moreover, when the stories the men had written were rated for sexual content (for example the word 'intercourse' scored five points and 'girlfriend' two) the sexual imagery score for stories of the men interviewed on the bridge was 50% higher than for the men on the park bench.

Source: Dutton, D.G. and Aron, A.P. (1974) Some evidence for heightened sexual attraction under conditions of high anxiety, *Journal of Personality and Social Psychology*, **30**(4): 510–17.

The men who were emotionally aroused merely by being on the suspension bridge were more attracted to a stranger than they would have been in a less aroused state. Being on an emotional high can have a major impact on our judgement (sexual attraction) and behaviour (calling up a stranger) in ways that we aren't consciously aware of. It's perhaps advisable therefore to avoid making important decisions in emotionally charged situations because the level of arousal can non consciously influence unrelated aspects of thinking and behaviour. For the social psychologist Timothy D. Wilson this and related research raises several issues which are as pertinent to the workplace as they are to wobbly bridges, summarised here as emotionality, inaccessibility and confabulation:

🔑 Key Facts No. 13: Emotionality and Rationality

Emotionality	Our perception, behaviour and judgement can be unconsciously affected by our emotional state.
Inaccessibility	Because we can't access our unconscious thoughts we may often make up reasons for our actions.
Confabulation	Our conscious verbal 'self' sometimes doesn't know why we do what we do and so has to make up an explanation that makes some semblance of sense.[7]

The justifications and explanations that we give – the stories that we tell ourselves – may make sense to our analytical mind but they might be far from the reality of our underlying motivations and intentions. Although we may not be able to do very much about it, the fact that we're aware that emotions can have powerful surreptitious, as well as overt, influence is a powerful insight into our own cognitive and emotional functioning.

The distinguished neurologist Antonio Damasio described emotions as chemical and neural responses produced by the brain. Emotions are objective facts: they can be seen with the naked eye (for example, a person's smile or frown) or measured using scientific instruments (for example, heart rate or blood pressure). Feelings, on the other hand, are our private mental representations of the physiological changes that take place as a result of an emotional response, for example, the feeling of fear, or of anger or love. By associating a feeling with a particular situation, memories that are tagged with a positive or negative feeling can help us to anticipate the good or bad outcome of similar situations in the future.[8]

The amygdala-induced emotional feelings of road rage are a fast, low-effort automatic response. Similarly the instinctive fear reaction to a snake-like object on a forest path is involuntary and lightning quick. Road ragers and hikers on forest paths don't premeditate their instinctive reactions – they just happen. Likewise, one of the hallmarks of gut feeling is that it's fast and spontaneous: we don't will it into action. But that's where the similarity ends; the feelings involved in intuition are quite different to those experienced in rage, anger, or love.

Road rage, snakes on paths and being suspended over canyons on rickety bridges are arousing situations which give rise to brain states and bodily responses that are accompanied by emotional feelings. They're distinguishable from intuitive feelings by their levels of intensity and duration – they're strong, sharp and short-lived peaks in our affective landscape, they create the impulse to act and have the power to move or excite us (literally and metaphorically) in particular ways ('emotion' is from the Latin *mōvere* – to move). Intuition is quite different: gut feelings and hunches are more subtle, longer lasting and less intense undulations in the landscape of our bodily feelings, and they don't rely on the same neural circuitry in the brain that leads to extreme emotional responses. If emotions are 'hot' and analyses are 'cool', intuitions are 'warm'.

An additional key fact that neurological research has revealed is that as well as being felt in the body intuitions can also be so subtle as to produce changes in the body that are outside of our conscious awareness but nonetheless able to influence the choices that we make. And while they may animate us or influence our decisions, unlike anger, fear, disgust or passion, they don't motivate us to fight, run away, be sickened, or fall in love. To understand intuitive feelings we have to take a closer look at the neuroscience of the intuitive mind.

THE SCIENCE OF THE INTUITIVE MIND – THE NEURAL GEOGRAPHY OF EMOTION

Modern imaging techniques allow neuroscientists to have glimpses inside the human brain in order to observe patterns of metabolic and neural activity. Two commonly used methods are functional magnetic resonance imaging (fMRI) and positron emission tomography (PET). The principle behind these technologies is called 'hemodynamics': when neurons fire they consume glucose and oxygen from the bloodstream, PET and fMRI images show where these substances are being carried to and consumed when the brain is engaged in different types of activity. Merely imagining physical activities can result in brain activation in movement-relevant areas even in people who are in a so-called 'vegetative state'. For example, in 2008 scientists from Cambridge and Belgium scanned the brain of a twenty-three year old woman who was in a coma as a result of a traffic accident. She was asked to imagine playing tennis or walking round her home while her brain was being scanned. The results – which startled the researchers – revealed that the same parts of her brain were activated as in healthy volunteers who were asked to imagine the same things.

As far as emotion is concerned neural scientists have found that two areas of the brain seem to be especially important – the amygdala and the prefrontal cortex (PFC) which is made up of orbitofrontal, ventromedial and dorsolateral sectors (see Figure 7.1). The PFC is where the brain represents the feelings (for example the feeling of 'approach to' or 'withdrawal from' a particular stimulus in our environment). Some neuroscientists think of this brain region as where our 'affective working memory' is located, the part of the brain where we 'listen' to our feelings. 'Affect' in this context refers to feelings, and 'affective working memory' as the place where we hold feelings in conscious awareness is analogous to ordinary working memory where we hold a piece of information while we consciously manipulate it, for example a seven-digit phone number.

Sources: Davidson, R.J. and Irwin, W. (1999) The functional neuroanatomy of emotion and affective style, *Trends in Cognitive Sciences*, **3**(1): 11–21; and Carter, R. (2000) *Mapping the Mind.* London: Phoenix.

We can learn to quiet down our emotional brain by keeping ourselves busy on non emotional mental tasks, whereas ruminating on things that make us unhappy can stoke the amygdala's affective fire. The fact that the amygdala is aroused in highly charged situations results in certain memories being tagged with

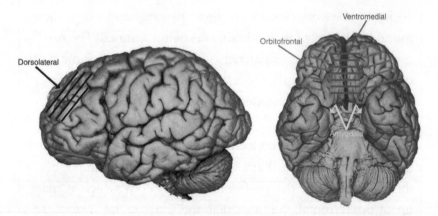

FIGURE 7.1 Sectors of human prefrontal cortex. Left: lateral view indicating dorsolateral cortical territory. Right: ventral view indicating ventromedial and orbitofrontal cortical territories. Also indicated are the amygdalae located on the medial margin of the temporal lobes. *Source:* Davidson, R.J. and Irwin, W. (1999) The functional neuroanatomy of emotion and affective style, *Trends in Cognitive Sciences*, **3**(1): 11–21. Reproduced by kind permission of Elsevier Science.

emotional significance, for example, for many people the events of 9/11 are very strongly tagged and people are often able to remember very vividly what they were doing on that occasion.

When Analysis and Intuition Break Down

Traditionally in business we think of the human mind as a place where feelings and intuitions are subservient to controlled, organised, analytical thinking – it's the way many managers have been trained and educated to think. Like the Prime Minister of a government or the Chief Executive of a large company the analytical mind has an executive function. It stands watch, ready to intervene and correct any affective excess committed by the intuitive mind. If this is the case what does neuroscience tell us about the biology behind this executive control function, and what happens when the 'president of the mind' is no longer able to function competently?

One of the distinctive features of rational planning is organization, and some of the most compelling evidence for the physical existence and location of the analytical mind's executive function is to be found in patients who've incurred damage to the dorsolateral prefrontal cortex: their behaviour becomes, in a word, 'disorganised'.[9] They experience difficulties in performing tasks that require planning, the use of working memory and the logical sequencing of actions; moreover they appear unable to check and inhibit their impulsive responses[10] – when analysis breaks down disorganisation and impulsivity reign.

But feelings are also 'data' just as much as facts and figures. In business they act as an alarm to signal avoidance, or as a beacon signalling attraction towards or away from a new business venture, a potential new hire, or an investment opportunity. As well as attracting us towards or repelling us away from a person, object or situation, feelings can also help to signpost the right direction and whittle down the range of options which can sometimes be overwhelming. Intuition is a filtering mechanism which makes the task of deciding more manageable. But what happens when intuition breaks down? Again we must look to evidence from the brain sciences to understand the mechanics of the intuitive mind.

THE SCIENCE OF THE INTUITIVE MIND – ANALYSIS PARALYSIS

The neurologist Antonio Damasio has treated hundreds of patients with brain lesions. One such patient from whom much was learned about the neural circuitry that connects decision making and feelings was a manager referred to as 'Elliot'.

Elliot's misfortune was that he developed a tumour along the mid-line region of his brain that eventually grew to the size of an orange and compressed his frontal lobes upwards. Although the meningioma tissue (tumour) itself was benign, unless removed it was likely to prove as fatal as a malignancy. The operation to remove the tumour, which also meant removing some of the surrounding frontal lobe tissue, was a surgical success. However, the effects on Elliot's personality and decision making were traumatic.

Before the illness Elliot was a good husband, father, an excellent manager and a role model with high personal, professional and social status. After the surgery he was able to read and classify documents with the same high level of knowledge and intelligence as he showed before. However, he could also suddenly and inexplicably become diverted into and engrossed by a minute and trivially detailed level of processing. He could spend entire days reading a single document and deciding on the criteria of how to analyse, process and classify it. What should have taken minutes could take hours or even days. Elliot lost sight of the bigger picture and ended up consumed by detail, obsessed with what for other people would be mind-numbing analysis. Aside from this Elliot could not make an effective plan for hours let alone months ahead; not only that, he collected junk, and eventually his employment was terminated. He ended by associating with disreputable individuals, made a bad second marriage and drifted through life. Elliot fell from grace and his whole life spiralled downwards.

The key to understanding Elliot's demise came from conversations with Elliot and his relatives and their perceptions of how his normal emotional functioning had profoundly altered post-surgery. They revealed someone who was emotionally mellower than previously, so much so that his emotions were a monotone showing little in the way of anger, impatience, sadness or frustration. By his own account things that once evoked emotions in him no longer did so. In decision-making tasks he could generate as many options as necessary but in his own words 'still wouldn't know what to do!' Analysis paralysis had gripped Elliot's neurological decision-making apparatus and he was bereft of his gut feelings.

Source: Damasio, A.R. (1994) *Descartes' Error: emotion, reason and the human brain.* New York: Penguin Putnam (pp. 34–51).

Brain scans revealed that Elliot's behaviour was associated with damage incurred during surgery to the ventro-medial prefrontal cortex (VMPC) region of his brain (see Figure 7.1). As a result he was capable of cold rationality but incapable of assigning emotional values to the different options. Because Elliot could not infuse gut feeling into his decisions his analytical mind was able to run riot. Damasio and his colleagues, including Antoine Bechara, have conducted numerous experiments in which they've compared the performance of VMPC-damaged patients like Elliot with people with intact VMPCs (referred to as 'normals').[11] One of the most well-known experiments is a fake betting task called the Iowa Gambling Task (IGT). In the IGT participants play using four decks of cards which are, unbeknownst to them, loaded – there are two 'bad' decks (A and B) and two 'good' decks (C and D). Participants are given $2000 in play money and they play the game under the guidance of an experimenter by turning over a card from one of the four decks over a run of 100 choices. The bad decks are loaded and much more risky, so that choosing mostly from them leads to losses and an eventual overall deficit. The good decks are loaded in the opposite way and much less risky: choosing mostly from them leads to gains and an overall profit.

In the experiment the two groups (VMPC-damaged and normals) were wired up to measure their skin conductance responses (SCRs), also known as micro-sweating – tiny tell-tale signs of emotional changes in the body landscape. After a number of card selections normals began to generate SCRs in the five-second window before selecting a card from the risky 'bad' decks. They also began to gravitate unconsciously towards the good decks. Normals had learned implicitly during their brief exposure to the game that decks A and B were risky; moreover, their bodies were aware of this fact even if they weren't. The VMPC damaged patients didn't generate any SCRs in anticipation of their risky choices, they made a loss even when they had realised consciously which decks were riskier. The normals were able to choose advantageously even though they didn't know why – their negative 'gut feelings' (as evidenced by micro-sweating) told them which decks to avoid. The normals' gut feelings were triggered automatically and didn't need to come into conscious awareness to have an effect on their gambling strategy (the SCRs were so subtle as to be undetectable by the participants and only picked up on by the sensitive measuring apparatus). These ground breaking experiments demonstrated clearly that gut feeling is a very real and measurable biological phenomenon. Even before we get a conscious hunch to avoid an unfavourable object, person or situation our intuitive mind can intervene and do the job for us by steering us subtly away.

Some of the strongest evidence for the power of the hunch in decision making comes from a closer look at the brains and behaviours of VMPC-damaged patients: they don't have the ability to generate any negative gut feelings. Their 'intuitive minds' have been compromised by brain damage to the extent that they don't generate the feelings that help normals to learn which situations in life are best avoided. As we witnessed in the case of Elliot and the IGT experiments the ventromedial sector of the brain's prefrontal cortex (PFC) is a crucial piece of neural hardware for effective decision making both in the lab and the real world of business organisations. The signals produced by the VMPC exert a powerful influence on decision making, but they don't necessarily register immediately in the conscious awareness; instead they show-up in bodily signals referred to by neurologists as 'somatic markers' (from the Greek *soma* – σῶμα – meaning 'body').

⚷ Key Facts No. 14: Damasio's Somatic Marker Hypothesis (SMH)

The somatic marker hypothesis (SMH) was developed by neurologist Antonio Damasio and his colleagues (including Antoine Bechara). The key features of the SMH were outlined by Damasio in his 1994 book *Descartes' Error: reason, emotion and the human brain.*

Before human beings apply cost benefit analyses (CBA) or reasoning to a decision, if a bad outcome associated with a given option comes to mind an unpleasant gut feeling is experienced.

The feeling is somatic (because it's in the body) and marks an image (images can be perceptual or recalled, and in a variety of sensory modalities, for example visual, auditory or tactile).

The somatic marker forces one's attention to the negative outcomes to which a given action, if followed through, may lead.

The somatic marker may lead to the rejection of a negative course of action or to the narrowing down of options allowing choice from fewer alternatives.

Rational CBA may still be applied after gut feeling has rejected certain options.

When a negative somatic marker is associated with a particular future outcome it functions as an alarm bell (and signals avoidance).

When a positive somatic marker is associated with a particular future outcome it functions as a beacon of incentive (and signals attraction).

Source: Damasio, A.R. (1994) *Descartes' Error: emotion, reason and the human brain.* New York: Harper Collins (pp. 173–5).

Somatic markers are involuntary, non-conscious, bodily signals that guide decision making in advance of conscious awareness. We tend to assume that when we make a choice we decide freely and consciously; research sheds some doubt on this and also raises some very significant questions: for example, is conscious free will an illusion (perhaps created by the conscious mind)? Perhaps the intuitive mind is more in charge than we might like to admit? If the intuitive mind is more than a mere passenger, who's in the driving seat in our personal and professional lives?

THE SCIENCE OF THE INTUITIVE MIND – NEUROBUSINESS

Neuromarketing, described by some as the 'love child' of neuro-science and marketing, provides corporate marketers with a tool that can get round the biases and unreliability of 'tick box' consumer surveys or the surreptitious tracking of purchasing habits with loyalty cards. It gets directly inside shoppers' skulls. For most businesses consumers' 'buy or not to buy' decision is crucial. From a psychological point of view such a decision boils down to a trade off for the consumer between the pleasure of acquisition versus the pain of paying. Researchers from three leading US universities used fMRI to scan participants' brains during a simulated shopping experience to see which parts of the brain were activated when products and prices were presented. By studying patterns of brain activation consumers' preferences (pleasure of consumption) for a product could be mapped on to quite different brain regions to those involved when consumers considered the pricing of products (pain of paying).

Neuroeconomics brings together conventional microeconomics with neurology with the aim of understanding the neural circuitry involved in economic decisions. For example, different brain regions are activated when financial decision makers contemplate risky and non risky decisions, and patients with damage to the ventro-medial pre-frontal cortex (VMPC) brain region behave as if they were ultra-rational *Homo economicus* able to coolly and calmly take decisions without any feelings at all.

Sources: Carr, N. (2008) Neuromarketing could make mind reading the ad-man's ultimate tool. *The Guardian*, Thursday 3rd April 2008; Goetz, J. and James, R.N. (2008) Human choice and the emerging field of neuroeconomics: a review of brain science for the financial planner, *Journal of Personal Finance*, **6**(4): 13–36; Knutson, B., Rick, S., Wimmer, E., Prelec, D. and Lowenstein, G. (2008) Neural predictors of purchases, *Neuron*, **53**: 147–56.

Neuromarketers claim that brain activations can be used to understand and predict consumers' purchasing decisions, and may eventually be used to help marketers design better campaigns and strategies for selling products and services. Neuroeconomists are particularly interested in the way the brain's rational and emotional circuits interact in financial decision making; perhaps one day they'll be able to help financial analysts understand when their emotions are likely to be a help and when they can be a hindrance. This area is controversial and some of its potential applications have caused voices to be raised in concern for the ethics of applying neuroscience to business management and the issue of 'mental privacy'.

As well as looking at applications in business neuroscience has concerned itself with learning what happens to the human brain as it interacts with the world, accumulates experiences and ages. Neuroscientific research into the way in which the human brain learns reveals a remarkable capacity for being shaped by learning.

For example, in areas as diverse as taxi driving and musical performance the human brain has shown a remarkable plasticity and capacity to acquire new expertise well into adulthood:

1. London taxi drivers have to memorise more than 25 000 street names and locations in order to get a licence. Their posterior hippocampus (important in the formation of new memories) is significantly enlarged and its size is proportional to their experience of taxi driving – prompting the headline that their 'brains grow on the job'.
2. The auditory cortex is 25% bigger in musicians than non-musicians.
3. Violinists, who use their left hand on the fingerboard of their instrument have an enlarged right sensori-motor cortex.
4. As little as two hours of piano practice per day over five days can result in signs of enlargement in the sensori-motor cortex.[12]

The neuroscientific good news is that the brain can change at any stage of life and these changes can take place much more rapidly than was ever thought possible. With an aging population and an older workforce once thought to be untrainable beyond a certain age this means we have to think again about pigeon holing older workers as having a 'sell by' date. The human brain doesn't, as was once thought, plateau once it reaches adulthood and then begin to atrophy downhill towards old age; it's able to grow new neurons, make new interconnections and go on developing further complexities.

The most important thing in order to have a continually learning brain is mental engagement. If we don't use our brains we run the risk of losing mental agility. Not only can we change our minds, we can change our brains as well. Because the intuitive mind is fuelled by learning, experience and expertise it actually gets stronger with age. In particular it appears to get better at intuitive pattern recognition – the basis for practical intuitions and 'street smarts'. We only need think of the great, and not so great, world leaders who have held important leadership roles in what for most people would be their dotage.

Emotion and Choice

Imagine that you recently returned from a holiday to Italy during which you bought a painting for $100. You arranged for it to be shipped home but when you opened the packaging you found that it'd been damaged beyond repair. Fortunately you'd taken out insurance, but to claim compensation you must take the painting in your car to the insurance office which is some miles away. If you go there you'll get the full $100 in compensation; if you don't you won't get a penny. Do you feel it would be worth making the trip?

This was the scenario that decision researchers Chris Hsee and Howard Kunreuther presented in an experiment to two groups of participants:

1. The first group were asked to imagine that they liked the painting very much, so much so that they fell in love with it at first sight and, even though it cost them $100, it was worth a lot more to them.
2. The second group were asked to imagine that they weren't all that keen in the first place about the painting, and that to them it was probably worth about the $100 they paid for it.

The two groups were then asked to say how many hours (maximum) they'd be willing to drive to the insurance office to claim $100 compensation.[13] How do you think the two groups responded?

The group who 'loved' the painting were willing to spend well over four hours driving to get their $100 compensation; the group who weren't all that crazy about the painting were willing to drive just under three hours to get their $100 back. In economic terms how can that be a rational choice? The painting was already lost and couldn't be replaced, so why should the group that loved the painting be willing to spend longer to get the same amount of money back? The answer is feeling, and more specifically the feeling of consolation for a loved object lost. The level of attraction that the money ($100 compensation) held for the two groups differed depending on the feeling that the painting evoked. The same phenomenon was witnessed in a similar experiment where people were willing to pay almost twice as much to insure a loved object than they were to insure an unloved object of the exactly the same monetary value.

It seems that when it comes to insuring loved objects economics and rationality can go out the window, instead emotion enters the fray as a powerful force for the alleviation of the pain of loss, or as a means of expressing affection for an object or person. And it's not only in buying insurance where emotion can influence economic decisions. Human beings' perceptions of how risky something is and its potential benefits are inversely related:

1. Things that are rated high on benefits tend to be rated as having lower risks, for example, if the benefit of nuclear power, or pesticides, or cosmetic surgery are depicted as high the associated risk is intuitively inferred to be low.
2. Things that are rated high on risk tend to be rated as having lower benefits, for example, if the benefit of nuclear power, or pesticides, or cosmetic surgery are depicted as low the associated risk is intuitively inferred to be high.

In other research financial analysts, whom pre-credit crunch we might have expected to be the epitome of rationality, judged an unfamiliar portfolio of assets perceived as generally 'good' as higher return *and* lower risk, whereas unfamiliar assets perceived as generally 'bad' were expected to provide lower returns *and* higher risks[14]. A management decision that's presented as high on benefits is more likely to be perceived as low on risk and vice versa.

Many of our judgements, both social and financial, are governed by a tendency of the intuitive mind to form an overall emotional impression (a 'halo') of something or someone as 'good' or 'bad' on the basis of partial information. This global judgement influences subsequent assessments of the associated risks and benefits[15] which are yoked together. If we like someone we're more likely to feel intuitively that they're trustworthy and competent, and as far as objects and situations are concerned consolation and attachment can bias our judgements. 'Likeability', in particular, is something that needs to be guarded against when making thin slice intuitive judgements, particularly in areas related to competence, reliability and trustworthiness (see Chapter 4). Human beings have been known to be deceitful (for example, by embellishing their résumés) and managers have been known to select more attractive applicants over the less attractive. Managers and leaders involved in selection need to base their decisions on a portfolio of hard evidence (résumés, test scores and aptitude tests) and soft evidence (including gut feeling) but also to be aware of the potential for bias and prejudice on their own part and the potential for deceitful behaviour on the part of others.

Feelings are an important tool in the armoury of marketing. For example, advertisers are well aware of the influence that positive haloes, emotional manipulation of overall impressions and positive images (sights, smells, sounds, tastes and touches) can have on consumers' purchasing decisions. The risk researcher Paul Slovic and his colleagues found that an advertisement for a brand of cigarettes called 'Kool Natural Lights' repeated the positively-haloed word 'natural' no less than thirteen times. The word 'natural', like similarly meaningless terms such as 'new' (what's wrong with 'old'?), 'improved' (was the product we've been buying all these years no good?), and 'environmentally friendly' (meaning?), when used in advertisements come with a halo that generates a favourable overall impression and creates a positive 'affective (emotional) tag' tied to the product in the intuitive mind of the potential purchaser.[16] Repeated exposure through the internet, radio, TV, magazines and product placement in movies reinforces the strength of the association. Goods and services don't just come with a price tag; some advertisers, manufacturers and vendors often also subtly append an affective tag in order to persuade you to buy something you don't really want or need, or to get you to pay more than something is actually worth.

The intuitive mind is fuelled by images and hence can be easily seduced by clever advertisers; conversely it's a poor performer when it comes to numbers that don't readily translate into an image. For example, it was found that people will rate a disease that kills 24.14% of the population as less dangerous than a disease that kills 1286 people in every ten thousand.[17] Images and the feelings that they evoke are the language of the intuitive mind, and if the intuitive mind can latch on to a feeling or a dramatic and vivid image (real people dying of diseases rather than cold 'per cents') it will use these as the basis for a potentially biased judgement and subsequent choice rather than a more accurate rational analysis of the facts and figures. Which of our two minds is being appealed to in a business communication depends on what's trying to be achieved. Government health departments in the UK have decided to fight fire with fire; they've supplemented the hard verbal message that 'smoking kills' with images of dead bodies and premature babies on packets of cigarettes in an attempt to appeal directly to smokers' intuitive minds and exert a stronger influence on their decisions.

EI and Intuition

The cover story of *Time Magazine* can often be taken as a barometer of what's relevant, topical and significant in current affairs. Typical stories include presidential elections, environmental crises, economic meltdowns, wars and terrorism. In October 1995 applied psychology made it on to the cover of *Time*: typeface six inches high proclaimed the following question: 'What's your EQ?' The quotient 'Q' in question wasn't the kind of intelligence that had dominated schooling and society for decades (IQ), rather it was something that a number of its proponents claimed 'can matter more than IQ' – Emotional Intelligence (EI).

EI – the skill of being able to identify, express, understand and regulate emotions not only in oneself but in others – began life in the psychology departments of universities in the 1980s. Notwithstanding EI's academic origins, the person most often associated in the mind of the general public with its promulgation and popularisation is Daniel Goleman. His book *Emotional Intelligence: why it can matter more than IQ* topped the *New York Times* best-seller list and spawned a host of follow-ups including *Destructive Emotions,* in conversation with the Dalai Lama. It's been claimed that between 85 and 90% of outstanding performance is due to EI. The psychologists Peter Salovey and John Mayer, who are credited with the inception of EI as a credible scientific subject, have distanced themselves from the more exaggerated rhetoric that surrounds EI and actively critiqued some of the more boastful claims.

The essence of EI is that people who are emotionally self-aware don't get engulfed by their emotions nor do they have a passive acceptance of them; instead they have the presence of mind and awareness to recognise their own emotional states as well as those of other people, and the skills to manage them productively.[18] The original EI 'tree' developed by Salovey and Mayer has four branches.[19] A fifth branch can be added to the EI tree that brings intuition into the picture. Someone who's emotionally and intuitively intelligent is able to do the following things routinely and competently.

🖋 **Application No. 14: The Branches of Emotional Intelligence (including intuition)**

Perceive emotions in themselves and others	For example, a company has just announced a major redundancy programme, the emotionally intelligent Peter is one of the lucky ones but his close friend Jack has had his contract terminated. Peter recognises Jack's state of shock and surprise from his facial expressions, tone of voice and body language; he also guiltily acknowledges his personal relief that he's survived the cuts.
Use their emotions in thinking	For example, Peter realises that his relief can be a positive source of energy and that he could use this to be of practical assistance to Jack and do what he can to help Jack talk about it and think ahead. He invites Jack for a coffee.

Understand emotions, emotional language and the signals conveyed by emotions	For example, Peter realises that Jack's current state is not going to be permanent and that other emotions are likely to follow, such as anger, resentment and acceptance; and knows what the signs are and is able to recognise them when they emerge during this process.
Manage emotions to achieve a goal	For example, Peter has accepted his own emotional reaction (a combination of guilt and relief), recognised the emotional state that Jack is currently in (low) and sets himself the goals of channelling his own energy into the goal of helping Jack come to terms with the situation and be of palpable assistance in helping him to move forward.
Distinguish between emotional feelings and intuitive feelings	Emotions and intuitions are both varieties of feeling but not only do they feel different, their underlying neural mechanisms aren't the same. For example, Peter recognises that he felt guilty relief (an emotional feeling) but he also had a vague sense for a long time that Jack was not that happy in his work (an intuitive feeling); perhaps this is an issue that he'll factor into his conversations with Jack when the time is right.

Basic skills for IQ-type intelligence are the abilities to read and write and do number skills. Similarly, the basic skills for intuitive intelligence are the abilities to distinguish between thoughts and feelings (which include emotional feelings and intuitive feelings), and distinguish between emotional feelings and intuitive feelings, and finally to express intuitive feelings[20].

Thinking and feeling aren't disconnected. For example, the mood that we happen to be in at the time can influence our thinking: if we're in a good (positive) mood we tend to give the intuitive mind a freer rein and act more on our feelings, whereas if we're in a bad (negative) mood we tend to engage the analytical mind in more conscious, conservative and effortful thinking. Decision makers who happen to be in a bad mood might sometimes suffer from over analysing reasons for their preferences, resulting in suboptimal decision outcomes, whereas decision makers who happen to be in a good mood might place too much uncritical reliance on their intuitions.[21]

For Charles Darwin (and many modern evolutionary psychologists) *Homo sapiens*' basic emotions are potent legacies of our species' evolution – they're adaptations to the forest and savannah environments that our ancestors inhabited where threats and opportunities existed at almost every turn. Basic human emotions can be identified through their expression (most obviously in the face) which signals our emotional state to others and communicates to them messages such as 'I need help' or 'back off!' Facial expressions for many of the basic emotions are universal across cultures and societies. For example, the psychologist Paul Ekman found that not only is anger expressed through a particular set of facial muscle configurations, but also that it's not quite so simple – according to Ekman there are over sixty subtly different expressions of anger.[22]

Not all basic emotions are expressed through facial expressions. For example in the modern digital world we can't always rely on face-to-face contact for the expression of an emotion, so we have to use tone of voice in a phone call, or proxies such as the smiley or not-so-smiley face symbols used in texting (for example, anger is :-| |) or the style of an e-mail (for example, 'netiquette' advises against the use of UPPER CASE letters as a recipient might construe this as anger or annoyance).

INTUITION WORKOUT No. 13: EMOTION OR INTUITION?

The fundamental building block of EI is the ability to read a person's emotional state from their facial expression, body language or tone of voice. Psychologists haven't agreed on an authoritative list of basic emotions, but if there were such a list it would probably include: anger; awe; contempt; disgust; distress; ecstasy; embarrassment; enjoyment; excitement; fear; grief; guilt; happiness; interest; joy; loathing; rage; sadness; shame; surprise. These basic emotions give rise to emotional feelings which are not the same as intuitive feelings, and it's possible to separate them by asking three simple 'yes/no' questions:

1. Is the feeling short and intense?
2. Is it one of the basic emotions?
3. Is the cause of and the reason for the feeling readily apparent?

'Yes' answers to all three questions signify an emotional feeling rather than an intuitive feeling. By separating emotions from intuitions we're getting closer to the essence of gut feeling.

Emotional feelings have advantages in many situations, for example where flight or fight is an appropriate response. In other situations extreme emotional reactions can be less helpful; for example, poker players are very wary about 'going on tilt', the situation where emotional reactions[23] (perhaps in pursuit of revenge or as a result of anger) prevail over the refined intuitive judgements that many expert players rely on. In the workplace extreme emotional reactions may be inappropriate and all too often destructive.

Words aren't the primary language of the intuitive mind, however they may sometimes be the only available way to express hunches and gut feelings. But words aren't always used as literal expressions. Metaphors are an equally valid way to express gut feelings ('It felt like a bright light', 'It felt like I was entering a dark tunnel', 'I sensed something was around the corner' and so forth). But even metaphors can fall short because the vocabulary of the intuitive mind is highly imagistic[24] – sounds, smells, tastes, touches as well as visual impressions are part of its language. Being aware of these types of images or bringing images into conscious awareness is as important as listening to bodily signals and messages. The power of the intuitive mind in creating images can also be used to mentally fast forward the 'movie in our heads' in order to visualise the imagined consequences of our actions and conjure not only where we might end up if we take particular personal or professional choices but also to get a sense of how we might feel in those situations.

INTUITION WORKOUT No. 14: GETTING TO GRIPS WITH GUT FEELINGS

Intuitions are feeling states which can be pinned down to a particular person, object or situation (*what* makes us feel the way we do); the reason for the intuition (*why* we feel the way we do) is less easily pinpointed. If there's a cause for a non-emotional feeling but no apparent reason this is a possible sign that intuition is at work.

We may not always have the words to express an intuition or be practised in doing so. An intuition lexicon can help in the development of a vocabulary of gut feeling. Here's a by no means exhaustive list of adjectives that could be used to describe positive and negative gut feelings and hunches.

A LEXICON FOR INTUITION	
NEGATIVE FEELING	POSITIVE FEELING
Anxious; challenged (negative); concerned; confused; dissatisfied; disturbed; doubtful; dubious; empty; frustrated; hesitant; hopeless; jumpy; lost; low; manipulated; odd (negative); offended; out of place; overwhelmed (negative); perturbed; pressurised; pushy; puzzled (negative); regretful; restless; sceptical; strange (negative); suspicious; tense; tentative; threatened; troubled; uncertain; uncomfortable; uneasy; unsettled; worried	Calm; captivated; certain; challenged (positive); comfortable; confident; contented; curious; excited; glad; good; hopeful; impressed; inspired; interested; intrigued; odd (positive); overwhelmed (positive); peaceful; pleasant; pleased; puzzled (positive); relaxed; relieved; restful; satisfied; self-confident; strange (positive); sure; tempted; trusted

Next time you experience an intuitive feeling which you need to express to yourself or to colleagues, but for which the words don't come easily:

1. Examine the feeling in your body (hunch, gut feeling, felt sense).
2. Is it positive (signalling attraction to a person, object or situation) or negative (signalling avoidance or withdrawal)?

3. Select the appropriate word or words from the intuition lexicon to help you to express how you feel.

It's also worth bearing in mind that words are the language of the analytical mind and also the conventional means of communication in business organisations. It's also possible to communicate intuitions through the more natural language of visual images. Creating an image can be an effective way to express a gut feeling, whether or not it's an acceptable mode of communication for the expression of gut feeling in the board room is a different matter, but it's not something that should be dismissed out of hand.

Describing intuitions is one thing, explaining them is another. Gut feeling is the outcome of complex early warning processes going on back stage of our conscious awareness. Don't be perturbed if the reasons for intuitive feelings aren't obvious or if you seem to have more negative intuitions than positive ones; gut feeling evolved in *Homo sapiens* to aid survival in hostile and threatening environments and may therefore have the habit of erring on the side of caution even in the modern, and seemingly more secure, world.

Who's There?

'Who's there' is the opening line of *Hamlet, Prince of Denmark*, one of the most existentially probing and significant works of art produced by the human hand. The French philosopher and mathematician Rene Descartes in his *Sixth Meditation* claimed that the mind and body are distinct: 'it is certain that I, that is to say my mind, by which I am what I am, is entirely and truly distinct from the body, and can exist without it'.[25] According to the Cartesian dualist view human beings are made up of two radically different constituents – a tangible material body inhabited by a ghostly immaterial mind.[26] The material body includes the brain, described by Darwin in *The Descent of Man* as 'the most important of all the organs' constructed on the same general type and model as other mammals and in which 'every chief fissure and fold' has 'an analogy in that of the orang [utan]'.[27] In contrast to the dualist

227

view, a monist believes that mind is a manifestation of matter, is embodied in the brain, and if parted from it is unable to exist.[28]

Antonio Damasio describes the human brain as having evolved the means to represent the 'self' in a multi-media, multi-sensory 'movie-in-the brain' which we call the 'mind' and which 'you' or 'I' have complete ownership of. We watch the movie, but in addition the fact of 'ownership' gives us an incentive to heed the warnings that the movie provides in order to avoid threats and pursue opportunities rather than dispassionately observing our own demise, a strategy which has clear survival advantages.[29] Damasio has predicted that by 2050 or thereabouts biology will have wiped out dualistic separations of body/brain, body/mind and brain/mind, which, far from excising the notion of 'mind', can only serve to enhance our awe and amazement at its capabilities.

In the meantime the idea of two minds embodied in one brain is not only elegant and appealing, it also provides a useful metaphor for understanding and managing the dynamic between thinking and feeling in leadership and management as well as in personal life. Questions of the relationship between brain and mind and whether two minds literally exist in one brain are quite different and much bigger issues and are beyond the modest scope of this book.

INTUITIVE INTELLIGENCE PRINCIPLE No. 7: EXPRESS YOUR INTUITIONS

Intuitive feelings are the cornerstone of intuitive judgements and decision making in management and leadership. Even though we can't be sure immediately that an intuitive judgement is correct, articulating intuitions and becoming better at doing so, especially in the workplace, is essential for three reasons:

1. It helps us to recognise, acknowledge and question our hunches and gut feelings.
2. It may lead to a better understanding of them.
3. We're social beings both in our personal and professional lives and we need to, or sometimes have to, justify and explain our intuitive judgements, decisions and actions to our friends, colleagues, bosses, shareholders and wider society.

NOTES

[1] 'Jury acquits OJ Simpson in a trail on road rage', retrieved on 13th January 2009 from http://query.nytimes.com/gst/fullpage.html?res=9C0DE2DC1231F936A15753C1A9679C8B63.

[2] Smart, R.G and Mann, R.E. (2002) Deaths and injuries from road rage: cases in Canadian newspapers, *Canadian Medical Association Journal*, **167**(7): 761–2.

[3] 'Road rage – what makes us do it?' retrieved on 13th January 2009 from http://www.telegraph.co.uk/motoring/safety/2743699/Road-rage—what-makes-us-do-it.html.

[4] Plutich, R. (1980) A general psycho-evolutionary theory of emotion. In Plutich R. and Kellerman H. (Eds) *Emotion: theory, research and experience, Volume 1: Theories of emotion* (pp. 3–33). San Diego: Academic Press.

[5] The Best Advice I Ever Got: Elon Musk. Retrieved on 29th January 2009 from http://money.cnn.com/galleries/2008/fortune/0804/gallery.bestadvice.fortune/17.html.

[6] 'Office rage and how to control it', retrieved on 11th January 2009 from http://www.businesslink.gov.uk/bdotg/action/detail?type=RESOURCES&site=181&itemId=5000683342.

[7] Wilson, T.D. (2002) *Strangers to ourselves: discovering the adaptive unconscious.* Cambridge, MA.: Belknap

[8] Damasio, A.R. (2001) Fundamental feelings, *Nature*, **413**: 781.

[9] Kimberg, D.Y., D'Esposito, M. and Farah, M.J. (1997) Cognitive functions in the prefrontal cortex – working memory and executive control, *Current Directions in Psychological Science*, **6**: 185–92.

[10] Stanovich, K.E. (2002) Is dysrationalia possible? In R.J. Sternberg (Ed.) *Why Smart People Can Be So Stupid* (pp. 124–58). New Haven: Yale University Press.

[11] Bechara, A., Damasio, H., Tranel, D. and Damasio, A.R. (2005) The Iowa Gambling Task and the somatic marker hypothesis: some questions and answers, *Trends in Cognitive Sciences*, **9**(4): 159–62.

[12] Blakemore, S.J. and Frith, U. (2005) *The Learning Brain*. Oxford: Blackwell.

[13] Hsee, C.K. and Kunreuther, H. (2000) The affection effect in insurance decisions, *Journal of Risk and Uncertainty*, **20**: 141–59.

[14] For familiar financial assets the relationship worked the other way round: information on risk and return determined the overall impression of an asset as 'good' or 'bad'.

[15] Dreman, D. (2004) The influence of affect in investor decision-making, *Journal of Behavioral Finance*, **5**(2): 70–4; Ganzach, Y. (2000) Judging risk and return of financial assets, *Organizational Behavior and Human Decision Processes*, **83**(2): 353–70.

[16] Slovic, P., Finucane, M., Peters, E. and MacGregor, D.G. (2002) The affect heuristic. In Gilovich, T., Griffin, D. and Kahneman, D. (Eds) *Heuristics and biases: the psychology of intuitive judgement* (pp. 397–420). Cambridge: Cambridge University Press.

[17] 1286 people in every ten thousand is 12.86 per cent, see: Yamagishi, K. 1997. When a 12.86% mortality is more dangerous than 24.14%, *Applied Cognitive Psychology*, **11**: 495–506.

[18] Matthews, G., Zeidner, M. and Roberts, R.D. (2002) *Emotional Intelligence: science and myth*. Cambridge, MA.: The MIT Press.

[19] Mayer, J.D., Roberts, R.D. and Barsade, S.G. (2008) Human abilities: emotional intelligence, *Annual Review of Psychology*, **59**: 507–36; Mayer, J.D., Salovey, P. and Caruso, D.R. (2008) Emotional intelligence: new ability or eclectic trait? *American Psychologist*, **63**(6): 503–17.

[20] Unlike basic emotions or intuitions a mood lacks a specific stimulus in the form of an object or person, instead they are more diffuse, less intense, can be longer lasting and function in the background of awareness but affect thinking and behaviour. Bless, H. and Schwarz, N. (1996) Mood: its impact on cognition and behaviour. In Manstead, A.S.R. and Hewstone, M. (Eds) *The Blackwell Encyclopaedia of Social Psychology* Oxford: Blackwell (p. 391).

[21] King, L.A., Burton, C.M., Hicks, J.A. and Drigotas, S.M. (2007) Ghosts, UFOs, and magic: Positive affect and the experiential system. *Journal of Personality and Social Psychology*, **92**(5): 905–19; de Vries, M., Holland, R.W. and Witteman, C.L.M. (2008) In the winning mood: Affect in the Iowa gambling task, *Judgement and Decision Making*, **3**(1): 42–50.

[22] Ekman, P. (1992) An argument for basic emotions. *Cognition and Emotion*, **6**: 169–200.

[23] Blake, C. (2008) *The Art of Decisions: How to manage in an uncertain world* (p. 48). Harlow: FT Prentice Hall.

[24] Vaughan, F.E. (1979) *Awakening Intuition*. New York: Doubleday.

[25] Descartes, R. (1641/1968) *Discourse on Method and the Meditations*, Translated and with an Introduction by F.E. Sutcliffe (p. 156). Harmondsworth: Penguin.

[26] Mautner, T. (Ed) (1996) *The Penguin Dictionary of Philosophy*, London: Penguin Books.

[27] Darwin, C. (1882) *The Descent of Man and Selection in Relation to Sex* (p. 6). London: John Murray.

[28] Dawkins, R. (2006) *The God Delusion* (pp. 179–80). London: Bantam Press.

[29] Damasio, A.R. (1999) How the brain creates mind, *Scientific American*, **281**(6): 112–17.

Chapter 8

THE INTUITIVE ENTREPRENEUR

In this chapter I'll explore the intuitive aspects of the entrepreneurial mind and how gut feeling enables business venturers to recognise and judge the viability of business opportunities that others may overlook. In addition to their alertness, intuitive entrepreneurs also have the in-depth knowledge that enables them to make sense of opportunities and the creative thinking style to make novel connections. The three mutually reinforcing elements of entrepreneurial DNA are alertness, expertise and creativity.

The former US President George W. Bush is reputed to have once said that 'The trouble with the French is they have no word for "entrepreneur"'.[1] It goes without saying that the origin of the word 'entrepreneur' is French. It's thought to have been first coined at the beginning of the 19th century by the French economist Jean Baptiste Say (1767–1832) and often taken literally to mean an adventurer or 'undertaker' (not in the funereal sense). For J.B. Say an entrepreneur was not a manager, rather he or she was someone who was able to appraise and forecast the potential outcome of a business idea, undertake business ventures (be an 'adventurer') and consequently, like all adventurers, take the risk as well. Whether the George W. Bush story is apocryphal or not, there's a serious point: entrepreneurs are vital to the sustainability and growth of any economy; in Say's words: 'A country well stocked with intelligent merchants, manufacturers, and agriculturists has more powerful means of attaining prosperity, than one devoted chiefly to the pursuit of the arts and sciences'.[2] But what kind of 'intelligence' singles out Say's adventurers; how are they able to judge the viability of a potential business venture; is there something unique about the entrepreneurial mind?

The Entrepreneurial Mindset

Entrepreneurs have a knack for sensing opportunities where others might see only chaos, contradiction and confusion.[3] The prototypical entrepreneur thrives on change, is adventurous, pursues opportunities, generates ideas and is proactive and innovative. In the uncharted territories of business which entrepreneurs seek to explore, historical precedents often don't exist and there may not even be clear criteria for success. At the risk of mixing metaphors, like a racing driver entering a sharp bend, business (ad)venturers have to 'skate where the puck's going, not where it's been'.

For many people the Indian-American venture capitalist and co-founder of Sun Microsystems Vinod Khosla epitomises and embodies the energy, creativity, technological innovation and entrepreneurship of California's Silicon Valley. Khosla has degrees in engineering and business from Carnegie Mellon and Stanford universities, and naturally he acknowledges the value of the technologist's mindset. However, he also recognises that being overly-analytical can have drawbacks: 'too mechanical a mindset can hurt'.[4] This view was echoed by Bob Lutz who, when in charge at US car giant Chrysler, said that: 'Numbers are a poor surrogate for imagination, intuition, judgement, critical thinking and leaps of faith.'[5] From the entrepreneurial mindsets of Khosla and Lutz two key ideas emerge.

Firstly, businesses have to be adaptable in order to navigate global business environment. This means that, unlike in the past when an entrepreneur might have been able to write a two-year business plan and be pretty confident of sticking to it, in Khosla's words now 'you have to change course all the time – you have to adapt not plan. The best you can do, I think, is [to] have a sense of direction – an intuition about where the big opportunities are'. Secondly, start-ups need to create a 'managed conflict' by way of the smart engineering of a business gene pool in order to ensure that intuition is part of the mix. But it doesn't have to be a shared intuition – a critical mindset with creative and constructive conflict is essential at the inception of a business venture.

The role of the leadership team and the boss is vital, they must integrate, reconcile and synthesise disparate intuitions and from this obtain a unique business angle based on a shared belief in something that others don't, won't or can't see.[6] It's what Larry Kramer of CBS Digital referred to as 'the knowledge base built in the business' which gives entrepreneurs themselves the confidence to 'believe something even when others don't'[7] and give their company the edge that's necessary in order to succeed in global markets.

To Plan or Not to Plan?

In spite of its undoubted benefits, one of the dangers of business planning is 'planning paralysis'. It's a potential danger because by the time a formal business plan has been researched, written and implemented the world may have moved on, the opportunity evaporated, or a competitor stepped into the breach. Founder and Chairman of the California-based software company Intuit, Scott Cook, recognises, perhaps not surprisingly, the value of intuition and judgement in business planning: 'If you use the spreadsheets to try to discriminate and predict which businesses will succeed and fail you'll be utterly off ... the failures had just as pretty spreadsheets as the successes'. Intuit lives by its name recognising the unique value of gut feeling in other aspects of business, for example, in closing sales: the best salespeople have an in-built early warning system that tells them when a client is playing games by withholding information that should be shared, playing one seller off against another, or using sellers as free research.[8] Cook's views are echoed by Kent Murdock, CEO of O.C. Tanner Company, a $300 million provider of employee recognition solutions based in Salt Lake City with several Fortune 100s on its client list: 'Numbers can give you seven ways to go, or tell you to do nothing. They show you the past. What creates value in an organization is uniquely human judgement, risk-taking, and intuition'.[9] Being slowed up by planning paralysis can be a hazard especially if the prevailing climate in an organisation is for analysis come what may. The gene pool of a business needs to be diverse enough to counter any tendencies towards analysis paralysis or the converse, intuitive excess.

THE SCIENCE OF THE INTUITIVE MIND – JUST DO IT?

Researchers at the Stockholm School of Economics and Case Western Reserve University, Ohio looked at whether it's better to 'plan or not-to-plan' in business start-ups. The arguments against business planning are that:

1. it's a distraction taking up time that could be better spent on doing;
2. the entrepreneurial environment is so dynamic that plans have a very short shelf life;

3. intuition makes planning redundant.

For business schools that push the mantra of 'plan-do-check' this is tantamount to heresy. The upsides of the 'planning before doing' orthodoxy are that:

1. assumptions can be surfaced and tested – time and money won't be wasted in learning through costly real-time mistakes;
2. processes can be better managed – resource shortages and operational bottlenecks can be avoided;
3. goals and progress towards them can be monitored – hence the old aphorism: 'if you don't know where you're going any road will get you there'.

A survey of two hundred new ventures in Sweden over their first two and half years found that although business planning is no guarantee of success, businesses which had formal plans were not only more likely to survive, business planning also speeded up their rates of product development.

An intriguing but potentially important aside pointed out by the researchers was that it wasn't clear from the research whether it was the quality of the plans that increased firms' likelihood of business survival or simply the process of planning itself and the communication and dialogue between managers that takes place as a result. It reinforces the point that it's only through effective dialogue that managers are able to articulate and share not only their formalised business plans but also their personal intuitions.

Sources: Delmar, F. and Shane, S. (2003) Does business planning facilitate the development of new ventures? *Strategic Management Journal*, **24**: 1165–85.

Make no mistake: formal business planning is invaluable, especially when start-ups are seeking venture capital or looking for a 'business angel', but it has to be practised skilfully leaving room for other complementary ways of moving a business forward. Plan, yes but don't blindly plan-to-do, have the presence of mind to plan-to-adapt. Moreover, there seems to be a myth, perhaps promulgated by the extreme factions both of the intuition and analysis fraternities, that intuition and planning are mutually exclusive opposites. They claim that, like oil and water, intuition and analysis don't mix: nothing could be further from the truth. It's perfectly possible to plan the implementation of an intuitive idea, something that many of the world's great innovating companies do as part of their normal day-to-day functioning in order to manage innovation projects. For example, this sentiment was echoed by Sony's Akio Morita, co-founder of a company with a record second to none for bringing inventive products to markets, who said that 'spontaneous intuition' is a vital part of the creative mix in innovation and new product development.[10]

Instinctive perception and intuitive appraisal is one of the defining characteristics of serial and corporate entrepreneurs such as Virgin's Sir Richard Branson. Over several decades Branson's business ventures have expanded from the modest beginnings of mail order vinyl records in the 1970s through to the travel and tourism, leisure and pleasure, shopping, media and communications, finance and money, and health businesses that comprise Virgin in the 21st century. Branson is undoubtedly an adventurer in every sense of the word; he attempted to break the record for a trans-Atlantic single-hulled sailboat crossing, and tried to circumnavigate the globe by balloon with Steve Fossett and Per Lindstrand. As far as business venturing goes Branson by his own admission relies more on 'gut instinct than researching huge amounts of statistics', and making up his mind 'within thirty seconds of meeting' someone doesn't just apply to people. It takes him a comparably short space of time to decide whether a business proposal 'excites' him or not.[11]

It's his instinctive perception that enables Branson to be mindful of opportunities that others are blind to. For example, when he moved away from the mail order business in the 1970s, looking for a retail space in London's Oxford Street, Branson spotted an unused first floor over a shoe shop and persuaded the owner to let him use it for free until a paying tenant could be found on the grounds that it would generate more business for the shoe shop. He signed Mike Oldfield and recorded *Tubular Bells* in 1973 after major record companies had turned the concept down; the album went on to sell over five million copies[12] (Branson has named one of Virgin Atlantic's Boeing 747 aircraft 'Tubular Belle').

Entrepreneurial Alertness

One of the keys to understanding the instinctive perception that many entrepreneurs have is captured in the idea of 'alertness'. Economists have known about 'alertness' for decades; for example, one of world's leading experts in this field, the economist Israel Kirzner, described it as 'an attitude of receptiveness to available (but hitherto overlooked) opportunities' that might inspire business activity. Kirzner's picture of the alert entrepreneur is of a person who doesn't, at least consciously, know what they're looking for, or who employs rigorous analytical search techniques; on the contrary, he or she is all the time scanning the horizon, not only ready and willing to make discoveries but also ready to be surprised. And even though the alert entrepreneur doesn't rely on deliberate search, neither does he or she indulge in pure guesswork or is at the mercy of lucky windfalls.[13] Instead, in the pursuit of creating and profiting from something new and valuable, a human quality much more complex and subtle than mere mechanics or pure chance is at work – intuition. For example, Coco Chanel, who with Chanel No. 5 gave the cosmetics business its most successful fragrance, didn't consider herself a business-woman in the sense of someone who understood the technical-ities of numbers; instead she had a sense both for the essence of making money and of feminine appeal, as she once told *Vogue* magazine: 'Fashion is not simply a matter of clothes. Fashion is in the air, borne on the wind. One intuits it. It is in the sky and on the road'. But great intuitors like Coco Chanel don't innovate in a void – they have deep reservoirs of experience, learning and skill to draw upon.[14]

Another unique feature of entrepreneurial alertness is the ability not only to see patterns where others see chaos, but also to make new connections that haven't been made before. The skill of intuitive pattern recognition isn't automatically available to every-one, but neither is it a special power: it comes with experience, practice, learning and constructive feedback. Seeing patterns that others miss is like any other form of expertise, it takes years to evolve. For example, Bill Gates' success can be attributed to many factors including background, personality, circumstances and motivation; to credit his or anyone else's entrepreneurial success to a single factor (such as intuition) is a gross over-simplification. Like other expert performers, ranging from Lewis Hamilton to W.A. Mozart, Gates had a passion and tenacity about his endeav-our from the outset. Although innate ability or 'genius' plays an important part, the head start that child and teenage prodigies get gives them a long lead-in time to develop knowledge and skill. Gates was fascinated by computers from the beginning; he dabbled with the technology at an early age, could program by the time he was in his teens and sold his first piece of software to a school for $4000.

Gates was ahead of the pack even before he went to university, nonetheless he went to Harvard but dropped out in his junior year to devote his time and energy to Microsoft. He built upon his expertise – Gates had the technical knowledge to write code, he knew what computers could do or had the potential to do, sensed what the market wanted and had a vision. Whether this exceptional mix was luck or judgement is impossible to say, but when asked in a CNN interview what or who was his sounding board for good ideas the response came back 'intuition': 'If I think something's going to catch on I trust my own intuition'. But Gates is also well aware that gut feeling is fallible, and acknowledges that it's 'often wrong, but my batting record is good enough that I keep swinging every time the ball is thrown'.[15]

Intuitive Connections

Wise business people know that blind instinct isn't to be trusted; the instincts that pay off for business people like Branson or Gates are honed to such a degree that they look like knee jerk reactions. In fact they're the tip of an iceberg of experience-educated informed intuition that gives an entrepreneur the core skills of being able not only to perceive and appraise opportunities but also to be adaptable in the face of challenge and change. That said, having reservoirs of knowledge and skill to draw on isn't enough to be an intuitive entrepreneur; a second factor is at work in the intuitive mind of the entrepreneur – creativity.

Creative leaps come about in many different ways ranging from pure chance, through dreams to formalised methods such as brain-storming or brain dumping. Whichever route they take creative entrepreneurs are able to connect things that were previously unconnected, links that after the fact seem obvious but at the time needed an extraordinary leap of imagination. When Charles Darwin published his theory of evolution by natural selection the biologist Thomas Huxley remarked after reading it: 'How extremely stupid of me not to have thought of that!' Some of the very best ideas seem obvious once they've been invented, for example we take the use of antiseptics in surgery for granted. Joseph Lister (1827–1912), made the now obvious discovery that micro-organisms travelled from surgeons' hands to the wound and not through some miasma of the air. But before Lister made this connection there was the saying that 'The operation was a success, but the patient died'[16] because it simply hadn't clicked with the medical profession in the 19th century that infections spread from hands that intended to heal.

Making novel connections seems to come naturally and fluently to some people (so-called 'divergent' thinkers). They're able to freely form associations, many of which turn out to be redundant, but nevertheless the sheer volume of combinations that a fertile mind produces is much more likely to throw up a truly novel idea than a mind that tends to make only conventional associations. Divergent thinkers have an aptitude for creativity – they can see novelty in the familiar. Creative people are also open to experiences, they are intellectually curious and have a heightened sensitivity – their openness leads them to explore the unfamiliar.[17]

There's little in the way of naïvety involved in consistent creativity, even though rookies may get a lucky hunch now and again and grab the headlines the people who consistently make breakthrough connections have the raw material to work with. For example Darwin, whose creative connections led to one of the most profound scientific breakthroughs of all time, had been meticulously amassing his observations of the natural world for decades before he had his insights or was prepared to publish them, especially in the light of the implications of his theory of evolution through natural selection for the prehistory of the human species.

INTUITION WORKOUT No. 15: TIME-OUT AND TEAM-UP

Creative connections take time to incubate. For example, in the human brain neural activations spread though the complex networks of associations in long-term memory, and once 'the dots have been joined up' the solution pop-outs in a 'Eureka!' moment.[18] But the connections aren't instantaneous, they may take hours, days, weeks or years to be made. Significant break-throughs can't be delivered on demand. Mental time-outs are vital for the slow thinking that is the machinery of creative thinking.

Creating personal time-outs from the pressures of the working day are also important. For example, Nell Minow, editor and co-founder of the Corporate Library, an independent source of information and analysis on corporate governance and execu-tive compensation, has built changing mental gear through time-outs into her working routine. She disciplines herself to take fixed days out 'to think out of another part of my brain and come back with a different perspective'.[19]

The value of teaming up with an unlike mind is one of the best business lessons for Zhang Xin, co-founder and CEO of Soho China, one of the leading developers of high-profile branded commercial properties in central Beijing. The unlike mind in this case is her husband and business partner Pan Shiyi: 'When you have two people trying to figure out problems together, one brings out new things in the other and vice versa.

Pan works in a very intuitive way even though he's the man. 'I believe in women's intuition, but I am also a product of my Western training [Cambridge, Goldman Sachs]. And so we approach decisions in very different ways and play different roles. He tends to come up with big ideas then I'm the one who goes around trying to test them. He's brilliant at sales. I worry about construction'.[20]

Two important lessons from business leaders for building the creative capacity of a business are:

Time-Out	Permit yourself the mental relaxation that's essential for ideas to incubate.
Team-Up	Find a business partner with a complementary thinking style to your own and put your two minds together.

What role does intuition play in the creative process? After all, when a clear solution to a problem suddenly emerges it's not a hunch or a gut feeling, there's nothing vague about it because the solution, or in*sight*, is clear to see. Intuition may not provide a solution but it can signpost a direction. For example, the pinnacle of scientific achievement is the Nobel Prize, not a place where we might expect to find intuition, but William Shockely, awarded the 1956 Nobel Prize in physics for inventing the transistor, was described by a fellow scientist as being 'phenomenal from the point of view of his physical intuition ... colleagues claimed that Shockely could *see* electrons. He had a tremendous *feeling* for what was going on inside silicon'.[21] He's not the only one, many other scientists including a number of Nobel laureates concur with this view, and no less a figure than Albert Einstein said that in scientific discovery 'The only really valuable thing is intuition'.[22]

In business management intuition can give entrepreneurs the wide angle peripheral vision to spot trends before they happen. According to decision researcher Paul Schoemaker, classic cases of business that had too narrow an angle of vision were IBM, Unisys and other mainframe manufacturers who were so focused on the current mainframe market that they couldn't see what was going on around the periphery in terms of the burgeoning home computer market. The crucial abilities are tuning into weak signals, separating them from the background 'noise', making sense of them and acting on them. Schoemaker's research suggests that less than 20% of global firms have the wide angle vision necessary to pick up on threats and opportunities.[23] This opens up opportunities for those firms and managers who are prepared to put their faith in the wide angle vision and holistic perception that the intuitive mind is capable of.

Seeing peripherally is something that a manager can work at, for example by being open to new experiences, reading widely, networking professionally and socially, scanning the boundaries of the organisation for new information, listening to customers and suppliers, looking at trends outside the core of the organisation's activities, watching where the competition is going and inculcating a spirit of curiosity in the organisation.[24]

Heroes and Hubris

Society sometimes depicts its entrepreneurs as risk-taking, wealth-creating heroes – lone 'go-with-your-gut' adventurers. For example, in Scotland, as in any economy, young fast-growing firms make their mark by creating jobs and wealth. In 1999 the 542 firms dubbed 'Local Heroes' by Scottish Enterprise had an average turnover of £2.92 million, employed 30 000 people between them and exported to the value of around £240 million per year.[25] For a relatively small country the figures are impressive, but was there a defining characteristic that singled out these entrepreneurs as 'heroes' in the local economy of Scotland? Were they heroes venturing on nothing more than gut instinct? Researchers from the universities of Leeds and Newcastle in the UK looked at the thinking styles of the small firm 'Local Heroes' and compared them with managers in large firms.[26] The 'Heroes' were quite unlike the regular middle and junior managers; instead they were much more like senior managers. What was it that singled the 'Heroes' and the senior managers out from the pack? Regular middle- and junior-ranked managers tended to be much more analytical in their approach to problem solving and decision making. 'Heroes' and senior managers were more intuitive than rank and file managers. Other research supports this view: small firms where intuitive owner managers were in charge tended to show better rates of growth over the longer term than firms where the predominant decision-making style was analytical.[27]

Everybody some time in their life takes risks of one sort or another. Many situations – driving a car or getting on an airplane – have levels of risk attached to them (in the USA respectively the risk of death from car driving is estimated at around one in 5000, and one in 11 million for flying in an airplane[28]). Some work situations have greater risks attached to them than others. For example, working in a public library is a relatively low risk work environment, as such it's likely to appeal to people who are risk averse. Fire-fighting, on the other hand, seems on the face of it to be a relatively higher risk profession; it's likely to appeal to someone whose personality isn't as risk averse as a librarian's. Managers also take risks, for example, who to hire and who to fire, how to spend scarce budgetary resources, whether to outsource activities and so forth. But are managers in general as risk-taking as entrepreneurs? The research evidence strongly suggests not. Entrepreneurs (defined as someone who independently owns and manages a small business) take significantly more risks than managers. Moreover, amongst entrepreneurs themselves those motivated by profit and growth take considerably greater risks than those whose motivation is to merely have an income. It seems likely that risk seekers will self select into entrepreneurial careers, and people who are more risk averse will self select into managerial careers.[29]

If that's the case, do risk seeking entrepreneurs see the risks objectively, or are they so over confident in their assessment of their own business venturing capabilities, or so in love with their idea, that they seriously over estimate their chances of success?

The rates of failure of business start-ups are high, for example in the UK as many as one in two fail within the first two years.[30] One reason that entrepreneurs may take an over optimistic view of their chances of success is that they take what decision researchers call the 'inside view' – a myopic focus on the abilities and the resources that they have irrespective of the crowd.[31] As a result they neglect the quality of the competition. The 'outside view' sees the forest rather than the trees. An entrepreneur with the outside view plays down the image they have and the stories they tell themselves about their own 'special' case, but by the same token doesn't ignore the harsh fact that many business start-ups fail. For example, a Walt Disney executive, commenting on the fact that on a given weekend with five new movies being released there can't be enough paying customers to go around, summed it up neatly when he said that: 'You think: "I've got a good story department, I've got a good marketing department, and we're going to go out and do this". And don't you think that everyone else is thinking the same way?'. An analytical mindset is a moderating influence because it has less of a tendency to overlook the statistical chances of success or failure.

Business venturers who keep on winning are likely to become increasingly self-confident, their batting averages become more and more impressive and a hubris of invincibility may prevail. Self confidence, even when justifiable on the basis of past successes, should be tempered with the bald facts of business success and failure, moreover as markets become increasingly competitive, to consistently keep on winning is likely to demand exceptional entrepreneurial skill and become increasingly tough. The intuitive mind, because it tends not to work all that well with abstract statistics, focusing instead on more tangible issues such as images and feelings, may be prone to the insider view and therefore under estimating the chances of a start-up failing and over estimating the chances of success.

Optimism and confidence are two of the features that distinguish entrepreneurs from managers, and without these vital ingredients entrepreneurial decisions couldn't be made, the analytical mind would be in the driving seat, prevarication is likely to prevail, opportunities would evaporate and first mover advantage would be lost. Analysis paralysis is not an option for business venturing. Intuitions, that present themselves in the form of metaphors, images and gut feelings, can provide the jolt that spurs entrepreneurs into action. The fact that entrepreneurs so often seem to go with their gut may also explain why they don't always make the best managers.[32]

Going with your Gut

We're largely unaware of creative intuition because it goes on backstage; only the outcome is posted into our conscious awareness as a gut feeling. For example, Starbuck's Howard Schultz described his feelings when on a visit to Milan – where there are literally hundreds of espresso bars – the entrepreneurial intuition of bringing Italian coffee house 'ritual and romance' to the US came to him: 'The vision was so overwhelming, I began shaking'.[33] When Schultz made this discovery in the early 1980s he was by no means a novice – his experiences in the coffee supply business meant he was able to draw on his expertise to come up with the vision of the all-American coffee house as a viable business opportunity. His intuitive mind produced a positive gut feeling signalling strong attraction to the idea. What began with Schultz's intuitive experience in Milan has become an organisation with more than 15000 retail locations in North America, Latin America, Europe, the Middle East and the Pacific Rim.

Most if not all personal and professional decisions elicit a feeling of some kind – totally cold, calculative rational decisions are few and far between and are often better accomplished by a machine rather than a human. Until recently emotions were thought to be an unnecessary distraction in the decision-making process – nothing more than a nuisance. Scientific research into the so-called somatic marker hypothesis (SMH) by the neurologist Damasio and his colleagues (see Chapter 7) has produced convincing evidence that emotions have evolved for a reason and that they are advantageous, indeed necessary, for decision making. Whether we like it or not emotions come into play in most business decisions, whether to hire or to fire someone, whether to invest or cut back – all are important choices with life changing consequences both for ourselves and others. The emotions that come into play in these situations can be consciously felt (as happiness or sadness, exhilaration or anxiety) or they can remain unconscious – either way they affect our decision-making behaviours.

THE SCIENCE OF THE INTUITIVE MIND – THE CURRENCY OF EMOTIONS

The neural circuitry that is an integral part of human decision making tags available options with positive and negative values which then sway our choices towards the options that are positively tagged and away from the options that are negatively tagged. This is nature's way of providing the 'go', 'stop' and 'turn' signals (gut feelings) that enable us to make the decision that's in our best interests. Without this system, we'd end up running a snail's-paced cost benefit analysis and would be likely to end up in a zone of indifference and frozen into indecision.

The brain may even have its own system for coding the value of the different options on a common scale – a neural 'currency' – which enables different options to be compared, for example money, food, sex, consumer goods and so forth. This makes sense because decisions rarely involve simple choices (for example, whether to have another glass of wine or not), they are more typically complex and multi-attributed. Neural-based accounting of options that conflict (for example, on the positive side the pleasure of the wine, on the negative side the financial costs and the health implications) result in an overall positive or negative emotional state associated with particular options which then sways our ultimate choice.

Source: Bechara, A. (2006) The neurology of emotions and feelings, and their role in behavioral decisions. In R. Parasuraman and M. Rizzo (Eds) *Neuroergonomics: The Brain at Work.* Oxford University Press (US). pp. 178–92.

The intuitive mind doesn't send out only positive vibes (for example, exhilaration and anticipation) that attract us towards particular options, it also sends out negative gut feelings (for example nervousness, doubt, anxiety) which signal 'avoid', or at least 'proceed with caution'. Nonetheless, one of the problems is that in entrepreneurship and business generally, negative instances of gut feeling decisions are much harder to pin down than positive ones. This is because the negative hunch tends to get hidden or forgotten about, after all who wants to dwell on a gut feeling that came to nothing? Entrepreneurs are essentially action and achievement oriented; they're likely to move on quickly from a negative hunch in search of the next positive opportunity in which they can invest their energies. That said the experience may be stored away subconsciously and emotionally tagged for future use should the same situation be encountered again.

Intuitive entrepreneurs aren't infallible, but by playing the long game they tend to have more successes than failures. The US logistics company FedEx is an example of a world class company that is a consummate player of the intuitive long game. For example, the embryonic idea that eventually became FedEx came to the company's chairman, president and CEO, Fred Smith, as a result of a paper he wrote in the 1960s for an economics class at Yale on the need for reliable overnight delivery in a computerised information age: 'As society automated, as people began to put computers in banks to cancel checks – rather than clerks – or people began to put sophisticated electronics in airplanes – society, and the manufacturers of that automated society, were going to need a completely different logistics system'. Smith didn't have a 'Eureka!' moment, instead he gradually became alert to the opportunities that FedEx eventually exploited, partly due to the fact that he was a charter pilot at a local airport. From hanging around other pilots he had first hand experience of the fact that a lot of airplanes up there were doing little more than flying replacement computer parts around the country. Smith could see that the world needed a completely different logistics system for delivering not only spare parts, but documents as well.[34]

Smith, who was named CEO of the year in 2004, had confidence in the concept and no doubt in his own mind that the idea was profound. Like many other successful entrepreneurs his gut check was an essential part of the mix, well aware that sometimes you can show the return on investment, at others you have to go with your gut – and that means taking risks and having the courage of your convictions. For example, in the early days of FedEx the Chief Finance Officer Alan Graf recalled one of the risks that Smith asked him to take: 'Fred called me into his office and said, "I need you to go down to Continental and buy some DC10s [wide bodied jets]"', with no marketing plan, no infrastructure and no pilots to fly the planes.

Any bet, especially one involving buying up jet aircraft, is by its nature risky. In the complex world that is business venturing, circumstances can conspire against a gamble and the world can change suddenly to knock what seemed only yesterday like a great idea completely off course. This is what happened to FedEx in the 1980s with its ZapMail concept based on the idea that with the Space Shuttle available to build very big antenna in space, a network of tiny satellite dishes on the roofs of clients' premises could be used to 'zap' images digitally across the globe on a satellite network. The satellites that were needed for the project were too big to go on a rocket, they had to go in the Shuttle. When the Challenger blew up on 1986 the business proposition became unviable overnight. For Smith it was never a 'bet the whole company' idea, but could have changed the face of the business under different circumstances. Nonetheless FedEx has assets of $25 billion and employs a quarter of a million employees around the globe; it's willing to take some entrepreneurial bets and its batting average means that it has many more successes than failures.[35] Moreover, if successful entrepreneurs make a bad gut call they usually know when to walk away; in the words of James H. Goodnight, chairman and CEO of SAS Institute, a $1 billion software company in Cary, N.C.: 'it's a lot cheaper to start a new hole than to keep digging a big one'.[36]

INTUITION WORKOUT No. 16: INTUITIVE HITS AND MISSES

Recall a decision you were involved in, where you had an intuitive 'hit' – in other words when your gut feeling worked well.

1. What was the decision?
2. What was the situation?
3. Who was involved?
4. What happened?
5. What feelings did you experience?
6. Why do you think it was a hit?

Recall a decision you were involved in, where you had an intuitive 'miss' – in other words when your gut feeling didn't work.

1. What was the decision?
2. What was the situation?
3. Who was involved?
4. What happened?
5. What feelings did you experience?
6. Why do you think it was a miss?

Do you detect any differences between your intuitive hits and misses? What was it about the hits that resulted in your gut feeling being on target? What was it about the misses that resulted in your gut feeling going awry?

If you repeat these questions in informal discussions with colleagues or other leaders and entrepreneurs do any patterns emerge?

Gut feelings that fail tend to become invisible, go underground and get forgotten. Tales of entrepreneurial success and failure underline the importance of balancing expertise, risk-taking and gut feelings in business venturing. Media boss Bob Pittman, in an interview for *Harvard Business Review*, cautioned fellow executives: 'don't fall in love with your decisions. Everything's fluid. You have to constantly, subtly make and adjust your decisions'. Pittman's advice underscores the traps that feelings can lay for the unwary. Mastering the skill of separating emotional feelings and intuitive feelings can be crucial because falling in love with a pet idea for a new product or service is not the same as having a positive gut feeling or hunch. Love and physical attraction are basic emotions and the emotional feelings that come with them are intense and powerful, but typically short-lived and likely to be biased in various ways. A major pitfall that business start-ups have to guard against, especially those founded by novices, is being seduced by their own idea. It's well known that strong positive feelings of attachment or wishful thinking may not only overpower the analytical mind, but masquerade as genuine intuitions. One consequence of this is that enthusiasm, optimism and passion can run riot and lead to over confidence and misguided estimates of the cost and time commitments and the customer base needed to turn an idea into a viable commercial enterprise. To fall foul of this is to become a victim of one of the enemies of good entrepreneurial intuition – emotional feelings. For experts and novices alike, emotion in business, whilst it is an invaluable source of motivation and energy, needs to be guarded against and filtered out if necessary.[37] Otherwise the feeble intuitions that result may turn out to be very costly indeed.

It's all in the Genes?

Scientific advances in areas such as evolutionary psychology, cognitive neuroscience and brain imaging are taking important strides forward in understanding the biological basis of the intuitive mind. One area of science that links together these different perspectives is genetics. Darwin didn't have the benefit of genetics to help him to explain how new species evolved and the breakthrough in this area came with the insights developed from the studies of plant breeding carried out by Austrian monk Gregor Mendel (1822–1884). Through a meticulous program of hybridisation he was able to show that certain characteristics in pea plants, such as height, could be inherited and passed down through the generations. Scientists were later able to explain Mendel's laws using the basic unit of inheritance – the gene.[38]

From a genetics perspective the 'recipe' for assembling a new entrepreneur is derived from the chromosomes of the maternal egg and paternal sperm of the yet-to-be business venturer. US entrepreneurship researcher Scott Shane and colleagues from the UK have applied the science of genetics to understanding what 'makes' an entrepreneur. They compared rates of entrepreneurship among more than 1200 pairs of twins in the UK. By looking at patterns of concordance (that is the numbers of pairs of twins in which both members are or are not entrepreneurs) Shane and his colleagues inferred that genetic factors accounted for nearly half of a person's propensity to become self-employed.

The same group of researchers has gone further by suggesting that the gene that's responsible for the regulation of dopamine in the brain might be implicated in how entrepreneurs spot business opportunities.[39] For example, research has shown that the neurotransmitter dopamine is associated with positive physiological sensations and reward, and dopamine levels in the brain affect how people react to success and failure, motivating us to get what we want but at the same time not avoiding what we fear.[40] People with a particular variant of the gene that regulates dopamine activity may show heightened alertness to opportunity-relevant information in the environment and the potential rewards this could bring. The genetically based characteristic could make them better at recognising business opportunities which, under favourable circumstances, would make them more likely than other people to undertake a business venture. That said it's early days for genetics research in management, and linking these two areas together is likely to prove more than a little controversial. But as we have seen neuro-economics, neuro-marketing and neuro-ergonomics have sprung up around the field of neuro-science, so perhaps it's only a matter of time before genetics will enable scientists to better understand the biology of entrepreneurship.

Whatever biology reveals in the future we know for certain that entrepreneurs have a powerful ability to intuit which enables them to perceive and evaluate potential business opportunities. Nonetheless, successful entrepreneurs aren't off the scale intuitives, rather they're cognitively adroit business people able to command intuitive and analytical mental gears. Business venturing is risky and neither intuition nor analysis will pay off 100% of the time. Intuitive entrepreneurs possess the three mutually reinforcing ingredients of the business venturer's DNA: alertness, expertise and creativity.

INTUITIVE INTELLIGENCE PRINCIPLE No. 8: GO WITH YOUR HEAD, YOUR HEART AND YOUR GUT

Being a successful entrepreneur is a delicate balance of expertise (head), passion (heart) and business instinct (gut). With too little head creative intuition doesn't have enough raw material to work with. With too little heart the passion and energy will be absent to carry the venture forward. With too little gut the ineffable sense of where the business opportunities are and how viable they are will be lacking.

NOTES

[1] 'George W. Bush; drawing to an end', retrieved on 17th January 2009 from http://www.timesonline.co.uk/tol/news/world/us_and_americas/us_elections/article5075878.ece.

[2] See the biography of J.B. Say ('JB Say the forgotten early Austrian') produced by the Ludwig von Mises Institute ('research and educational centre of classical liberalism, libertarian political theory, and the Austrian School of economics'). Link: http://mises.org/about/3242#45. Last accessed 17th January, 2009.

[3] Timmons, J.A. (1989) *The entrepreneurial mind.* Andover MA: Brick House Publishing: p. 1 emphases added.

[4] Gangemi, J. (2006) Vinod Khosla talks shop, *BusinessWeek.* http://www.businessweek.com/smallbiz/content/oct2006/sb20061004_513595.htm.

[5] 'Got guts?' *Inc,* (1999), March: pp. 50–7, (p. 54).

[6] Champion D. and Carr, N.G. (2000) Starting up in high gear, *Harvard Business Review,* July–August: 93–100.

[7] Becker, A. (2006) Kramer's latest platform, *Broadcasting and Cable,* August 28: 30.

[8] Anthony, S. (2008) Three questions every innovation-minded CEO should ask, *Chief Executive,* November/December 2008; Boress, A.S. 'Six best practices for closing more sales', retrieved on 23rd January 2009 from http://accountant.intuit.com/practice_resources/articles/practice_development/article.aspx?file=ab_sixbestpractices.

[9] How to revolutionize your business, *Chief Executive,* March 2005.

[10] Morita, A. (1991) 'Selling to the world: the Sony Walkman story', In J. Henry and D. Walker (Eds) *Managing innovation*, London: Sage Publications, pp. 187–91 (p. 191).

[11] Branson, R. (2005) *Losing my virginity: how I've survived, had fun and made a fortune doing business my way*, London: Virgin books: pp. 120 and 152.

[12] Branson op cit.; Bolton, B. and Thompson, J. (2004) *Entrepreneurs: talent, temperament and technique*. Oxford: Elsevier Butterworth-Heinemann.

[13] Kirzner, I.M. (2000) *The Driving Force of the Market: essays in Austrian economics.* (p. 19). Abindgdon: Routledge.

[14] Landrum, G.N. (2004) *Entrepreneurial Genius: the power of passion.* Burlington, Ontario: Brendan Kelly Publishing (p. 57).

[15] 'A one on one interview with Bill Gates', retrieved on 17th January 2009 from http://archives.cnn.com/2002/TECH/industry/02/28/gates/index. html; Bolton, B. and Thompson, J. 2004. *Entrepreneurs: talent, temperament and technique.* Oxford: Elsevier Butterworth-Heinemann.

[16] Arunakul, N.K. (2003) Dr. Joseph Lister: the founder of antiseptic surgery, *Primary Care Update*, **10**(2): 71–2; 'The discovery of the obvious – Joseph Lister', retrieved on 17th January, 2009 from http://longstreet. typepad.com/thesciencebookstore/2008/03/great-simple-id.html.

[17] King, L.A., McKee Walker, L., Broyles, S.J. (1996) Creativity and the five factor model, *Journal of Research in Personality*, **30**: 189–203;

[18] Jung-Beeman, M., Bowden, E.M., Haberman, J., Frymiare, J.L., Arambei-Liu, S., Greenblatt, R. et al. (2004) Neural activity when people solve verbal problems with insight. *Public Library of Science Biology*, **2**: 97.

[19] The Best Advice I ever Got: Nell Minow: Retrieved on 29th January 2009 from: http://money.cnn.com/galleries/2008/fortune/0804/gallery. bestadvice.fortune/24.html.

[20] The Best Advice I Ever Got: Zhang Xin. Retrieved on 29th January, 2009 from http://money.cnn.com/galleries/2008/fortune/0804/gallery. bestadvice.fortune/13.html.

[21] Moore, G.E. (2001) The accidental entrepreneur. http://nobelprize.org/ cgi-bin/print?from=%2Fnobel_prizes%2Fphysics%2Farticles%2Fmoore% 2Findex.html. Last accessed 19th January 2009.

[22] http://www.einstein-quotes.com/.

[23] 'Thinking your way to Growth', retrieved 17th January 2009 from http://executiveeducation.wharton.upenn.edu/wharton-at-work/0808/thought-leaders1-0808.cfm.

[24] Day, G.S. and Schoemaker, P.J.H. (2006) *Peripheral Vision: detecting weak signals that will make or break your company.* Boston, MA.: Harvard Business Press.

[25] '30,000 jobs created by Scotland's 542 Local heroes', retrieved on 17th January 2009 from http://www.scottish-enterprise.com/sedotcom_home/about-us/se-whatwedo/news-se-about-us/news-se-about-us-details.htm?articleid=14828.

[26] Allinson, C.W. Chell E. and Hayes, J. (2000) 'Intuition and entrepreneurial performance', *European Journal of Work and Organizational Psychology,* **9**(1): 31–43.

[27] Sadler-Smith, E. (2004) Cognitive style and the performance of small and medium sized enterprises, *Organization Studies,* **25**: 155–82.

[28] 'Airplane disasters and plane crash statistics, retrieved on 26th January 2009 from http://www.fearlessflight.com/airplane-disasters-plane-crash-statistics.

[29] Stewart, W.H. and Roth, P.L. (2001) Risk propensity differences between entrepreneurs and managers: a meta-analytic review, *Journal of Applied Psychology,* **86**(1): 145–53.

[30] 'Business failure', retrieved on 26th January 2009 from http://www.thetimes100.co.uk/theory/theory–business-failure–320.php.

[31] Camerer, C. and Lovallo, D. (1999) Overconfidence and excess entry: an experimental approach, *American Economic Review,* **89**(1): 306–18.

[32] Busenitz, L. and Barney, J. (1997) Differences between entrepreneurs and managers in large organizations: biases and heuristics in decision making', *Journal of Business Venturing,* **12**: 9–30.

[33] 'Interview: King Bean', *Your Company,* 1998, April/May, 8(3), (emphases added).

[34] The Great Innovators: Fred Smith on the birth of FedEx. *Business Week* 20th September 2004.

[35] Ibid.

[36] 'Finding the secret sauce for success', retrieved 26th January 2009 from http://findarticles.com/p/articles/mi_m4070/is_202/ai_n8576053/pg_1?tag=artBody;col1.

[37] Baron, R.A. and Ensley, M.D. (2006) Opportunity recognition as the detection of meaningful patterns: evidence from comparisons of novice and experienced entrepreneurs. *Management Science*, **52**(9): 1331–44; Hyatt, J. (2001) The death of gut instinct, *Inc*, January: 38–44.

[38] Ridley, M. (1999) *Genome: the autobiography of a species in 23 chapters*. London: 4th Estate.

[39] 'Much of entrepreneurial drive is genetic', retrieved 26th January 2009 from http://blog.case.edu/case-news/2006/04/13/much_of_ entrepreneurial_drive_is_genetic_new_study_finds; Nicolaou, N. and Shane, S. (2009) Can genetic factors influence the likelihood of engaging in entrepreneurial activity? *Journal of Business Venturing*, **24**: 1–22.

[40] American Academy of Neurology (30th April 2007). Dopamine-related Drugs Affect Reward-seeking Behavior. *ScienceDaily*. Retrieved 26th January 2009, from http://www.sciencedaily.com/releases/2007/04/070427072318.htm.

Chapter 9

INTUITIVE LEADERSHIP

In this chapter I'll propose three attributes of intuitive leadership – 'doing things right' (based on the idea of informed intuitive expertise), 'doing right things' (based on the idea of a moral instinct) and 'right direction' (the vision and the strategy taken in pursuit of a vision). The chapter will conclude by raising questions about what it means to 'do the right thing' in business and what role leaders play in the pursuit of 'good business'.

Intuitive leaders 'do things right' and 'do right things'. They combine the virtues of being 'smart' (doing things right) and 'moral' (doing right things)[1]. An intuitive leader who does things right (is 'smart') has the intelligence, knowledge, skill and judgement to intuitively solve a problem or take a decision. Unlike an inexperienced novice leader, an experienced intuitive leader is smart because he or she is able to take into account the subtleties and nuances of particular situations. But being able to intuitively 'do things right' isn't enough. It's possible for a leader to be smart and inspire her or his followers to do things right (and by that I mean with intelligence, knowledge, skill and judgement), but it may not be the 'right' thing to do. Business and human history is replete with examples of leaders who from their own point of view did things 'right', they managed to capture the hearts and minds of followers (sometimes numbering millions), but were themselves morally corrupt: a missing dimension was moral intuition.

As well as having the virtues of being 'smart' an intuitive leader also has moral virtue – he or she does right things based on a moral instinct that signals what ought to be done for the greater good. Because leaders by definition can't exist in a vacuum – they're part of a community – there has to be a trade off between their own interests and those of their followers. Empathy and altruism are important ingredients of the moral mix.

The idealised intuitive leader is 'smart' (he or she intuitively does things right) and possesses moral virtue (he or she instinctively does the right thing). Smartness and moral virtue are symbiotic. Balanced intuitive leadership is not possible without 'smarts' and morals. Leadership that's unbalanced is likely to be 'dumb' or amoral or both.

As well as the smart and moral dimensions in business there also has to be vision, strategy and direction in intuitive leader- ship – business leadership is not an end in itself. Leaders must generate excitement, passion and optimism, create security, coop- eration and trust and build the capacity amongst followers to anticipate the future and pursue a shared vision. Planning ahead isn't the same as seeing ahead, and it's impossible for leaders or followers to plan ahead if they can't see ahead. Not only do leaders create the conditions for the journey they also see ahead and set the direction and inspire others to follow their lead. Strategy can and should be informed by rational analysis, but the intuitive mind provides an instinctive sense of direction that forms the basis of a vision. Intuitive leaders see ahead and set the right direction (see Figure 9.1).

Intuitive leadership combines 'doing things right' (smarts), 'doing right things' (morals) and 'following right direction' (strategy).

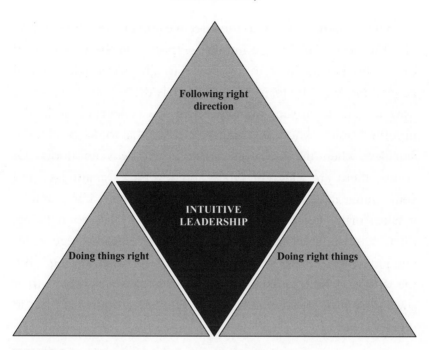

FIGURE 9.1   The elements of intuitive leadership

Doing Things Right

'Doing things right' is another way of saying 'doing-with-expertise' or being smart (and as we'll see isn't the same as being 'intelligent'). Expertise in the context of the intuitive mind doesn't necessarily mean something remote and cerebral (but it can be). An intuitive expert is able to do things with skill, judgement and, seemingly, low effort – they're smart. This can be in any walk of life and in any aspect of business from the boardroom downwards. Most people who've had good education and training, experienced enough tough challenges and had good feedback on their performance are likely to have developed the ability to be smart in some aspect of their life.

Everyday experts are vital to the effective and efficient functioning of a business. We can see intuitive expertise in the experienced CEO who knows how to handle a tough shareholder annual general meeting, the team leader who has the sensitivity to know how to handle an emotionally distressed colleague, or in the unruffled janitor who knows automatically what to do to calm the situation when the elevators break down between floors. Of course there are different types and levels of 'smartness', and some things take a lot longer to master than others. For example, it takes many years of training to become a high court judge, pilot, neurosurgeon or CEO – the intelligence, knowledge, skills and judgement involved are complex and the stakes are high. But the janitor and the judge are both smart because each have their own version of intuitive muscle power, they're both smart but in different ways.

Colin Powell, former US Secretary of State and four-star military leader understands the value of intuitive muscle power built up over years of experiencing tough challenges: 'we all have a certain intuition and the older we get the more we trust it'. He too calls it 'informed intuition'. For Powell one measure of being an intuitive leader is the ability and confidence to rely on a 'gut check'. In Powell's terms an intuitive leader looks hard at the evidence that's being presented by the people under his or her command and asks 'I know what I'm *supposed* to feel about this. Now what do I *really* feel about this? Do I believe this reality?'

When Powell flew to Tehran in 1978 to assess the precarious situation of the US-backed Shah of Iran before he was deposed by revolutionary fundamentalists led by the Ayatollah Khomeini, the Shah treated Powell to an elaborate military pageant, lavish dinners, parades and impressive shows of air strength. Powell's finely tuned intuitive mind wasn't misled by the charade: he felt that something was 'amiss', that he'd witnessed a façade prepared to conceal the frightening reality of the situation. Sure enough there was a revolution three months later, the Shah's regime collapsed, he was deposed and fled to Egypt, and Powell's hosts were summarily executed. One of the 'Powell Principles' is to look at what the data's telling you but question if it's the same thing that your gut's telling you, and if not why not?[2]

Informed intuition amongst military leaders isn't unique to Colin Powell; for example, Lieutenant General 'Hal' Moore, whose Vietnam War experiences were chronicled in the 2002 film *We Were Soldiers* starring Mel Gibson, knew that he'd never have all the information needed to remove uncertainty on the battlefield. Moore saw the initial plan as a 'springboard into action' and advised his commanders to trust their intuitive instincts: 'they are the product of your education, training, reading, personality and experience'.[3]

Intuition is only part of the leadership mix, and leadership in military and political contexts, as elsewhere, is often built on mutually beneficial relationships between leaders. For example, Winston Churchill is seen by many as being an archetypal intuitive leader. Indeed, 1st Viscount Alanbrooke, his Chief of the Imperial General Staff in World War Two, with whom he had a not untroublesome working relationship, said of him 'planned strategy was not his strong card. He preferred to work by intuition'. However, their combined styles created a synergy, Alanbrooke provided a counterweight of rationality and pragmatism to Churchill's more instinctive and impulsive style.[4]

It's not only in the international political arena, the battlefield or the boardroom where informed intuitive leadership comes to the fore, or where the person doing the leading has formal authority as politician, military general or manager. Intuitive leadership looms large in other situations and in circumstances in which the person doing the leading doesn't have a formal authority role. For example, intuition can turn out to be a life saver in the medical and health care professions. Picture the scene: the emergency department of a busy hospital. An experienced nurse, let's call her Jane, is presented with a new patient – a seven month old baby boy accompanied by his babysitter who's deeply concerned although there are no obvious symptoms of an illness to go on. Jane heeds the babysitter's concerns and takes a look at the child – one glance is enough, her stomach 'turns over'. To check her gut feeling she does the routine tests – but nothing unusual shows up, nonetheless against all protocol she tells the doctor in charge that she's taking the child to the resuscitation area of the ward straight away. The doctor asks why, but all Jane can offer is that 'he needs to be there'.

Two hours later the child was in theatre undergoing major surgery for heart failure caused by a previously undetected heart wall defect. When asked how she knew it was the right thing to do Jane said: 'I could not provide any answer … I just had a sense of knowing that something was seriously wrong'. Without intuitive leadership borne out of years of intensive training and experience of real-life events with real-life consequences the child in this case most probably would not have survived – Jane's intuitive 'smarts' translated into courageous leadership behaviour and saved the child's life.[5]

In cases of intuitive leadership it's hard to single out intelligence, or knowledge, or skill or judgement as a single factor that enables intuitive leaders to do things right. Intelligence, knowledge, skill and judgement are all vital ingredients in the mix that is expert intuition. Ask an intuitive leader how he or she does what he or she does and often you'll get a dumbfounded response or a quizzical look – the knowledge and skills that are the bedrock of expert intuition can't always be articulated – instead they're held tacitly in the intuitive mind and manifest themselves in actions rather than words.

The idea of 'tacit knowledge' helps to explain this phenomenon. 'Tacit' means 'implied but not stated explicitly'. For example, conversation contains elements that are tacit; things that are read between the lines of what's said or inferred from other modes of communication, such as body language. Sometimes we can choose to be tacit by keeping quiet or expressing our views implicitly, for example by saying 'Have you ever thought about doing that in a slightly different way?' rather than being brutally honest and saying 'I think you're wrong' or 'You're incompetent' (in other words it's possible to have too much honesty). But in other situations being tacit isn't something over which we have conscious control. For example, many people can ride a bicycle and know (tacitly) which way to turn the handlebar to prevent themselves from falling off the bike if it starts to go off balance. To explain in words rather than actions which way to turn the handlebar to stay upright on a wobbly bike isn't an easy task. It's something that bike riders do expertly and intuitively, but can't articulate easily. The idea of 'tacitness' was encapsulated neatly by the philosopher Michael Polanyi when he said: 'we know more than we can tell'.[6] Tacit knowledge is vital for coping with and adapting to the challenges of daily life – it's what makes us smart and without it we'd be unable to function in the real world. The psychologist Robert J. Sternberg distinguishes 'book smarts' (knowledge and skill that's explicitly stated in the written or spoken word) from 'street smarts' (knowledge that's tacit and embodied in 'doing').

Book smarts are in the domain of academic learning and academic problems. Book smarts are based on knowledge that was created by someone else in the past (perhaps hundreds of years ago) and represent someone else's thoughts and experiences. We become book smart by going to school and college, and by educating ourselves through various media (books, TV, internet and so forth).

Street smarts, on the other hand, are in the domain of real-world experience and real-world problems. Street smarts embody knowledge that's personal (we acquire it ourselves, usually with the help of others), contextualised (what works in one situation doesn't necessarily work in another), based on experience (it accumulates over time) and, most importantly, it's action-oriented (it helps to solve real life problems).

Book smarts help us to solve academic problems, puzzles that have been formulated by other people, they're well defined, all the information needed to solve them is available, and they usually have a right or a wrong answer. The problems that street smarts help solve are messy, often without a single right way to get to the answer or even a definite right answer. For example, a manager might learn how to conduct a selection interview by reading a 'how to' book or attending an HR training course, but it's only by interviewing real candidates for real jobs that he or she will develop the street smarts needed to become a competent, and ultimately intuitive and effective selection interviewer.[7]

Street smarts are also deep smarts. The term 'deep smarts' was coined by Dorothy Leonard of Harvard Business School and Walter Swap of Tufts University. 'Deep smarts' are expertise based on tacit knowledge, real life experiences, they're more about 'know-how' (street smarts) than 'know-what' (book smarts).

Leaders who're equipped with deep smarts can 'see the forest and the trees', they're able to make swift, expert decisions that turn out not only to be good but wise. Deep smarts are the closest thing to practical wisdom, and they're the kind of thing that intuitive leaders have in abundance.[8]

INTUITION WORKOUT No. 17: WHAT ARE YOUR STREET SMARTS?

As a leader (or manager) what are your three most important 'street smarts' that followers respect you for and which inspire in them trust and confidence (in other words in what areas does your expertise lie which qualifies you to lead people at work)? List them on Figure 9.2.

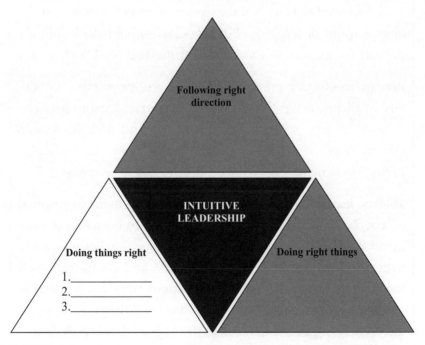

FIGURE 9.2   What are your street smarts?

None of this is intended to undermine the value of book smarts – they're vital. The best book smarts have an intrinsic and enduring value whereas street smarts are valuable only so long as they're practically useful. Book smarts and street smarts don't inhabit different worlds, they're mutually reinforcing. Book smarts provide the foundation for street smarts; street smarts help us to make sense of and know when and how to apply book smarts in an intelligent and discerning way. Throughout the course of our personal and professional lives book smarts and street smarts interact and help to build knowledge, skill, judgement and, ultimately, practical wisdom.

THE SCIENCE OF THE INTUITIVE MIND – STREET SMARTS PAY OFF

Tacit knowledge (TK) is the essence of 'street smarts' and the engine room of intuition. But does having and deploying TK pay off for leaders and managers in the real world?

Researchers from a number of US universities and the US Military Academy at West Point looked at the relationship between military leaders' scores on a test of TK and their leadership effectiveness. The first problem that TK researchers face is pretty fundamental: if TK is 'tacit' how can it be measured?

Military leaders' TK was assessed by asking them to respond to a series of scenarios (for example, how to deal with a commander who's a 'shoot the messenger' type, soldier insubordination, or communicating the mission) and comparing their judgements with those of military experts (majors and lieutenant colonels) who had TK in abundance. If their responses to the scenario agreed with those of the experts they were deemed to have expert levels of TK.

The research with soldiers at West Point confirmed the importance of TK: leaders who had higher levels of TK were judged to be more effective as military leaders. What surprised them was the fact that TK didn't seem to be as strongly related to experience as might be expected. And although the old aphorism that 'experience is the best teacher' holds some truth, it's much more likely that it's the quality of the experience and what one learns from it that matters rather than simple tenure – 'more' is not necessarily 'better'.

The same type of research but this time looking at managers' TK revealed:

1. no relationship between TK and intelligence as traditionally measured by IQ-type tests. IQ smart people aren't necessarily street smart (this isn't the same as saying that IQ smart people can't be street smart);
2. higher levels of TK were associated with managers' annual percentage salary increase (based on merit) and success in generating new business.

The evidence from the TK research suggests strongly that intuitive 'street smarts' have real consequences for leadership and managerial performance both in military and business organisations.

Sources: Hedlund, J., Forsythe, G.B., Horvath, J.A., Williams, W.M., Snook, S. and Sternberg, R.J. (2003) Identifying and assessing tacit knowledge: understanding the practical intelligence of military leaders, *The Leadership Quarterly,* **14**: 117–40; Sternberg, R.J. and Hedlund, J. (2002) Practical intelligence, *g* and work psychology, *Human Performance,* **15**(1/2): 143–60; Wagner, R.K. and Sternberg, R.J. (1985) Practical intelligence in real world pursuits: the role of tacit knowledge, *Journal of Personality and Social Psychology,* **49**(2): 436–58.

The best leaders have a smartness that's fuelled by their practical intuitions. They demonstrate consistently the ability to do things right. Intuitive leaders can respond flexibly depending on the situation, and whilst not being infallible, they're expert performers and the best of them combine intuition with the charisma to capture the hearts and minds of followers. A leader's ability to be smart helps to build trust. But trust is built on a broader foundation than the mere perception of a leader as competent; the qualities that create trust between followers and a leader include the leader's ability and demonstrable benevolence and integrity.

✎ Application No. 15: Creating Trust Between Leaders and Followers

Ability	Setting a clear direction and having expert knowledge.
Benevolence	Creating a supportive environment and coaching followers.
Integrity	Demonstrating accountability, shared values, justice and fairness.[9]

The idea of personal qualities and virtue as vital ingredients of good leadership isn't new. In fact it can be traced back at least 2500 years to ancient Greece. Aristotle (384–322BC) identified the character and virtues needed by an idealised good statesman or citizen who played an active and productive part in his or her community. For Aristotle the good of the community was the greater good, and this aspect of his philosophy makes the virtues doubly important in leadership. The foundation of the virtuous mind (Aristotle's equivalent of 'smarts') is intelligence (*nous*), overlain on this is knowledge (*episteme*) and expertise (*techne* – technical art or skill), the prudence to balance our interests with those of others (*phronesis*) and finally, the capstone of all the virtues, wisdom (*sophia*) cultivated over the course of one's lifetime. From an Aristotelian perspective experienced and competent leaders are smart, prudent and wise.

🗝️ Key Facts No. 15: Intuitive Leadership from an Aristotelian Perspective

Smart	Effective leaders base their intuitive responses on intelligence (*nous*), knowledge (*episteme*), and skill (*techne*).
Prudent	Compassionate, benevolent and empathetic leaders balance their own best interests with those of their followers and the wider society through prudence (*phronesis*).
Wise	Intuitive leaders know that they don't know everything and become 'smarter' with experience and age on their journey towards wisdom (*sophia*).

But if becoming smart is a matter of practice (like an archer becoming better at hitting the target through practice), given what happens to the brain over the course of the human life span (it inevitably deteriorates) the growth of leadership wisdom with age would appear to be paradoxical.

It's a biological fact that our brains decline with age but we somehow have the potential to become smarter and wiser. For example, younger people tend to come up with major intellectual breakthroughs that require a lot of 'computational power'. Einstein was in his mid-20s when *Special Relativity* was published in 1905. As we get older mental decline sets in; older people may be able to remember The Beatles, Bob Dylan and the Vietnam War but they tend to forget where they've left their spectacles. Political leaders are a case in point: they tend to be old by the time they reach office and far from immune to the effects of neurological decline. Ronald Reagan showed signs of Alzheimer's disease while still in office, the autopsy of Stalin's brain revealed arteriosclerosis and Chairman Mao suffered from the neuro-generative disease amyotrophic lateral sclerosis. But as the clinical neuro-psychologist Elkhonon Goldberg points out, despite these very real neurological infirmities Reagan, Stalin and Mao were able to remain in charge and very capable of taking potentially momentous decisions. Political leaders develop street smarts and deep smarts which enable them to be wily if not always wise. Complex patterns of perception, recognition and response enable experienced, aged leaders to function effectively and hold on to power even in the face of a decline in their cognitive analytical capabilities. This is testimony to the power of the intuitive mind: it is much less prone than its analytical counterpart to the ravages of age.[10] In Goldberg's words the history of leaders such as Reagan 'show with dramatic clarity that the machinery of pattern recognition [the intuitive mind] can withstand the effects of aging on the brain to a remarkable degree' and give them a significant advantage over their 'computationally nimble but less "pattern-recognition-enabled" [i.e. younger] colleagues'[11].

Irrespective of age intuitive leaders have the power to inspire liking, trust and loyalty and sometimes even awe, they're role models for followers and fledgling leaders; for these reasons intuitive leaders carry a heavy weight of responsibility on their shoulders. People defer to 'experts' and are influenced by them, we only need to think of how many times we see on TV 'an interview with an expert' in connection with a newsworthy story. Expert opinions in media reports are valuable currency since they can sway public opinion by crucial percentage points. For this reason the street smart leader can be a potent force in business and society. But intuitive followers aren't easily fooled and displays of a leader's expertise have to be authentic. Anything less is not only morally indefensible, but in the final analysis counterproductive because it exposes leaders who are charlatans to terminal undermining. Intuitive followers can instinctively sniff out purveyors of snake oil and 'quack' medicine, and tough real world challenges have a habit of peeling away the layers of a charade to reveal if there's a fraudster beneath the slick veneer.

On the positive side, intuition can be an indispensable guide to building business relationships and trust in leadership as Joanna Shields, founder of the popular social networking website BeBo, explained in an interview for *Fortune Magazine*: 'I go back to things my dad said: "Your career is long and the business world is small. Always act with integrity. Never take the last dollar off the table"'. For Shields this advice was critical in the deal to sell BeBo to AOL: 'You can always do a slightly better deal, but that incremental dollar or windfall is not worth creating an imbalance that affects the relationship. You have to have the intuition to know when to say "I'm going to make sure that we walk away feeling like we've both done well"'.[12]

Intuitive leaders with their power to command trust, loyalty and following can be potentially dangerous to themselves and society if they lack prudence, morality and a concern for the greater good. Such people can be deluded into thinking that they're doing the right thing. In the words of the English poet John Dryden (1631–1700) 'Great wits are sure to madness near allied, and thin partitions do their bounds divide'. A thin partition that divides good leaders from wicked leaders is the moral sense of 'doing right things'. Substituting 'leader' for 'wits' and 'evil' for 'madness' in Dryden's line encapsulates one of the enduring leadership perils of our species. In the absence of a moral compass to direct expert intuition towards what is 'right' the more sinister aspects of intuitive leadership may emerge where guile supplants wisdom. The smarts that develop with age need not be exclusively benign and the litany of evil witnessed throughout human history shows what can happen when leaders are unable or choose not to follow a moral instinct for justice and fairness and do the right thing.

Doing the Right Thing

What is clear by now is that to be effective intuitive leaders have to be much more than well-schooled experts who by dint of their experiences can instinctively deploy informed intuition. Intuitive leaders have another equally critical dimension which if absent has the power to inflict permanent damage on employees, companies, entire industries and national economies. Like an earthquake it sends shockwaves around the world that reverberate long after the event itself; society has to live with its damaging consequences and the lives of millions are changed forever by it. Intuitive leaders need to show an ethical imperative based on a moral instinct for doing the right thing.

The epitome of flawed leadership in the corporate world is Enron – a byword for scandal and immorality. Under the leadership of Kenneth Lay and other senior executives Enron's market value grew from £2 billion in 1985 to $70 billion in 2001 and the company paid grossly inflated levels of remuneration to its smart young executives; for example, the head of Enron's Portland office was paid a $5 million annual bonus in 2001. Wind the clock back to the early 1980s, Enron was the US's biggest gas pipeline company run by experienced street smart managers, but change was on the horizon. From the mid-80s the company pursued growth by embarking on an aggressive strategy of expansion and diversification into everything from water to broadband and weather forecasting. Bright but inexperienced young men and women with business school degrees were recruited to spearhead the expansion – a management and HR strategy likened by some to allowing 'a bunch of kids to run loose without adult supervision'.[13]

In spite of this, ex-Enron employee turned whistleblower, Lynn Brewer, saw many of the attributes of good leadership in the company: bold market-leading vision; employees who were inspired to execute the vision; culture to support innovation and change; and smart high-performing staff. However, what Enron lacked corporately was the intuitive sense of 'doing the right thing' – demanding honesty and integrity of its executives, leaders and employees rather than countenancing employees in the selfish pursuit of what was beneficial to them.[14] In 2004 in a speech at the University of Colorado Brewer urged students to heed their own moral instinct and, unlike the large number of Enron employees whom she claimed knew and went along with what was going on, have the courage to act because 'what each of you ha[ve] inside is intuition, and if something doesn't feel right, it's up to you to stop it'.[15] Regrettably Enron was not unique, it was the tip of an iceberg of unethical business behaviour including everything from irresponsible selling to tax evasion and fraud borne out of ignorance of or disrespect for an instinctive morality.

THE SCIENCE OF THE INTUITIVE MIND – THE MORAL LAW WITHIN

A research team led by the biological anthropologist Marc Hauser explored how intuition influences moral judgement by looking at ordinary people's responses to trade-offs in hypothetical life-or-death situations. Here are the scenarios the researchers used, often called 'the trolley problem' (a thought experiment in ethics originally developed by the British philosopher Philippa Foot):

1. You're a passenger on an out-of-control train. You can let the train hit five individuals on the track ahead of you and kill them, or you can pull a lever and turn the train down a side track towards a single individual and kill him. Is it morally right for you to turn the train onto the side track and kill one man or let the train run on and kill five?
2. You're standing on a footbridge above a railroad track, and stood next to you is a heavy man. Suddenly an out-of-control train approaches. You can allow the train to run underneath you and hit five people on the track ahead killing them instantly, or you can shove the heavy man on to the track which will kill him but stop the train and save the five. Is it morally permissible for you to shove the man into the path of the on-coming train?

There's little difference from the analytical mind's perspective between the two scenarios: in both of them one person dies to save five. We might therefore expect people, if they make a rational, analytical moral judgement, to respond in the same way to both scenarios. But this is far from what people actually say they would do. In the first scenario 85% of people said that it was morally right to pull the lever. In the second scenario only 12% of people said it was right to shove the man on to the track.

If you said 'yes' to Scenario 1 and 'no' to Scenario 2 what was your reasoning? When Hauser and his colleagues asked people 'why?' most people were unable to give a sufficient justification, typical responses were: 'I don't know how to explain it', 'It struck me that way', and 'It was a gut feeling'. Scientists call it 'moral dumbfounding' and put it down to an instinctive moral aversion that most human beings have to manhandling an innocent person in a way that would result in their death. It's an intuitive moral gut reaction that overwhelms any weighing-up of pros and cons.

When similar research was conducted using fMRI scanning the rational areas of participants' brains were activated in Scenario 1 whereas the emotional areas were activated in Scenario 2. Similar areas of the brain (the medial frontal cortex) are involved in the production of the gut feelings that people experience when playing the gambling task in Antoine Bechara's and Antonio Damasio's experiments that were the basis for the somatic marker hypothesis (SMH) (see Chapter 8). People who've incurred damage to this part of their brain are more likely to endorse pushing the heavy man in front of the train – their judgements are more coldly utilitarian and less emotion-ally influenced than those of people whose emotional hard wiring is intact.

Sources: Hauser, M., Cushman, F., Young, L., Jin, R.K-X. and Mikhail, J. (2007) A dissociation between moral judgements and dissociations, *Mind and Language,* **22**(1): 1–21; Koenigs, M., Young, L., Adolphs, R., Tranel, D., Cushman, F., Hauser, M. and Damasio, A.R. (2007) Damage to the prefrontal cortex increases utilitarian moral judge-ments, *Nature,* **446**(7138): 908–11; Pinker, S. (2008) The moral instinct, *New York Times,* 13th January.

Both in personal and professional life tension arises between the push of the analytical mind towards the ideal of rationality ('sacrifice one life for five'), and the pull of the intuitive mind to an instinctive moral centre of gravity ('could you really push a person standing next to you under a train?'). In many situations an elemental sense of right and wrong prevails and gut feelings, rather than the reasoning of the analytical mind, determine our actions.

To understand what it takes to show intuitive moral leadership we can again wind the clock back to ancient Greece, this time in the 8th century B.C. In Homer's epic poems the *The Iliad* and *The Odyssey* the mythical heroic leaders such as Achilles and Odysseus were defined by their virtuous behaviour: Odysseus was depicted as having the virtues of 'patience', 'nobility' and 'nimble wittedness', whilst Achilles (a mere mortal) was nothing less than 'god-like'. Several hundred years later in the philosophy of Aristotle the practice of moral as well as intellectual virtue (smarts), not just on the battlefield but in life more generally, was essential to the functioning of civilised society. To be 'virtuous' as a leader or a citizen in ancient Greece meant firstly doing what was right, and secondly avoiding excesses; for example, the virtue of 'courage' was deemed the right thing to do, and it lay between the to-be-avoided extremes of 'rashness' (excess of courage) and 'cowardice' (deficiency of courage). Applying Aristotle's philosophy to leadership we find three important issues at work.

Application No. 16: Leadership Virtue, Practice and Habit

Virtue	Leaders should behave virtuously because it's right to do so.
Practice	Only by practising doing virtuous things do leaders habituate the virtues.

Habit	Virtuous leadership if practised well and long enough becomes intuitive (habituated). A leader's instinctive and public response to a situation gives a window into how virtuous they really are.[16]

Aristotle's philosophy is as relevant to business leaders in the 21st century as it was to the citizens of Athens over two thousand years ago. Not only do intuitive leaders habituate the virtues through practice they also have a responsibility towards their followers and the wider community (the firm and the society). Within the Aristotelian doctrine it's better to achieve the good of the community as a whole than that of the individual leader him or herself.

Of the twelve moral virtues identified by Aristotle, 'courage' (avoiding rashness and cowardice), 'temperance' (avoiding licentiousness and insensibility), 'proper ambition' (avoiding want of ambition or over ambition) and 'truthfulness' (avoiding boastfulness and understatement)[17] seem especially relevant to leadership in the 21st century. Take the so-called 'credit crunch': it was tales of excess and greed where profits and personal wealth creation were pursued blatantly for their own sake, society itself was complicit. The Aristotelian moral virtues were largely conspicuous by their absence. According to Lord Turner, head of the UK's banking regulator the Financial Services Authority speaking in 2009, nobody seemed to realise that the pieces of the jig-saw which were about to fall into place (current account deficit, rapid credit extension, unsustainable house price rises, a complex international market in mortgage-backed securities and irrational exuberance in the market price of credit), meant that 'the whole system was fraught with market-wide, systemic risk'[18] – echoes perhaps of Huxley's words after reading Darwin's *Origin of Species*: 'how stupid of us all not to realise that'.

Is it really the case that most people didn't see the credit crunch coming? Was there a collective blind-sight or did those involved choose to exercise financial myopia? Was the credit crunch a financial 'Eureka!' moment for insiders, commentators and regulators, or did the smart people in the money game intuitively know what was coming? A financial sector fuelled by the excesses of acquisitiveness and personal wealth, ignited by failures in an international lending system so complex that it was alleged to be beyond the intellects of the smartest and most expert minds in the business, and the lack of an ethical imperative rebounded badly and resulted in an economic melt-down and world-wide recession. At the end of the day when a leader's, company's or society's intuitive moral compass goes haywire their intellectual virtues are thrown into confusion. In the money game the bankers and financiers ended up outsmarting themselves, but the taxpayers bankrolled the bail out.

Do we still trust bankers as a result? Trust was broken in Enron, and it became a very fragile commodity in the 'credit crunch', but it's the vital element of leadership. Leaders who possess charisma can deploy it to inspire the trust and followership of groups, organisations and even whole nations through the eloquence of their rhetoric and skills of persuasion. Followers trust leaders with their jobs, careers, money and even their lives. When a leader is privileged with followers' trust there's no guarantee her or his actions will be morally justifiable. The employees and shareholders of companies such as Enron misguidedly placed their trust in a company which lied about its profits, concealed debts so that they didn't show up in company accounts and whose auditors deliberately destroyed the evidence by shredding documents.[19] Similarly, before the credit crunch home owners put their trust in financial advisors' exhortations that the market was sure to deliver year-on-year growth in house prices. In retrospect this was a bubble that had to burst, and society apparently failed to recognise that both its judgement and trust was misguided.

Against this backcloth the spectrum of virtues that guard against moral bankruptcy and which are vital to leaders in the 21st century include some or all of the following (but this is not an exhaustive list, and their relevance will depend on the situation).

✐ **Application No. 17: A Selection of Leadership Virtues**

Altruism	Courage
Commitment	Creativity
Dependability	Honesty
Integrity	Intelligence
Initiative	Loyalty[20]

Virtuous behaviour balances excess and deficiency. For example, the virtue of courage lies between rashness (the vice of excess) and cowardice (the vice of deficiency). Following this line of thought (from Aristotle) it is possible therefore to have an excess of honesty, for example, giving a colleague overly candid feedback on their performance or potential may only serve to insult and de-motivate them. Through experience and practice leaders can develop the intuitive sense of what the 'golden mean' is and what the right thing to do is in each situation based on their intuitive appreciation of the context. One of the pioneers of intuition in management, the AT&T executive Chester Barnard writing in the 1930s echoed Aristotle when he called this an 'artistic principle' for management, this skill of attaining proportion between extremes through constant practice.[21]

INTUITION WORKOUT No. 18: WHAT ARE YOUR
MORAL IMPERATIVES?

What are the three most important moral imperatives for you
as a leader (or manager)? List them on Figure 9.3.

Whether some virtues are more important than others depends
on the situation, moreover finding the 'golden mean' and balancing the different and sometimes conflicting virtues is not always
an easy task. Nevertheless we have little choice: at the end of the
day our intuitive moral instinct is part of human nature, it has
evolutionary roots that enabled our ancestors who lived in relatively large social groups compared to other primates to be altru-
istic and survive in harsh, threatening environments.[22] Although
it is far from infallible, for business leaders in the modern world

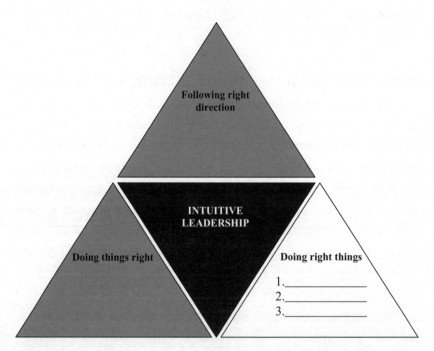

FIGURE 9.3   What are your moral imperatives?

who aspire to be virtuous intuitive morality and moral conduct are indispensable for two reasons – they help them to know what to do and how to do it:

✎ **Application No. 18: The What and How of Doing Right Things**

What to do	The moral instinct tells them intuitively where to look and reveals what the moral target is.
How to do it	Through learning, practice and experience the virtues of smartness and morality become habituated and guide their conduct automatically; and over time leaders become more skilled at hitting the moral target.

In addition to doing things right and doing right things (ideals which can apply to any member of society) there is, in business, a third essential ingredient of intuitive leadership – vision.

Right Direction

Leaders who intuitively do things right are in command of the operational details, they have the street smarts and the informed intuitions to know what normally works and are able to carry it through by their actions. But intuitive leaders are also people who see the forest as well as the trees, they grasp the big picture, lead in the right direction and are driven by the 'right vision'. They establish a picture of the future for the business in their own minds and have the skills to be able to communicate it to followers.

Establishing a direction can be as much an intuitive act as an analytical one. For example, Motorola is a world leader in global communications and has been at the forefront of telecommunications innovation for decades. It made the equipment that carried the first words from the Moon and was responsible for the development of the first handheld portable cell phone in 1983. In 2007 the company's net sales were $36.6 billion with $4.4 billion expenditure on research and development. Motorola was founded by Paul H. Galvin in 1928 as the Galvin Manufacturing Corporation. Galvin was successful because he was prepared to follow his instinct, be bold and go against conventional wisdom by grasping at 'straws in the wind' or 'gems in the junk pile'. Moreover Galvin was prepared to fund these ideas before traditional market analyses had been completed. Car radio (dismissed as being 'unsafe – how could anyone drive a car with a radio in it?') and cell phones (doubts were expressed that people would pay four to six times the cost of their monthly telephone bill for the privilege of having a mobile phone in their pocket) were intuitive directions that Motorola sensed 'on the wind' and followed through.[23] Galvin's and Motorola's anticipations paid off and helped create the communication technologies we now take for granted in the 21st century.

The skill of intuitively anticipating where businesses and markets are headed is crucial for Eddie Lampert, chairman and CEO of ESL Investments and chairman of Sears Holdings. Lampert recounts the best advice that he ever got was when playing football in the yard with his father who taught him the 'sixth sense' to be where the ball was going to be before the ball itself got there. He translates this lesson to business: 'Anticipation is key to investing and to business generally. You can't wait for an opportunity to become obvious', you have to think ahead and anticipate people's behaviour, and in order to anticipate you have to keep practising and preparing.[24]

Intuitive leaders, like successful entrepreneurs, read faint signals in the business environment and anticipate and adapt. The process begins with an instinctive perception of a business opportunity, is followed by an intuitive appraisal of its viability and finally an evaluation of whether or not it's worth the risk. Speed of response gives first-mover advantage, and in a fast-moving business world that places a premium on creativity and innovation, whilst it may be much harder to lead than to follow, in the long run businesses that lead will always have the edge over the trailing pack. For this reason alone companies can't afford to be without intuitive leaders who have a sense for 'right direction'. Faint signals, no matter how dim, stand a better chance of being picked up by well-attuned and experienced intuitive minds vigilant for the right direction. A former vice-president of the French MNC L'Oréal recognised that decision-making intelligence requires a fine balancing of two seemingly contradictory capabilities, intuition and rationality: the first one allows executives to pick up on important but weak signals; the second enables executives to act on them. The former CEO of the same company saw the challenge for executives as a matter of imagination and intuition in equal parts: 'It is intuition [when one asks] "what do these brands *have* that just might seduce the world?" But also in terms of imagination, [by asking] "what could they *become* to seduce the world?" '[25]

THE SCIENCE OF THE INTUITIVE MIND – PROFITING THROUGH INTUITION

The acid test for 'going with your gut' in management is 'does being intuitive bring results?' Whilst it's never easy to give a hard and fast 'yes' or 'no' answer to this type of question in a context as complex and dynamic as business, there is some hard evidence that relying on the intuitive mind to guide the direction of a firm can be *associated* with better firm performance and competitive advantage.

For example, senior managers' use of intuition in decision making has been found to be associated positively with business performance in US firms operating in unstable environments, whilst in stable environments the reverse was true. Moreover, participants in the research didn't see it as a sixth sense, rather as one of them commented, gut feeling is 'a subconscious derivative of the accumulation of years of management experience' and an MBA although it can provide the tools 'is no substitute for management experience'.

In a study of the relationship between CEOs' decision-making style and financial performance in a sample of US non-profit organisations it was found that higher levels of CEO intuition were correlated positively with business performance. The researchers explained their findings: 'reliance on an intuitive decision style, bolstered by a storehouse of tacit organisational knowledge acquired over time [in other words "deep smarts"] serves to actually enhance organisation performance'.

Sources: Khatri, N. and Ng, H.A. (2000) 'The role of intuition in strategic decision-making', *Human Relations*, **1**: 57–86; Ritchie, W.J., Kolodinsky, R.W. and Eastwood, K. (2007) Does executive intuition matter? An empirical analysis of its relationship with non-profit organization financial performance, *Non-profit and Voluntary Sector Quarterly*, **36**: 140–155.[26]

As well as the imperatives of smartness and morality, intuitive leadership also has a strategic imperative – sensing a vision of the future, articulating the vision and charting a direction. Intuition enables leaders to sense and explore a range of possible futures, how they and their followers feel about them (do they 'feel right'), and anticipate and plan for them. In the oil crisis of the 1980s mentally fast forwarding to construct a range of possible futures enabled Royal Dutch Shell to override the business-as-usual and analytical mindsets which many of its competitors were stuck with. The technique of 'scenario planning' allowed Shell to combine leaders' intuitions with formal analyses to create an expanded world view that anticipated new and previously unforeseen circumstances. One such 'visit to the future' was led by Shell's Head of Planning Arie de Geus: the scenario asked what the right directions for Shell might be if the 'end of world' situation of oil prices falling from $28 a barrel to $15 became reality? Scenario planning is business crystal balling without the mystique, and when the price actually fell to $10 a barrel Shell's leadership had already visited this future in its collective mind and intuited its response. Shell's competitors who didn't have the 'sixth sense' advantage of scenario planning fared less well, for example, one major oil company had to let 15000 employees go in the wake of the 1986 oil price collapse.[27]

The issue of 'right direction' raises a fundamental question for business leaders: 'right direction for whom?' Do leaders lead companies with the intention of personal gain, profitability, shareholder value, longevity or sustainability? How can the needs of and responsibilities towards the shareholders and the larger social system be reconciled with the question of 'right direction' and 'right intention'? Where is the moral high-ground for business and how can leaders and managers capture it? The answers to some of these questions already exist on our supermarket shelves.

Doing the right thing is the intention at the heart of the Fair Trade Foundation which began life in the 1980s under the initiative of the Dutch development agency Solidaridad, and the first Fair Trade coffee ('Max Havelaar' brand) was named after a fictional Dutch character who opposed the exploitation of coffee pickers in the Dutch colonies. The Fair Trade Foundation was formalised in 1992 by CAFOD, Christian Aid, Oxfam, Traidcraft and the World Development Movement. Its intentions are to get 'better prices, decent working conditions, local sustainability, and fair terms of trade for farmers and workers in the developing world' and to address 'the injustices of conventional trade, which traditionally discriminates against the poorest, weakest producers'. The intentions of the movement are to:

1. address the iniquities of the present global trading system which privileges large agribusinesses;
2. bring about the redistribution of wealth on a global scale.

One of the ways in which this intention is translated into action is by requiring companies to pay sustainable prices (which must never fall lower than the market price). But the world has a long way to go. Raw statistics make scale of the challenge all too apparent: the total value of Fair Trade business was estimated in 2002 to be US$500 million compared to US$45000 million for Tesco, the UK's largest food retailer.[28]

INTUITION WORKOUT No. 19: WHAT ARE YOUR STRATEGIC IMPERATIVES?

What are the three most important strategic imperatives for you as a leader (or manager)? List them on Figure 9.4.

The issues of 'right things', 'right intentions' and 'right actions' are amongst the most difficult and pressing questions for business leaders to formulate and face, let alone answer. We may intuit the existence of such questions and our personal, organisational and societal shortcomings. As we know, human beings along with their primate cousins have the potential to engage in deceitful behaviour, whether this manifests as the minor embellishment of

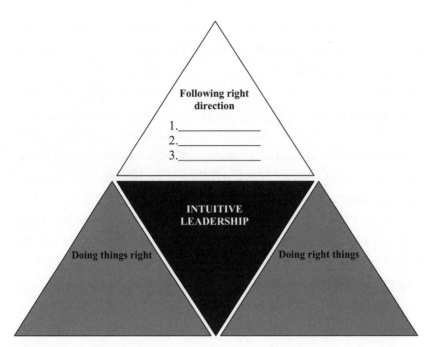

FIGURE 9.4 What are your strategic imperatives?

a résumé, blatant white collar crime or something even more serious. Nonetheless, our instinctive sense of right intentions and right actions may cause the intuitive mind to post a nagging doubt into our conscious awareness, but other more pressing emotional or practical issues may repress these intuitions. Such issues often have a habit of hanging around, they lurk and they, or their consequences, are likely to emerge at some point in the near or distant future. They can be addressed, and through the right combination of intuitive and analytical intelligences leaders and followers may formulate and seek answers to the most fundamental business questions of all: 'what is the "right" thing to do?' and 'what is "good" business?'

Leaders deploy intuitive judgement day-in day-out, and informed intuition is important both for the inception and the longer term survival of businesses. Intuitive decision making is not only connected to performance in profit-driven enterprises it 'works' in non-profit organisations also and isn't merely a servant to the pursuit of financial gain. But as we've seen when a leader's intuitive compass fails to function or to be heeded wrong things may be pursued in wrong ways for the wrong reasons: the consequences can be dire. The existence of an evolved moral instinct which leaders feel compelled to follow is consistent with empathy and altruism underpinned by instincts of justice and fairness. This is the essence of intuitive leadership and it inspires the trust, respect and cooperation of followers. What are your street smarts, moral instincts and strategic sense which enable you to do things right, do right things and follow right direction (Figure 9.5)?

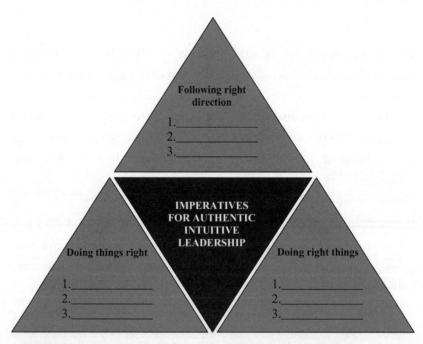

FIGURE 9.5   Your imperatives for intuitive leadership

> ## INTUITIVE INTELLIGENCE PRINCIPLE No. 9: DO THINGS RIGHT, DO RIGHT THINGS AND FOLLOW RIGHT DIRECTION
>
> Intuitive leadership is about:
>
> 1. doing things right (street smarts);
> 2. doing right things (moral instinct);
> 3. following right direction (strategic sense).
>
> When all three are present intuitive leadership is intellectually, morally and strategically complete. When one or more is missing opportunities are created for the void to be filled with smart, moral or strategic imperatives:
>
> 1. Smart: doing right things and following right direction, but not doing things right – leadership needs to develop a smart imperative.
> 2. Moral: doing things right and following right direction, but not doing right things – leadership needs to develop a moral imperative.
> 3. Strategic: doing things right and doing right things, but not following right direction – leadership needs to develop the vision of a strategic imperative.
>
> These three imperatives are the starting points for individual and collective introspection, reflection, inquiry and dialogue, and the development of an authentic intuitive leadership in the business organisations of the 21st century.

NOTES

[1] A virtue can be defined as habitually (intuitively) doing, through practice, what is 'right'. The term 'smart' as used here can be taken as broadly equivalent to the term 'intellectual virtue' (from Aristotle). 'Smart' doesn't mean 'clever' or 'polished', instead it refers to 'practical

intuitions' or 'intuitive expertise' developed over many years of learning, training and real-world experiences and deployed, in the main, non-consciously.

[2]Harai, O. (2003) *The Leadership Secrets of Colin Powell.* New York: McGraw-Hill (p. 84).

[3]McMaster, H.R. (2008) Adaptive leadership: Harold G. 'Hal' Moore (p. 220). In Laver, H.S. and Matthews, J.J. (Eds) *The Art of Command: military leadership from George Washington to Colin Powell.* Lexington, KY: The University Press of Kentucky (pp. 209–30).

[4]Rogers, C.T. (1994) Intuition: an imperative of command, *Military Review,* **74**(3): 38–50 (p. 39).

[5]Lyneham, J., Parkinson, C. and Denholm, C. (2008) Intuition in emergency nursing: a phenomenological study, *International Journal of Nursing Practice,* **14**: 101–8.

[6]Blackman, D. and Sadler-Smith, E. (2009) The silent and the silenced in organisational knowing and learning, *Management Learning,* **40** (in press); Cook, S.D.N. and Brown, J.S. (1999) Bridging Epistemologies: The Generative Dance Between Organizational Knowledge and Organizational Knowing. *Organization Science,* **10**(4): 381–400; Polanyi, M. (1966) *The Tacit Dimension.* London: Routledge and Kegan Paul.

[7]Hedlund, J., Forsythe, G.B., Horvath, J.A., Williams, W.M., Snook, S. and Sternberg, R.J. (2003) Identifying and assessing tacit knowledge: understanding the practical intelligence of military leaders, *The Leadership Quarterly,* **14**: 117–40.

[8]Leonard, D. and Swap, W. (2005) *Deep Smarts: how to cultivate and transfer enduring business wisdom.* Boston, MA.: Harvard Business School Press.

[9]Burke, C.S., Sims, D.E., Lazzara, E.H. and Salas, E. (2007) Trust in leadership: a multilevel review and integration, *The Leadership Quarterly,* **18**: 606–32.

[10]Goldberg, E. (2005) *The Wisdom Paradox: how your mind can grow stronger as your brain grows older.* London: Free Press.

[11]Goldberg pp. 71–2.

[12]The Best Advice I ever Got: Joanna Shields. Retrieved on 29th January from http://money.cnn.com/galleries/2008/fortune/0804/gallery.bestadvice.fortune/16.html.

[13]Bolman, L.G. and Deal, T.E. (2003) *Reframing organizations: artistry, choice and leadership*. San Francisco: Jossey-Bass (pp. 394–5).

[14]Harari, O. and Brewer, L. (2004) If Colin Powell had commanded Enron: the hidden foundation of leadership, *Business Strategy Review*, **15**(2): 37–45.

[15]'Ex-Enron exec urges students to avoid ethical errors', retrieved 1st January 2009 from http://www.colorado.edu/academics/honorcode/ files/Ex-Enron%20exec%20urges%20students%20to%20avoid%20 ethical%20errors.pdf.

[16]Clemens, J.K. and Mayer, D.F. (1999) *The Classic Touch: lessons in leadership from Homer to Hemingway*, Chicago: Contemporary Books.

[17]Vardy, P. and Grosch, P. (1999) *The Puzzle of Ethics*. London: Fount.

[18]'City watchdog – banking system needs profound change', retrieved 1st January 2009 from http://business.timesonline.co.uk/tol/business/ industry_sectors/banking_and_finance/article5564878.ece.

[19]BBC News (22nd August 2002) Enron scandal at-a-glance. Retrieved on 29th January 2009 from http://news.bbc.co.uk/1/hi/business/ 1780075.stm.

[20]Godin, S. (1995) *Wisdom Inc.: 30 business virtues that turn ordinary people into extraordinary leaders*. New York: Harper Collins; Solomon, R.C. 1993. *Ethics and Excellence: cooperation and integrity in business*. Oxford: Oxford University Press.

[21]Barnard, C.E. (1938) *The Functions of the Executive*. Cambridge, MA: Harvard Business School Press, p. 322.

[22]This type of instinct is not uniquely human, a variety of it can be seen in our primate cousins, for example, rhesus monkeys in the lab will endure hunger rather than pull a level that gives them food and another monkey an electric shock. See: Pinker, S. 2008. The moral instinct, *New York Times*, 13th January.

[23]Winston, M.G. (1997) Leadership of renewal: leadership for the 21st century, *Business Forum*, Winter: 4–7.

[24]The Best Advice I Ever Got: Eddie Lampert. Retrieved on 29th January 2009 from http://money.cnn.com/galleries/2008/fortune/0804/gallery. bestadvice.fortune/9.html.

[25]Robert Salmon, former vice-president of L'Oréal (http://www.refresher. com/!signals); Lindsay Owen-Jones, Chairman and Chief Executive Officer of L'Oréal in *Business Week Online*, 28th June 1999.

[26] *Note*: both of the studies described were correlational, this means they looked at statistical associations. One of the limits of such studies is that correlation or association between two variables (for example intuition and performance) doesn't necessarily reflect causation (intuition doesn't necessarily cause enhanced performance).

[27] Van der Heijden, K., Bradfield, B., Burt, G., Cairns, G. and Wright, G. (2002) *The Sixth Sense Accelerating Organizational Learning through Scenarios*. Chichester: John Wiley and Sons; pp. 238–9; De Geus, A. (1997) *The Living Company*. Cambridge, MA.: Harvard Business School Press.

[28] Jaffee, D. (2007) *Brewing Justice: fair trade coffee, sustainability and survival*. Berkeley: University of California Press; Moore, G. (2004) The Fair Trade movement: parameters, issues and future research, *Journal of Business Ethics*, **53**: 73–86; What is Fair Trade? FAQs Retrieved on 30th January 2009 from http://www.fairtrade.org.uk/what_is_fairtrade/default.aspx.

Chapter 10

INTUITIVE INTELLIGENCE

'So if the states of mind by which we reach the truth are science, prudence, wisdom and intuition; and if it cannot be any one of the [first] three of them, namely prudence, science, and wisdom: what remains is that the state of mind that apprehends first principles is intuition.' Aristotle, The Nicomachean Ethics (Book iv: 152)

Leaders and managers understand how the world is now and how it might be in the future using two systems of thinking and reasoning – the analytical mind and the intuitive mind. Evolution has hard wired the human brain to run the complementary functions of these two systems in parallel. The mental models that the systems use – their 'software' – are uploaded and constructed actively over many years of learning and experience. They're deployed by the intuitive mind when the need arises to take decisions in complex, time-pressured and judgemental situations.

A model is a representation of something – people, systems, events and relationships. Mental models are our simplified, internal representations of the external world. They're patterns made up of 'memory objects', including facts we've acquired, 'know how', episodes in our lives, narratives we create, images we store (in a variety of sensory modalities) and the feelings that are attached to these objects. Mental models are vital for making sense of the world and they become richer and more complex as we gain experience. Their down side is that they're incomplete and can become outdated. When mental models no longer make sense they may require anything from a minor refinement to a radical overhaul.[1]

What are the consequences of harbouring incomplete or outdated mental models, and, on the other hand, what are the benefits of constantly updating our mental models and keeping the hard wiring and software of the intuitive and analytical minds finely tuned?

The Credit Crunch

We need look no further than the 2008 Credit Crunch for a vivid illustration of the consequences of deploying an incomplete, over-simplistic or outdated mental model as a proxy for a complex, dynamic and unpredictable reality. Prior to the shock of 2008 the mental model for millions of homebuyers was that property purchase was a one-way bet, a risk-free investment. As a result millions of ordinary people borrowed heavily, sometimes up to 125% of property value on the back of a globalised and arcane financial system that permitted a blend of capricious lending and irresponsible borrowing. A property bubble was growing on both sides of the Atlantic with record house price rises reported regularly in the media month on month.

But there's no such thing as a one-way, risk-free bet. 'Bet' means an agreement to pay if you're wrong (and vice versa). The mental model was 'borrow and buy'; the reality turned out to be 'balloon and bust'. During the boom years there were occasional 'party poopers' who were using a radically different mental model. They were often depicted as pessimistic doom-mongers, who didn't buy into the same mind set as the majority of bankers and politicians. An article in *The Times* of London in October 2008 called 'Ten people predicted the financial meltdown' quoted several prominent naysayers. For example, in a veiled reference to banking bosses who'd patently overstretched their expertise and capabilities, Christopher Wood, Chief Strategist of Asia-Pacific broking firm CLSA, commented in 2007: 'Some institutions have been behaving like leveraged speculators rather than banks. The UK economy is heading for a sharp shock. It just remains to be seen how bad [it will be]'. It was a shock for many bank customers in the UK to learn that a number of banking executives grilled by a Parliamentary Committee in 2009 had no formal banking qualifications. Evidence of the value of genuine expertise was to be found in the comments made at a 2006 IMF fund meeting by NYU economics professor Nouriel Roubini. He announced the looming crisis to a host of largely deaf ears prophesying that an impending once-in-a-lifetime housing bust in the US would mean that 'Homeowners would default on mortgages, trillions of dollars of mortgage-backed securities would unravel worldwide and the global financial system would shudder to a halt'.[2]

Inferences made by managers and leaders built on robust intuitions have the potential to lead businesses and societies institutions in the right direction. But intuitions are feeble when they lack expertise (is it right for the head of a bank to have no formal banking qualification?) or are contaminated with wishful thinking (for example, who wouldn't like to think that their assets can just keep on growing with no pain and all the gain?), or the vulgarities of greed (witness the size of the bonuses, pay-offs and pensions paid to a number of bank employees). In spite of what the growth statistics were saying – for example year-on-year record house price rises – was it reasonable to expect them to go on growing at such rates when in the UK the cost of a starter home was four to five times average the income of first time buyers? Doesn't a basic intuition, or even common sense, tell us all that this was unsustainable; furthermore doesn't a fundamental moral instinct send a signal that this was an unjust and unfair situation for societies that pride themselves on being property owning democracies?

When we need to find direction or take action the installed version of our mental model, with all its assumptions and expectations, provides a comforting, sometimes compelling, and certainly convenient way to make sense of the world and make predictions. But the map in any mental model isn't literally 'the territory', it's a representation of something that appears to be 'out there' which can be viewed through rose tinted spectacles (as it was in the boom) and can change in the blink of an eye (as it did in the bust). The territory is constantly changing, and consequently managers' and leaders' mental models need to be constantly updated and the system upgraded to reflect the way the world *is*, not how it *was*, or how he or she'd *like* it to be.

If intuition is a vital asset then becoming intuitively intelligent requires managers and leaders to constantly update their knowledge base (through on going professional education and training), extend themselves outside of their comfort zone (taking on new and challenging assignments) and question their assumptions (both at the level of detail and as a whole through narrow angle and wide angle lenses). In this respect a manager or leader builds informed intuitions in an act of *becoming* intuitively intelligent, but never *becomes* intuitively intelligent in the dynamic and turbulent world of business and economics.

The Miracle on the Hudson

Some of our intuitive capacities, such as the capability to experience and express a moral instinct, come hard wired and pre-loaded (analogous to the microchips and operating systems on a PC when it leaves the factory), but our informed intuitions begin their life in the analytical mind and are sustained by it. Through education and training, and repeated exposure, practice and feedback in tough and challenging situations knowledge and skill crosses over the mental divide and becomes, in the words of Nobel Laureate Herbert Simon, 'analyses frozen into habit and the capacity for rapid response through recognition', and which send out powerful affective cues as signals for action. We need look no further than the Hudson River in New York for a vivid illustration of the benefits for leaders and managers of constantly updating our mental models and keeping the software and hard wiring of the intuitive and analytical minds finely tuned.

On the afternoon of Thursday 16th January 2009 a US Airways Airbus A320 took off from New York's La Guardia airport. A minute after take-off Flight 1549 collided with a flock of Canada Geese and lost all engine power. The plane couldn't make it back to La Guardia or to the next nearest airfield at Tetboro, New Jersey. In a split second the pilot, flying over one of the most densely populated places on Earth, took the only reasonable decision available to him: land the plane in the icy waters of the Hudson River. What followed was a remarkable display of skill, courage and automated expertise. Passengers were advised to brace for a hard landing, and the plane was guided down, nose slightly up, onto the Hudson in what was as near perfect a landing as was humanly possible. The aircraft bobbed around on the water but remarkably stayed afloat whilst a small armada of New York Waterway commuter ferries, tugs and Coastguard vessels moved in to rescue terrified passengers who began swarming onto the aircraft's wings,[3] images of which were being beamed around the world within minutes of it happening.

The pilot who turned a potential 'Tragedy on 34th Street' into the 'Miracle of the Hudson' was Captain C.B. 'Sully' Sullenberger, who had intuitive intelligence in abundance. Once he made the decision to land on the Hudson Sullenberger embarked on one of the most awkward and difficult manoeuvres that any pilot is likely to face in their whole careers. That said, it would have been hard to find a more expert performer than Sullenberger to bring off the miracle escape. He had over forty years of flying experience, he got his pilot's licence at age fourteen, was a former USAF fighter pilot, served as a flight instructor and Airline Pilots' Association safety chairman, had taken part in several USAF and National Transportation Safety Board (NTSB) accident investigations, studied the psychological responses of flight crews in emergencies and, more than appropriately for this incident, is a certified glider pilot.[4]

The 'textbook' model for landing on water requires the flight crew to: ensure the undercarriage is up (for a smoother landing) and air conditioning is turned off (to equalise cabin and outside pressures); slow down the aircraft; fly into the wind; fully extend wing flaps; get rid of as much fuel as possible; slow down enough but not stall; make sure the wings are perfectly level (any deviation would cause one to clip and cartwheel the plane); lower the tail end keeping the nose at an angle of 12 degrees; and finally gently skim the surface of the water until the plane comes to a halt (at which point it's likely to start to take on water) and then implement emergency evacuation procedures.

These daunting requirements, allied to the fact that a fully laden A320 weighs in excess of seventy-five tonnes and can carry almost 200 passengers, give an indication of the expertise that Sullenberger, over many years on the flight deck, compressed into a decisive intuitive response that could be accomplished in a matter of seconds[5] with no room for prevarication, hesitancy, recklessness or weakness. When the decision researcher Gary Klein set out to study the decisions of experienced fire fighters in emergency situations Klein knew that they couldn't systematically weigh up all the available alternatives – it simply wasn't an option. Klein thought they might come up with two leading options and compare these: to his surprise this hunch was wrong – the more experienced fire-fighters (more than twenty years in the job) came up with only a single option, in their own minds they didn't *consider* anything they just *acted*.[6] Captain Sullenberger, in one of the first interviews given after the incident, said that at the time 'The physiological reaction I had to this was strong, and I had to force myself to use my training – and force calm on the situation'. The questions and 'what ifs?' only started in the days following the emergency landing, but in the moment of taking the decision there were no 'ifs and buts', the decision to land on the Hudson was 'the only viable alternative … the only level, smooth place sufficiently large to land an airliner was the river'.[7]

To say that Sullenberger had the 'right stuff' for this emergency is an understatement. His leadership and courage was perfectly suited to the circumstances, and was exercised without any trace of rashness. He had the professionalism and a lifetime of preparation for this incident (which hopefully most pilots will never have to face). The combination of the right person and the right conditions led to a happy outcome for all and provides exemplar of intuitive expertise that will be admired by generations of pilots to come.

To be deployed intelligently, intuition should be used by the right person, at the right time, under the right conditions and for the right reasons. What's 'right' in any given management or leadership situation is a matter of experience, judgement and ultimately, wisdom. Making right judgements demands a synthesis of analysis and intuition. Intuitive intelligence in professional contexts cannot exist without finely tuned intuition and a rigorously developed analytical mind.

Developing Intuitive Intelligence

Intuitive intelligence is the capacity to understand, apply and develop one's intuitive judgement. Intuitive intelligence has three components:

Understanding intuition	Knowledge of what intuition is and how the intuitive mind works.
Intuitive expertise	High levels of knowledge and skill in your chosen professional field.
Intuitive self-awareness	Appreciating what happens when you intuit, and how you can make more effective use of intuitive judgement and create the conditions for intuitions to flourish in personal and professional life.

We'll now look at each of these three components in turn.

Understanding Intuition

It's possible, and not uncommon, for people to confuse intuitions with other 'Is' – particularly insight and instinct. Becoming intuitively intelligent starts by grasping what intuition is, and what it is not.[8]

🔑 **Key Facts No. 16: The Three Is**	
Intuition isn't instinct	'Instinct' per se refers to innate, automatic biological responses (for example, the homing instinct in some birds) whilst intuitions are affectively-charged judgements that arise through rapid, non-conscious and holistic associations in response to complex, judgemental situations[9] – quite different from autonomous, instinctive responses.

Intuition isn't insight	When insight occurs a problem solver moves from the position of 'not knowing' to 'knowing' and being able to articulate the solution. An intuition of an impending solution may occur prior to the insightful moment – intuition may be an intimation that insight is about to happen. Some intuitions never emerge as insights, but remain as feelings of attraction or avoidance, which are verified or refuted only with the unfolding of events. Intuition allows us to *sense* connections; insight allows us to *see* connections.
Intuitive feelings aren't emotional feelings	Intuitive feelings differ from emotional feelings. The feelings associated with fear, for example, are typically intense bursts – they are emotional but do not persist. 'Gut feeling', on the other hand, is less intense and typically manifests as feelings of anxiety, disquiet or possibility.

One instinct that Homo sapiens is probably unique in possessing is the moral instinct, described by Marc D. Hauser as 'a faculty of the human mind that unconsciously guides our judgements concerning right and wrong' and which, across human history, has manifested itself in various codes: 'hurt not others in ways that you yourself would find hurtful' (Buddhism) or 'do not unto others what you would not have them do unto you' (Taoism), or put even more simply: 'do as you would be done by'.

Intuitive Expertise

Experts in any field ranging from management to musical performance have an extensive database of knowledge and skill held in long-term memory. These patterns make up mental models of the world built up through formal learning, exposure to challenging real-world problems and feedback. Under the right conditions managers and leaders progress from being novice to expert:

🔑 Key Facts No. 17: Novice/Expert Differences

Novice Leaders and Managers	Deploy rules and procedures in a formulaic and un-nuanced way without taking the subtleties of the context into account. A novice is able to follow a recipe but struggles if the recipe book or the right ingredients aren't available.
Expert Leaders and Managers	Have the ability to perceive and discriminate between a large number of contextual variables and exhibit a fluidity of performance which is as 'easy' to execute as it is difficult to articulate[10]– experts often know what to do (especially in time pressured situations) without knowing how or why they know.

Experts' ease of performance is borne out of many years, consisting of thousands of hours, of learning and experience. Estimates vary, but expertise researchers often use the rule-of-thumb of ten years or 10000 hours of practising in a particular domain before expert levels of performance can be attained. Expertise expert K. Anders Ericsson is firmly of the view that experts are 'made' more than they're 'born', and that not all practice makes perfect. Deliberate, focused and sustained efforts to do something that one cannot currently accomplish well or do at all extends one's performance, rather than routinely practising what can already be accomplished.[11]

Arie de Geus, the former head of planning at Royal Dutch/Shell, once observed that one of the most surprising things in management is that we experiment with reality. Contrast this potentially dangerous form of 'play' with that of the golfer on the practice green or the tennis player on the practice court (or pilot rehearsing an emergency landing in a flight simulator): they get as many chances as they want or need to perfect their swing or stroke, and it doesn't matter on the practice grounds if they get it wrong. Management and leadership can learn from what happens on sports practice grounds and in musical conservatories. These are safe environments where skills can be improved and new and relevant skills acquired.

Coaching and feedback are vital for the development of good intuitive judgement. On the sports practice ground and in the conservatories expert coaches analyse performance and give candid feedback on how to improve. Without the right kind of feedback it is possible for bad intuitions to go unchecked – a perilous state of affairs both for the individual and the organisation that they are a part of. The decision researcher Robin Hogarth distinguishes between kind and wicked feedback environments and the very different kinds of learning they engender.

🔑 Key Facts No. 18: Kind and Wicked Learning Environments	
Kind learning environments	Lead to the development of good intuitions as a result of relevant and accurate feedback and extensive personal experience.
Wicked learning environments	Lead to the development of bad intuitions as a result of irrelevant and misleading feedback and limited personal experience.

In management the acquisition of intuitions in kind learning environments with focused deliberate practice outside of one's comfort zone in simulated and real settings with ongoing precise, relevant and candid feedback is likely to lead to the ability to exercise intuitive judgements which feel right but – since intuition does not come with any guarantee of success – may nonetheless be fallible.[12] It's important for managers to be able to practice without the fear that making mistakes may cost them, their employees, their customers or their businesses dear.

Intuitive Self-Awareness

Management and leadership has traditionally down played the significance of intuition, publicly at least. One unfortunate consequence of this is that intuition tends to be ignored, overlooked, downgraded or kept firmly in the closet. As a result leaders and managers, even though they inevitably experience intuition, often feel uncomfortable in admitting to its existence or in embracing it when it occurs. In order to capitalise on one of our most important assets it's vital that intuition is brought into the open and scrutinised in order to develop managers' and leaders' awareness of how their intuitive mind functions. Intuitive self-awareness may be achieved by an acceptance of intuition, creating the conditions for intuitions to flourish and harmonising intuition and analysis.

Acceptance of intuition: the simplest way to accept intuition is to reflect on it from an inner perspective by asking two questions:

1. What happens when you intuit (how does it feel for you)?
2. What happened on occasions in the past when you intuited (what were the outcomes when you relied on intuitive judgement; when did it help, when did it hinder; do you consider intuition your friend or foe, powerful or perilous)?

A more rigorous approach to intuitive reflection involves documenting intuitive episodes in a journal, diary or log book and simple protocols can be used which enable the systematic analysis of intuition.

✎ Application No. 19: An Intuition Log

When and where	Where and when did the intuition occur?
Strength and clarity	What was the strength and clarity of the gut feeling or hunch?
Form	What form did the intuition take (was it an image, a metaphor or a bodily sensation)?
Utility	How useful or effective did the intuition prove to be?

More extensive tried and tested guidelines for journalling intuitions have been developed by one of the pioneers of intuitive management Professor Bill Taggart (see the 'Intuitive Self' project web site at http://www.the-intuitive-self.org). This type of journalling approach has been evaluated and shown to be an effective way of developing leaders' and managers' intuitive awareness.[13]

Creating the conditions: one of the most important ways of creating the conditions for intuitions to arise (recall that they cannot be forced, but proxies can be created via the imagined events of a mental simulation) is through the process of 'quieting' the (analytical) mind. The assumption behind this is that the voice of the intuitive mind (including subtle bodily sensations) may be drowned out by the constant verbalisations of the analytical mind (what the instigator of intuitive management, AT&T's Chester Barnard, referred to as the 'incessant din of reasons'). There are a variety of methods available for 'quieting' ranging from simple physical and mental relaxation and 'switching off', to outright meditative and contemplative techniques rooted in Eastern philosophies such as Buddhism. Such techniques are becoming increasingly common and accepted in the West and in business organisations and are no longer thought of as 'far out' or 'New Age'.[14] Related to the idea of 'quieting the mind' is the notion of mindfulness.

Mindfulness involves cultivating a sense of heightened awareness, savouring the things of the here and now and encompasses three attitudes of mind:

✎ Application No. 20: The Attitudes of Mindfulness	
Meta-aware	Not just doing something but also being aware of what you are doing and how you are doing it.
Undistracted	Your mind isn't bogged down in the constant stream of stimuli that are vying for attention.
Non judgemental	You adopt the position of being a neutral observer of things that are going on around you.

Being mindful can help to release the mind from its dependence upon habitual and 'sticky' thinking. It's a way of: examining things in your environment that you might automatically take for granted; shifting ones perceptions and perspective. Cultivating mindfulness comes through slowing down the onrush of mental activity and focusing attention on the world of sensations. Mindfulness training can improve observational skills and enrich and alter your direct perception of the world as it currently is and can counteract the all too frequent hijacking of thoughts by emotions, fears, prejudices and biases.

Harmonising intuition and analysis: a fundamental precept of the 'two minds model', with which this book began, is that the intuitive mind and the analytical mind each have a vitally important role in thinking, reasoning, creativity judgement, decision making and moral action. Consequently it's important that managers are aware of the strengths and the limitations of each mind and are able to use them as checks and balances on each other.[15] The ultimate goal is the ambidexterity of mind discussed in Chapter 2 – the ability to 'switch mental gears'.[16]

Intuitive Wisdom

The psychologist Robert J. Sternberg demonstrated considerable wisdom when he commented that to understand wisdom fully and correctly probably requires more wisdom than any of us have: 'we can't quite comprehend the nature of wisdom because of our own lack of it'. For one of the earliest Greek philosophers, Socrates,[17] wisdom was ultimately a transcendent state of being – impossible to touch in this world because the soul that aspires to wisdom is entombed in a physical body which impedes its flight. At a more practical level Aristotle's view was that a human being must possess wisdom in order to achieve happiness (εὐδαιμονία, *eudaimonia*). In Aristotelian philosophy happiness isn't a hedonistic, pleasure-oriented, here-one-minute gone-the-next condition, rather it's a state of 'flourishing and completeness',[18] but to reach the condition of eudaimonia a person has to be virtuous: 'we praise a wise man on the grounds of his state of mind; and those states that are praiseworthy we call "virtues"' (Aristotle, *The Nicomachean Ethics*).

We may turn to Buddhism for a down-to-earth, here-and-now centred view of the state of mind and virtues that a wise person may possess. His Holiness the 14th Dalai Lama, Tenzin Gyatso, who describes himself as a 'simple Buddhist monk', considers 'wise discernment' to be the adjusting of our virtues (for example, for Buddhists a cardinal virtue is 'non-harming') to the situations we find ourselves in. Wise discernment involves being constantly vigilant and adjusting the excesses of our perceptions and actions so that they're neither too narrow minded or short sighted and that our motives are genuinely compassionate in their nature to all beings. Our moral knee jerk reactions speak much louder than words. Through our spontaneous intuitive reactions we reveal our intuitive intelligence and intuitive self. If our general habits and dispositions are 'unwholesome' this will be reflected in our spontaneous actions which will be unwholesome and destructive.[19] A virtuous intuitive self is cultivated through openness and honesty about our motives and actions. Being open, honest and vigilant is governed by the irrefutable intuitive principal of 'do unto others as you would have them do to you'. For intuitive managers and leaders this generosity and compassion extends not only to people but also to business (of which people are the essence) and the environment (the fundamental condition for human existence). The Dalai Lama attributed the global recession of 2009 to unlimited greed, a lack of transparency and lies. He offered spirituality as a source of containment, truthfulness, honesty and morality and as a way to combat the uncontrolled material development and exploitation of nature that's causing serious environmental degradation,[20] likely to be the major problem facing humanity long after the credit crunch has become just one more chapter in the economic history books.

INTUITIVE INTELLIGENCE PRINCIPLES No. 10: BE TRUE TO YOUR INTUITIVE SELF

Intuitive intelligence is not simply a process of the accumulation of knowledge, skill and experiences, they have to be made sense of and constructive feedback from bosses, peers, employees and followers on how a manager or leader is performing produces a better informed and more refined intuitive judgement. Over time 'intuitive muscle power'[21] builds and managers and leaders become intuitively 'wiser' with age. The intuitive mind is embodied in our brains but also in our bodies and expresses itself in the 'head', 'heart', 'hands' and 'gut' of our intuitive self:

Head (intuitive knowledge)	The repertoire of learning and knowledge which forms the bedrock of informed intuition.
Heart (intuitive feelings)	The connection with the voice of the intuitive mind, and heeding of its signals for avoidance or attraction.
Hands (intuitive skill)	The ability to do things right in complex, judgemental and often time pressured situations.
Gut (intuitive moral instinct)	The instinctive sense of what's right. Knowing when one's actions and one's internal moral compass are out of kilter. Acceptance of the fundamental principles of justice and fairness which engender feelings of empathy and compassion towards one's fellow human beings.

The intuitive self is our most vital asset; the intuitive mind is a system that under the right conditions can constantly be upgraded; we never achieve a finished state of 'being intuitive'; through the experience of living and learning and by being true to our intuitive self we 'become intuitive' and begin to 'apprehend first principles'.

The ten principles of intuitive intelligence are:

Principle 10	Be true to your intuitive self.
Principle 9	Do things right, do right things and follow right direction.
Principle 8	Go with your head, your heart and your gut.
Principle 7	Express your intuitions.
Principle 6	Develop expertise.
Principle 5	Beware of feeble intuitions.

Principle	4	Count on first impressions and make first impressions count.
Principle	3	Don't mix up your I's.
Principle	2	Switch mental gears.
Principle	1	Acknowledge the intuitive mind.

NOTES

[1] Klein, G. (2003) *Intuition at work*. New York: Doubleday.

[2] 'Ten people who predicted financial meltdown' retrieved on 27th February 2009 from http://timesbusiness.typepad.com/money_weblog/2008/10/10-people-who-p.html.

[3] 'Pilot is hailed after jetliner's icy plunge' retrieved on 27th February 2009 from http://www.nytimes.com/2009/01/16/nyregion/16crash.html?pagewanted=2&_r=1.

[4] 'Profile: Chesley B. Sullenberger' retrieved on 27th February 2009 from http://news.bbc.co.uk/1/hi/world/americas/7832642.stm.

[5] 'How do you land a plane on water?' retrieved on 27th February 2009 from http://news.bbc.co.uk/1/hi/magazine/7833317.stm.

[6] Klein, G. (2003) *Intuition at Work*. New York: Doubleday.

[7] 'Chesley B. Sullenberger III talks of Hudson River drama in first interview', retrieved on 19th April 2009 from http://www.timesonline.co.uk/tol/news/world/us_and_americas/article5697690.ece; 'Crew of plane that landed in Hudson gives first TV interview', retrieved on 19th April 2009 from http://www.guardian.co.uk/world/2009/feb/09/flight-1549-crew-sullenberger-interview.

[8] Hogarth, R.M. (2001) *Educating Intuition*. Chicago: University of Chicago Press; Sadler-Smith, E. (2008) *Inside Intuition*, Abingdon: Routledge; Sadler-Smith, E., and Shefy, E. (2004) The intuitive executive: understanding and applying 'gut feel' in decision-making, *The Academy of Management Executive*, **18**(4): 76–92.

[9] Dane, E. and Pratt, M.G. (2007) Exploring intuition and its role in managerial decision-making. *Academy of Management Review*, **32**(1): 33–54.

[10] Dreyfus, H.L. and Dreyfus, S.E. (1986) *Mind over Machine: The power of human intuition and expertise in the era of the computer.* New York: Free Press.

[11] Ericsson, K.A., Prietula, M.J. and Cokely, E.T. (2007) The making of an expert, *Harvard Business Review*, July–August: 114–21.

[12] Hogarth, R.M. (2001) *Educating Intuition.* Chicago: University of Chicago Press.

[13] Sadler-Smith, E. and Shefy, E. (2007) Developing intuitive awareness in management education. *Academy of Management Learning and Education*, **6**(2): 1–20.

[14] Sadler-Smith and Shefy (2007) op cit.

[15] Sadler-Smith, E. (2008) *Inside Intuition*, Abingdon: Routledge.

[16] Louis, M.R. and Sutton, R.I. (1991) Switching cognitive gears: From habits of mind to active thinking. *Human Relations*, **44**: 55–76.

[17] The literal meaning of 'philosopher' is wisdom (sophia) loving (philo).

[18] Sternberg, R.J. (2003) *Wisdom intelligence and creativity synthesized.* Cambridge: Cambridge University Press.

[19] Dalai Lama XIV Bstan-'dzin-rgya-mtsho (2000) *Ancient wisdom: modern world.* London: Abacus.

[20] 'Tibetan Spiritual leader the Dalai Lama today said the main cause of global financial meltdown is unlimited human greed. Retrieved on 2nd March 2009 from: http://www.dalailama.com/news.335.htm.

[21] This is Klein's view of intuitions as skills that can be acquired and strengths that can be expanded through exercise. See: Klein, G. (2003) *Intuition at Work.* New York: Doubleday.

INDEX

Index compiled by Annette Musker

Also by this author

Learning and Development for Managers
Perspectives from Research and Practice

Eugene Sadler-Smith

Paperback | 488 pages | ISBN: 978-1-4051-2982-4

A John Wiley & Sons, Ltd., Publication